April DeConick is Assistant Professor
in the Department of Religion, Illinois
Wesleyan University, Bloomington,
Illinois, USA.

JOURNAL FOR THE STUDY OF THE NEW TESTAMENT SUPPLEMENT SERIES
157

Executive Editor
Stanley E. Porter

Sheffield Academic Press

Voices of the Mystics

Early Christian Discourse in the Gospels of John and Thomas and Other Ancient Christian Literature

April D. DeConick

Journal for the Study of the New Testament
Supplement Series 157

Copyright © 2001 Sheffield Academic Press

Published by
Sheffield Academic Press Ltd
Mansion House
19 Kingfield Road
Sheffield S11 9AS
England

www.SheffieldAcademicPress.com

Typeset by Sheffield Academic Press
and
Printed on acid-free paper in Great Britain
by Biddles Ltd,
Guildford, Surrey

British Library Cataloguing in Publication Data

A catalogue record for this book is available
from the British Library

ISBN 1-84127-190-X

April D. DeConick, *Voices of the Mystics*

ISBN 1 84127 190 X

Errata (errors which entered the manuscript, post final proof)

p. 16, item 2, *for* 'What are the religious traditions that the author uses to build his or her ideology? What does her or she draw from the general religious environment...', *read* 'What are the religious traditions that the author uses to build his ideology? What does he draw from the general religious environment...'.

pp. 87-88, *note 4 on p. 88 should be attached after* 'Thomas's teacher' *p. 87 line 15. There is no note on p. 88.*

p. 143, line 7, the reference is to the *'Dialogue of the Savior'* and not to the *'Gospel of the Savior'*.

p. 144, line 4, the reference is to the *'Gospel of the Savior'* and not to the *'Dialogue of the Savior'*.

CONTENTS

ACKNOWLEDGMENTS

This book weaves together a large portion of the research that I have produced since the publication of *Seek to See Him* in 1996. Some of the research was delivered orally in various presentations to the Thomasine Traditions Group and the Early Jewish and Christian Mysticism Group, both of the Society Biblical Literature. I wish to thank all those members of these groups who offered me their comments and criticisms as well as the members of both steering committees who gave me invaluable opportunities to test out my ideas in public forums. So I extend my thanks especially to Jon Asgeirsson, Risto Uro, Tjitze Baarda and Elaine Pagels of the Thomasine Traditions Steering Committee and Christopher Morray-Jones, Alan Segal, Jim Davila, and Phil Munoa of the Early Jewish and Christian Mysticism Steering Committee.

Some of the sections contained within this monograph were published in earlier versions since 1996. Chapter 2 includes a brief section on journeys through the celestial Temple which is also found in my article, 'Heavenly Temple Traditions and Valentinian Worship: A Case for First-Century Christology in the Second Century', in C.C. Newman, J.R. Davila, and G.S. Lewis' volume, *The Jewish Roots of Christological Monotheism: Papers from the St. Andrews Conference on the Historical Origins of the Worship of Jesus* (JSJSup, 63; Leiden: E.J. Brill). Chapter 3 represents a more substantially developed form of my article, '"Blessed are those who have not seen" (Jn 20.29): Johannine Dramatization of an Early Christian Discourse', in J.D. Turner and A. McGuire's volume, *The Nag Hammadi Library After Fifty Years: Proceedings of the 1995 Society of Biblical Literature Commemoration* (Leiden: E.J. Brill, 1997). Chapter 6 includes a short summary of my article on the *Dialogue of the Savior*: 'The Dialogue of the Savior and the Mystical Sayings of Jesus', *Vigiliae christianae* 50 (1996). It should also be noted that portions of Chapter 4 synthesize my previous research on the *Gospel of Thomas* found in my various publications up through 1996.

This book developed out of two observations that kept surfacing in my work: the lack of a solid methodology to investigate 'intertraditions'; and the absence of a sense of the historical contexts and settings for the extracanonical literature. In addressing these issues, I have had many pleasant conversations with others who helped to point me in new directions. So I would especially like to thank Vernon Robbins for the many conversations that we have had about Rhetorical Criticism and developing a methodology for studying intertraditions. I am also indebted to Ismo Dunderberg for discussing with me issues about the relationship between John and *Thomas*. I extend my warmest gratitude to Paul Mirecki who asked me to consult with him about a 'new' gospel that he had come across in the Berlin archives: the *Gospel of the Savior*. Because of my previous work, he thought that I might be 'very interested' in his text. So he sent me pre-publication copies of his transcriptions in the spring of 1998. The text turned out to be more than I could ever have dreamed of.

I'd like to thank Alan Segal, Gilles Quispel, Tjitze Baarda and Jarl Fossum for reading various versions of this monograph and offering me their comments and insights. This monograph has been enriched because of them.

My deepest thanks to Illinois Wesleyan University, which awarded me the 1999–2000 Illinois Wesleyan University Junior Faculty Leave. This grant has given me invaluable time and financial resources to complete this book.

Finally, I'd like to thank Professor David Terrell to whom this book is dedicated for getting me into all of this in the first place.

April D. DeConick
29 February 2000

ABBREVIATIONS

ABD	David Noel Freedman (ed.), *The Anchor Bible Dictionary* (New York: Doubleday, 1992)
AGJU	Arbeiten zur Geschichte des antiken Judentums und des Urchristentums
ANRW	Hildegard Temporini and Wolfgang Haase (eds.), *Aufstieg und Niedergang der römischen Welt: Geschichte und Kultur Roms im Spiegel der neueren Forschung* (Berlin: W. de Gruyter, 1972–)
APOT	R.H. Charles (ed.), *Apocrypha and Pseudepigrapha of the Old Testament in English* (2 vols.; Oxford: Clarendon Press, 1913)
ARW	*Archiv für Religionswissenschaft*
BBB	Bonner biblische Beiträge
BCNH	Bibliothèque Copte de Nag Hammadi
BH	A. Jellinek (ed.), *Bet ha-Midrash* (6 vols.; Jerusalem: Wahrmann, 3rd edn, 1967)
BHT	Beiträge zur historischen Theologie
Bib	*Biblica*
BJS	Brown Judaic Studies
BSac	*Bibliotheca Sacra*
BVC	*Bible et vie chrétienne*
BZNW	Beihefte zur ZNW
CH	*Corpus Hermeticum*
CMC	*Cologne Mani Codex*
CSCO	Corpus scriptorum christianorum orientalium
EPRO	Etudes préliminaires aux religions orientales dans l'empire Romain
ETL	*Ephemerides theologicae lovanienses*
EvT	*Evangelische Theologie*
FRLANT	Forschungen zur Religion und Literatur des Alten und Neuen Testaments
HNT	Handbuch zum Neuen Testament
HR	*History of Religions*
HSM	Harvard Semitic Monographs
HSS	Harvard Semitic Studies
HTR	*Harvard Theological Review*
HUCA	*Hebrew Union College Annual*

ICC	International Critical Commentary
JAOS	*Journal of the American Oriental Society*
JBL	*Journal of Biblical Literature*
JewEnc	*The Jewish Encyclopedia*
JJS	*Journal of Jewish Studies*
JR	*Journal of Religion*
JSJ	*Journal for the Study of Judaism in the Persian, Hellenistic and Roman Period*
JSJSup	Supplements to the *Journal for the Study of Judaism*
JSNTSup	*Journal for the Study of the New Testament*, Supplement Series
JSQ	*Jewish Studies Quarterly*
JTS	*Journal of Theological Studies*
Judaica	*Judaica: Beiträge zum Verständnis des jüdischen Schicksals in Vergangenheit und Gegenwart*
KD	*Kerygma und Dogma*
LAE	*Life of Adam and Eve*
LCL	Loeb Classical Library
LSJ	H.G. Liddell, Robert Scott and H. Stuart Jones, *Greek–English Lexicon* (Oxford: Clarendon Press, 9th edn, 1968)
Neot	*Neotestamentica*
NHMS	Nag Hammadi and Manichean Studies
NHS	Nag Hammadi Studies
NovTSup	*Novum Testamentum*, Supplements
NRT	*La nouvelle revue théologique*
NTAbh	Neutestamentliche Abhandlungen
NTOA	Novum Testamentum et orbis antiquus
NTS	*New Testament Studies*
Numen	*Numen: International Review for the History of Religions*
NumenSup	*Numen: International Review for the History of Religions*, Supplement
OTP	James Charlesworth (ed.), *Old Testament Pseudepigrapha*
PG	J.-P. Migne (ed.), *Patrologia cursus completa...Series graeca* (166 vols.; Paris: Petit-Montrouge, 1857–83)
PGM	K. Preisendanz *et al.* (eds.), *Papyri Graecae Magicae* (2 vols.; Stuttgart: Teubner, 2nd edn, 1973–74)
PVTG	Pseudepigrapha Veteris Testamenti graece
PW	August Friedrich von Pauly and Georg Wissowa (eds.), *Real-Encyclopädie der classischen Altertumswissenschaft* (Stuttgart: Metzler, 1894–)
RB	*Revue biblique*
RechBib	Recherches bibliques
REG	*Revue des études Grecques*
Rel	*Religion*
RevQ	*Revue de Qumran*

RSR	*Recherches de science religieuse*
SBLDS	SBL Dissertation Series
SBLSP	SBL Seminar Papers
SBT	Studies in Biblical Theology
SC	Sources chrétiennes
SJLA	Studies in Judaism in Late Antiquity
STDJ	Studies on the Texts of the Desert of Judah
StTh	*Studia theologia*
SVTP	Studia in Veteris Testamenti pseudepigrapha
Synopse	P. Shäfer, *Synopse zur Helchalot-Literatur*
TDNT	Gerhard Kittel and Gerhard Friedrich (eds.), *Theological Dictionary of the New Testament* (trans. Geoffrey W. Bromiley; 10 vols.; Grand Rapids: Eerdmans, 1964–)
TRu	*Theologische Rundschau*
TS	*Theological Studies*
TSAJ	*Texte und Studien zum Antiken Judentum*
TU	Texte und Untersuchungen
UUÅ	Uppsala universitetsårsskrift
VC	*Vigiliae christianae*
VCSup	Supplements to *Vigiliae christianae*
VTSup	*Vetus Testamentum*, Supplements
WUNT	Wissenschaftliche Untersuchungen zum Neuen Testament
ZNW	*Zeitschrift für die neutestamentliche Wissenschaft*
ZTK	*Zeitschrift für Theologie und Kirche*

[ ]	Reconstruction of words in lacunae
( )	Clarification of ambiguities in the text or antecedents

Chapter 1

TRADITIO-RHETORICAL CRITICISM: A METHODOLOGY FOR EXAMINING THE DISCOURSE OF INTERTRADITIONS

> Ideology does not just concern people;
> it concerns the discourse of people
> (Vernon Robbins).

Traditio-rhetorical Criticism is an approach to literature that focuses on reconstructing the exchange and modification of religious traditions as they are discussed, evaluated, and textualized. This approach pays close attention to the details of the text and to the traditions of the people who wrote the text.

The hyphenated prefix 'traditio-' refers to the traditions that express the self-understanding of a community of people: their sense of the past, their systems of religious belief, and their manner of conduct. These traditions are passed down from generation to generation in the form of stories, sayings, myths, creeds, liturgical statements, and so on. At certain moments in the history of the community, their oral traditions are textualized, crystallizing the community's ideology at a particular stage.

The term 'rhetorical' means the way in which the language in a text is used as a means of *communicating among people*. One of its main concerns is to reconstruct the topics within a text in order to understand the text's thought, speech, stories, and arguments.[1] Its focus is language that is used by people to establish bonds, to identify opponents, to negotiate shared interests, to pursue self-interests, and to offer a new perspective.[2]

---

1.   B.L. Mack, *Rhetoric and the New Testament* (Minneapolis: Fortress Press, 1990).

2.   V.K. Robbins, *Exploring the Texture of Texts: A Guide to Socio-rhetorical Interpretation* (Valley Forge, PA: Trinity Press International, 1996), p. 1.

Taken together, this type of textual analysis is a hermeneutic that seeks to understand the discourse which ellicited the textualization and creation of an ideology. Furthermore, Traditio-rhetorical Criticism has the goal to reconstruct the modified ideology in relation to the religious traditions of the people involved.

Thus the four main questions of Traditio-rhetorical Criticism are:

1. What is the situation that has ellicited the development of a particular ideology in a text? In other words, who or what is the author responding to in the creation of his stance? Can we reconstruct the voices of discourse buried in the text?
2. What are the religious traditions that the author uses to build his or her ideology? What does her or she draw from the general religious environment of Judaism and the ancient world at large? What does he draw from the religious environment of his opponents? What does he draw from the religious environment of his own community?
3. In what ways has the author modified these religious traditions in order to provide new meaning within a traditional structure, a structure that remains comprehensible to his audience?
4. What is the most probable reconstruction of the author's ideology and its meaning, a reconstruction that makes sense given the discourse and the traditions of the people involved?

In order to answer these questions, I have found the work of Robert Wuthnow to be particularly helpful because it establishes boundaries and outlines the characteristics of the textualization of discourse. He published his theory in 1989 in his voluminous work, *Communities of Discourse*, where he analyzes the interaction between ideology and social structure in the Reformation, the Enlightenment, and European Socialism.[3]

Although credited with offering a functional model for examining the textualization of discourse, Wuthnow contributes nothing new to the idea that social conditions are transformed into ideology in the textualization process. In New Testament research, this is an old idea grounded in the brilliant research of Rudolph Bultmann and his students who demonstrated that the needs of the religious community became layered

---

3. See especially his 'Introduction: The Problem of Articulation', *Communities of Discourse* (Cambridge, MA: Harvard University Press, 1989), pp. 1-22.

in the texts it wrote. Therefore the texts primarily voice the experience of the Church and are only secondarily about the events of Jesus which they describe.[4]

According to Wuthnow's model for examining the textualization of discourse, one must first identify the 'social horizon'. This is the actual social experience(s) that produce(s) the ideology. Wuthnow reminds us that ideology exists within the dynamic context in which it was produced and disseminated. It should not be abstracted from this concrete setting. Moreover, the development or transformation of ideology subsumes discourse, whether the verbal or the written, the informal or the formal, the ritual or the conceptual. It is only when we acknowledge these concrete, living and breathing communities that their discourse and their process of articulation can become meaningful in the interpretative process. It must be recognized, however, that the process of textualization of ideology is itself selective and transformative so that the actual social horizon and the social world represented in the text may only resemble each other partially. Struggles between different social classes or political parties in the real world may differ in part from those found in the narrative or in the theoretical representation of these conflicts.

Second, he points to the 'discursive field' that defines the range of the problem between the two factions. This is done on a symbolic level where actual features of the social horizon are incorporated at the textual level as symbolic acts and events. The real opposition between the factions is dramatized. Such dramatizations provide a contrast to the social horizon, thus evoking for the author a space for his creative reflection.

Third, there is 'figural action' which is representative of the solution to the problem. Figural action provides the solution that makes sense when given the problems that have been identified. Sometimes the aid of 'figural characters' is employed. Such characters have been abstracted from the social horizon and are framed within a generalized discourse that pulls the characters beyond their immediate situations.

---

4.   See particularly Bultmann's article 'The Study of the Synoptic Gospels', in *Form Criticism: Two Essays on New Testament Research* (trans. F.C. Grant; New York: Harper & Row, 1966), pp. 11-76; *idem, Die Geschichte der Synoptischen Tradition* (Göttingen: Vandenhoeck & Ruprecht, 1921); and *idem, The Theology of the New Testament* (trans. K. Grabel; London: SCM Press, 1955).

Wuthnow's model falls short in the language of religious communities where the scaffolding provided for these discourses was the broader religious environment of the contemporaneous world. The communities engaged in these discourses were certain to articulate closely enough with the ideology of this religious environment so as not to become irrelevant, abstract, or unrealistic to their audience. But, by implication, they also were evoking space in which their own creative reflections could take root. They were, thereby, disarticulating themselves with this environment as well. Any model that may be developed to talk about Traditio-rhetorical Criticism must allow for this connection with the broader religious environment.

The work of Vernon Robbins is also useful in the construction of Traditio-rhetorical Criticism because he is to be credited with one of the first attempts to develop an multilayered language to address the combination of rhetorical and social concerns. According to Robbins, 'socio-rhetorical criticism integrates the ways people use language with the ways they live in the world'.[5] Thus Robbins identifies multiple textures in texts. Of particular relevance to this study are his discussions of intertexture, ideological texture, and sacred texture.

Robbins divides his notion of intertexture between oral–scribal intertexture (how a text configures or reconfigures language from other texts), cultural intertexture (how a text interacts with cultural knowledge of various kinds), and the ideological texture of texts (that the ideology is representative of the community not simply the author). One of the assumptions of socio-rhetorical interpretation is that 'a person's ideology concerns her or his conscious or unconscious enactment of presuppositions, dispositions, and values held in common with other people'. It is not very satisfactory to speak about one person's ideology since this is not so much the subject of ideology as of psychology.[6] According to John Elliot, 'Ideologies are shaped by specific views of reality shared by groups—specific perspectives on the world, society, and man [human beings!], and on limitations and potentialities of human existence'.[7] At the heart of the matter is Robbins's statement that ideo-

---

5.   Robbins, *Texture*, p. 1. See also his *The Tapestry of Early Christian Discourse: Rhetoric, Society and Ideology* (London: Routledge, 1996); Robbins, 'The Dialectical Nature of Early Christian Discourse', *Scriptura* 59 (1996), pp. 353-62.

6.   Robbins, *Texture*, p. 95.

7.   J. Elliot, *A Home for the Homeless: A Social-Scientific Criticism of 1 Peter, Its Situation and Strategy* (Philadelphia: Fortress Press, 1990), p. 268.

logy 'concerns people's relationship to other people. But, ideology does not just concern people; it concerns the discourse of people'.[8]

The principles of Traditio-rhetorical Criticism have also been informed by the work of Peter Berger and Thomas Luckmann in their book on the sociology of knowledge. We learn from them that as institutions form, so does a common stock of knowledge,[9] the summation of 'what everybody knows' about their world.[10] This stock is an integration of rules of conduct, maxims, morals, values, beliefs, and myths.[11] This knowledge becomes the standard or canon by which everything is measured. Any radical deviance from this stock knowledge is viewed as a departure from reality and is explained as mental instability, immorality, or ignorance.[12] One of the consequences of the formation of institutions is the possibility that 'subuniverses' of meaning develop within particular groups. The result? Conflict and competition between the groups.[13]

When one applies this perspective to early Christian texts, a constellation of interpretative moments appears. Twenty years ago, this was beginning to be recognized in the research of John Gager who asserted that within early Christian texts was embedded conflict of the most intense level involving competing ideologies or competing views of the same ideology. He determined three critical moments in early Christian history: (1) conflict with Judaism over the claim to be the *true* Israel; (2) conflict with paganism over the claim to have *true* wisdom; and (3) conflict among different Christian communities over the claim to possess the *true* faith of Jesus and the apostles.[14]

Thus, the model of Robbins needs to be expanded, in my opinion, to include the arena 'intertraditions'. This is an arena where specific language connections cannot be identified, but where we can see that people appear to be consciously talking to one another in their texts. The authors are using texts to dramatize actual dialogues which were

8. Robbins, *Texture*, p. 110.
9. P. Berger and T. Luckmann, *The Social Construction of Reality: A Treatise in the Sociology of Knowledge* (New York: Doubleday, 1966), pp. 53-85.
10. Berger and Luckmann, *Social Construction*, p. 65.
11. Berger and Luckmann, *Social Construction*, p. 65.
12. Berger and Luckmann, *Social Constuction*, p. 66.
13. Berger and Luckmann, *Social Construction*, p. 85.
14. J. Gager, *Kingdom and Community: The Social World of Early Christianity* (Engelwood Cliffs, NJ: Prentice–Hall, 1975), p. 82.

engaging their communities. Thus we do not necessarily find the text recontextualizing statements from another text, but we hear voices reverberating aspects of a common discourse.

The recent work of Cameron Afzal has identified what I call 'inter-traditions' as 'communal icons' which he defines as 'patterns of the imagination that participants in communal conversation can assume they have in common'.[15] The communal icons are 'configurations of symbols' that can be 'manipulated by individuals and groups in order to change how a community perceives aspects of reality embodied in the constituent symbols'.[16] Afzal correctly notes that the use of images in a text 'depends on the prior knowledge of these images by his audience'.[17] Thus, the communal icon represents 'a pattern of thought that an author inherits by virtue of participation in society'.[18] This means that such icons are a 'repository' at the disposal of authors. While writing, the author assumes that his intended audience also has knowledge of these patterns of thought. His text, therefore, does not simply 'reproduce' the communal icons, but the text may in fact be written to modify or destroy the icons. In this way, the reality of the reader is subtly manipulated.[19] For Afzal, the interpretative process means that we must try to understand the communal icons which the author had assumed on the part of his audience or the text will remain impenetrable to later readers.[20] Moreover, if we focus on the relationship between texts with reference to their use of communal icons, we do not need to establish direct literary dependence of one Christian text upon another in order to draw meaningful conclusions.[21]

In order to achieve this end, I find that a Traditio-rhetorical model needs to be created. In this model, first we must define three horizons:

---

15. C. Afzal, 'The Communal Icon: Complex Cultural Schemas, Elements of the Social Imagination (Matthew 10:32//Luke 12:8 and Revelation 3:5, A Case Study)', in V. Wiles, A. Brown, and G. Snyder (eds.), *Putting Body and Soul Together: Essays in Honor of Robin Scroggs* (Valley Forge, PA: Trinity Press International, 1997), pp. 1-79 (58).
16. Afzal, 'Communal Icon', pp. 58-59.
17. Afzal, 'Communal Icon', p. 63.
18. Afzal, 'Communal Icon', p. 65.
19. Afzal, 'Communal Icon', p. 68
20. Afzal, 'Communal Icon', p. 79.
21. Afzal, 'Communal Icon', p. 64.

1. the Religio-Historical Horizon
2. the Author's Traditio-Religious Horizon
3. the Opponents' Traditio-Religious Horizon

Second, we must identify the Point of Discourse between the author's community and the opponents' community. Third, we must trace the Interpretative Trajectory of the Point of Discourse as the author's own creative thinking elevates it to new meaning. And finally, we must reconstruct the Synthetic End Point, the author's newly fashioned ideology.

The Religio-historical horizon is the general religious environment in which the author and his community lived and breathed. In the case of early Christianity, this would include Judaism and the Hellenistic religious environment. The author, when textualizing his ideology, must articulate coherently with this environment even when reinterpreting particular symbols and images. Otherwise, his writing would be incomprehensible and unpersuasive to his audience. Thus, for the author's Interpretative Trajectory to become meaningful to us, it is essential to reconstruct the Religio-historical Horizon. For us to truly engage in the discourse of the author, his community, and the opponents' community, we must first recognize the manner in which the general religious environment had addressed previously the topic of dispute or how it had developed similar traditions in order to answer a comparable question.

The Author's Traditio-religious Horizon and the Opponents' Traditio-religious Horizon point to the Christian heritage of the particular communities engaged in discourse. These horizons represent particular myths, rituals, stories, and ideologies that belong to the rich traditions of their individual Christian communities. For example, does the text belong to the Jamesian community? Or does it represent Pauline traditions? Is it reflective of the Johannine trajectory? Or the Thomasine?

In order to better understand these horizons, they can be mapped in three-dimensional space as the x, y, and z axes (see Figure 1).

On our map, the Point of Discourse should be located at the intersection of the three horizons, indicating that the Point exists only because there is discourse between two communities located within the general religious environment. This also means that the new ideology of the author would not have been created without the intersection of these three horizons at a certain moment in history (see Figure 2).

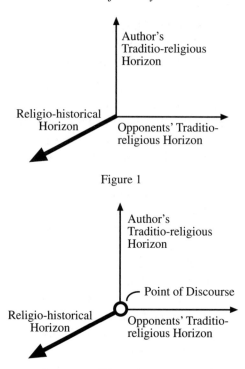

Figure 1

Figure 2

The Interpretative Trajectory is the movement of the Point of Discourse from its starting point to its end point by the creative force of the author. As the author reinterprets the Point of Discourse, he does so in relation to the three horizons, his own creative reflections opening up space for the movement of the Point within the horizons. In this way, the Point of Discourse is reinterpreted while at the same time maintaining connections and relevance with its traditional heritage.

This Interpretative Trajectory ends in a synthesis that mediates the contemporary reality of the dispute and the creative reflections of the author. Thus the Synthetic End Point provides the author's solution, his new ideology. This ideology will make sense when given the identified Point of Discourse and the peculiar horizons.

The Interpretative Trajectory and the Synthetic End Point can be added to the map in a direction reflective of the particular solution in a given text. Thus the solution may be represented in relative proximity to the traditions of the author, opponents, or general religious environment in each case studied (see Figure 3):

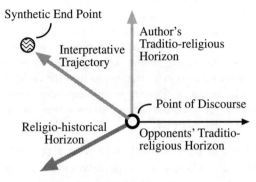

Figure 3

It should be noted that discourse embedded in texts does not always have to result in an Interpretative Trajectory and a Synthetic End Point. There may be cases where the author might choose to ignore his opponent's case rather than modify the disputed ideologies as I will argue John does. Or he might simply build a case to maintain the status quo altogether or present his alternative model forthright without reference to his opponents. Or he might try to conceal material that would support his opponent's position. Or he might condemn his opponent's system outright. As Traditio-rhetorical Criticism is developed and applied to different texts, the variety of responses an author may use against his opponents must be taken into consideration and sophisticated tools created in order to identify and analyze these specific situations.

The present monograph seeks to apply this new methodology to the Gospels of John and *Thomas*. The study of the Gospel of John in particular has a long history examining its origins and speculating about the community responsible for its composition. For the present study, several scholars merit special mention. The first is Xavier Léon-Dufour. In his article on Jn 2.19-22, he pioneered the conclusion that passages in the Gospel of John purport theologies which are directly relevant to the spiritual needs of the *author's* own community.[22] But it was not until J. Louis Martyn's significant work, *History and Theology in the Fourth Gospel*, that the subject was examined in detail. Martyn, in fact, makes it his primary goal:

22. X. Léon-Dufour, 'Le signe du temple selon Saint Jean', *RSR* 39 (1951/52), pp. 155-75.

> Our first task…is to try to say something as specific as possible about the
> actual circumstances in which John wrote his Gospel. How are we to
> picture daily life in John's church? Have elements of its peculiar daily
> experiences left their stamp on the Gospel penned by one of its mem-
> bers? May one sense even in its exalted cadences the voice of a Christian
> theologian who writes *in response to contemporary events and issues*
> which concern, or should concern, all members of the Christian
> community in which he lives?[23]

Martyn goes beyond previous scholars who proposed theories about
John's origins and audience since he advocates that passages in the
Fourth Gospel tell stories about actual events in the experience of the
community. Such events have been dramatized as episodes in the life of
Jesus.[24] He believes that the key to unlocking the meaning of the Fourth
Gospel is:

> to take up temporary residence in the Johannine community. We must
> see with the eyes and hear with the ears of that community. We must
> sense at last some of the crises that helped shape the lives of its mem-
> bers. And we must listen carefully to the kind of conversations in which
> all of its members found themselves engaged.[25]

Even though Martyn asks of the Johannine text questions similar to
those asked by previous scholars (e.g. What is the identity of the
author's audience? Jewish or Gentile? What is the geographical location
and life situation of the author and his audience?),[26] he differs from
them because he works with the realization that the various questions
do not necessarily have one answer. The Johannine text has a long oral
and compositional history spanning a time when the Johannine community encountered significant problems and experienced significant
alterations in its population and theology. Martyn compares the Fourth

---

23. J.L. Martyn, *History and Theology in the Fourth Gospel* (Nashville: Abingdon Press, 2nd edn, 1979), p. 17.

24. He develops these ideas in his articles collected in *The Gospel of John in
Christian History* (New York: Paulist Press, 1979).

25. Martyn, *History and Theology*, p. 18.

26. For example: C.K. Barrett, *The Gospel of John and Judaism* (London:
SPCK, 1975); C.H. Dodd, *The Interpretation of the Fourth Gospel* (Cambridge:
Cambridge University Press, 1953); W.C. van Unnik, 'The Purpose of St. John's
Gospel' (TU, 73; Berlin, 1959), pp. 382-411; J.A.T. Robinson, 'The Destination
and Purpose of St. John's Gospel', in R. Batey (ed.), *New Testament Issues* (New
York: Harper & Row, 1970), pp. 191-209; and R. Brown, *The Gospel According to
John* (2 vols.; New York: Doubleday, 1966, 1970).

Gospel to an archaeologist's tell. By this he means that there are numer-
ous strata that 'reflect communal interests, concerns, and experiences'.[27]
The literary history reflects the history of a single peculiar community
over a period of years. Martyn explains that it is possible 'to draw from
the *Gospel's literary history* certain conclusions about the *community's
social and theological history*'.[28]

Martyn is particularly interested in probing the moment in the history
of the Johannine community when it experienced a rupture between its
Jewish origins and its increasingly Christian population. Thus he starts
building his investigation with the healing story of the blind man in
Chapter 9, a healing story which he understands to be a dramatization
of the experience of the community. The main actors actually represent
characters from the community's experience: Jesus is a latter-day
Christian prophet; the blind man is a Christian convert; and the San-
hedrin is the 'Gerousia' or local Jewish city council. This chapter, Martyn argues, reflects 'actual experiences of the Johannine community',
particularly it reflects 'experiences in the dramatic interaction between
the synagogue and the Johannine church'.[29] Martyn goes on, it seems
too quickly, to connect this dramatization with the famous insertion into
the Eighteen Benedictions of the clause expelling the so-called 'Here-
tics' (85–90 CE). His identification, however, in this dramatization of
the rupture with the Jewish community is sound. So significant are his
works that they have provided the foundation for the research of succeeding generations of Johannine scholars.

In 1966, Wayne Meeks took yet another gigantic step forward in
thinking about the process of the textualization of ideas. At the beginning of his study, he hoped to contribute 'new information to the widely
discussed but far from resolved question of the Johannine "background"' by focusing his attention upon 'one limited constellation of
ideas and imagery which perhaps characterized the groups toward
which the evident polemic and apologetic elements of John were directed'.[30] But what he achieved was far more since he was able to conclude
convincingly that at least part of the ideology presented by the Johannine author was the result of a dialogue between the Johannine

---

27. Martyn, *Gospel of John in Christian History*, p. 90.
28. Martyn, *Gospel of John in Christian History*, p. 91.
29. Martyn, *History and Theology*, p. 37.
30. Wayne Meeks, *The Prophet-King: Moses Traditions and the Johannine
Christology* (NovTSup, 14; Leiden: E.J. Brill, 1967), p. 1.

Christians and new converts from the Jewish and Samaritan communities who revered Moses. His famous study, *The Prophet-King*, concludes that the Christology presented in John was shaped 'by interaction between a Christian community and a hostile Jewish community
whose piety accorded very great importance to Moses and the Sinai
theophany, probably understood as Moses' ascent to heaven and his
enthronement there'.[31]

Such studies left the door open for Raymond Brown who must be
credited with popularizing the notion of the textualization of the Johannine community's experience in various literary strata of the Fourth
Gospel. He understood that the Fourth Gospel 'indirectly gives us in-
sight into that community's life at the time when the Gospel was written'.[32] Through source analysis, he believed that the Gospel could
reveal something of the community's history, especially if the recover-
able pre-Gospel sources or traditions were shaped at an earlier stage in
the life of the community.[33] Even with a limited methodological scope,
Brown was able to develop from very complex materials a fairly cred-
ible model of four phases in the life of the Johannine community.

Over the years, the study of the Gospel of John has collided with
research on the *Gospel of Thomas*. Even though past research has in-
dicated that a connection exists between the Gospels of John and
Thomas, the actual relationship has not been worked out satisfactorily.
Although several scholars noted relatively early on in research on
Thomas that certain *Thomas* logia have Johannine parallels,[34] the relationship between these two Gospels was not the subject of any study
until Raymond Brown published his now famous article, 'The Gospel
of Thomas and St John's Gospel'.[35] This article is essentially an attempt
to lay out all of the parallels between sayings in the two traditions and
'to investigate how much use, if any, *GTh* makes of the Johannine

31. Meeks, *Prophet-King*, p. 318.
32. R. Brown, *The Community of the Beloved Disciple: The Life, Loves, and
Hates of an Individual Church in New Testament Times* (New York: Paulist Press,
1979), p. 17.
33. Brown, *Community of the Beloved Disciple*, pp. 17-18.
34. J. Doresse, *L'Evangile selon Thomas ou les paroles seecrètes de Jésus*
(Paris: Librairie Plon, 1959), pp. 236-40; R. Grant and D. Freedman, *The Secret
Sayings of Jesus* (Garden City, NY: Doubleday, 1960), p. 109; R. Kasser, *L'Evangile selon Thomas* (Neuchâtel: Delachaux & Niestlé, 1961), pp. 167-68.
35. R. Brown, 'The Gospel of Thomas and St John's Gospel', *NTS* 9 (1962/63),
pp. 155-77.

writings and, in particular, of St John's Gospel'.[36] Underlying this statement is Brown's now antiquated opinion that *Thomas* is a late deviant Gnostic document.[37] Even with this assumption, Brown still struggles to prove his hunch, admitting 'that there is not a single verbatim citation of John' in the *Gospel of Thomas*.[38] In the end, he posits that there must have existed a Gnostic-like source that functioned as an intermediary source between the Gospels of John and *Thomas*.[39] Therefore, *Thomas* is 'ultimately (but still indirectly) dependent on John itself'.[40]

Since Brown's article, investigations of the relationship between these two texts continued to center on parallels in the sayings traditions. Based on source criticism, Gilles Quispel's work has explored possible connections between these two traditions at the level of a common Jewish-Christian gospel.[41] The form critic, Helmut Koester has argued that several of the discourses in John can be understood as interpretations of a tradition of sayings which *Thomas* has preserved. John, however, often uses different hermeneutic principles from *Thomas* when he is creating his variants of these traditional sayings.[42] In a more recent work, Koester analyzes a series of christological, soteriological

36. Brown, 'Thomas', p. 156.

37. For a complete discussion on *Gos. Thom.* and Gnosticism, see A.D. DeConick, *Seek to See Him: Ascent and Vision Mysticism in the Gospel of Thomas* (VCSup, 33; Leiden: E.J. Brill, 1996), pp. 3-27. Most recently, A. Marjanen has summarized the scholarly debate in 'Is *Thomas* a Gnostic gospel?', in R. Uro (ed.), *Thomas at the Crossroads: Essays on the Gospel of Thomas* (Studies of the New Testament and Its World; Edinburgh: T. & T. Clark, 1998), pp. 107-39.

38. Brown, 'Thomas', p. 175.

39. Brown, 'Thomas', p. 177.

40. Brown, 'Thomas', p. 176.

41. G. Quispel, 'John and Jewish Christianity', in *idem*, *Gnostic Studies* (2 vols.; Nederlands Historisch-Archaeologisch Instituut te Istanbul, 34; Leiden: E.J. Brill, 1975), II, pp. 210-29; *idem*, 'Love Thy Brother', in *idem*, *Gnostic Studies*, II, pp. 169-79; *idem*, 'Qumran, John and Jewish-Christianity', in J. Charlesworth (ed.), *John and the Dead Sea Scrolls* (New York: Crossroad, 1991), pp. 144-46.

42. Refer to his 'Dialog und Spruchüberlieferung in den gnostischen Texten von Nag Hammadi', *EvT* 39 (1979), pp. 532-56; H. Koester, 'The History-of-Religions School, Gnosis, and the Gospel of John', *StTh* 40 (1986), pp. 115-36; Koester, 'Gnostic Sayings and Controversy Traditions in John 8:12-59', in C.W. Hedrick and R. Hodgson, Jr (eds.), *Nag Hammadi, Gnosticism, and Early Christianity* (Peabody, MA: Hendrickson, 1986), pp. 97-110; Koester, *Ancient Christian Gospels: Their History and Development* (Philadelphia: Trinity Press International, 1992), pp. 113-24.

and anthropological sayings in John and *Thomas*. He concludes that the author of John 'critically interpreted' a tradition of sayings that has been preserved in the *Gospel of Thomas*. By reinterpreting these sayings, the Johannine author was 'rejecting' the theology of these Thomasine sayings. According to Koester, it is the soteriology of the Thomas Christians which was particularly troublesome to John, a soteriology that John reinterprets.[43]

More recently, two studies have moved beyond the discussion of sayings parallels to more provocative hypotheses. Hans-Martin Schenke has advanced the theory that the Beloved Disciple of the Johannine tradition may have been modeled off the Syrian apostle, Judas Thomas.[44] Even though his specific arguments are doubtful, he must be credited with the vision of an interaction between these texts at more than the level of the sayings tradition. This idea has informed the recent book by James Charlesworth who proposes the novel, albeit unconvincing, thesis that Thomas is the Beloved Disciple in the Fourth Gospel, an identification which later influenced the portrayal of Thomas in the literature of the 'Thomas School'.[45] Ismo Dunderberg has written a balanced critique of Schenke's and Charlesworth's hypotheses, concluding that 'neither of these suggestions is entirely convincing' because 'there is no sufficient proof for regarding Thomas as *the* historical model for the Beloved Disciple, not to speak of their complete identification'.[46]

Jesse Sell has even been more courageous and has argued that the *Gospel of Thomas* has been directly influenced by the *Gospel of John*.[47] He states that the sayings parallels are so extensive between these two Gospels, that Brown's intermediary Gnostic text would have to have been a text of a nearly complete Gospel of John.[48] In particular, he identifies eight sayings in *Thomas* (Prologue; L. 8, 13, 28, 38, 43, 91, and 92) that 'display the sort of echoes of Johannine ideas and vocab-

43. Koester, *Ancient Christian Gospels*, pp. 113-28.

44. See his, 'The Function and Background of the Beloved Disciple in the Gospel of John', in Hedrick and Hodgson, Jr (eds.), *Nag Hammadi*, pp. 111-25.

45. J.H. Charlesworth, *The Beloved Disciple Whose Witness Validates the Gospel of John?* (Valley Forge, PA: Trinity Press International, 1995).

46. I. Dunderberg, '*Thomas* and the Beloved Disciple', in Uro (ed.), *Thomas at the Crossroads*, pp. 65-88 (66).

47. J. Sell, 'Johannine Traditions in Logion 61 of The Gospel of Thomas', *Perspectives in Religious Studies* 7 (1980), pp. 24-37.

48. Sell, 'Logion 61', p. 28. Sell hears in *Gos. Thom.* 'echoes' of 53 verses from 17 different chapters of John (p. 27).

ulary' which make it impossible for Sell to deny 'the probability of some direct influence of "John itself " on GT'.[49] The same conclusion has been drawn by Miroslav Marcovich who believes that *Thomas* was inspired by John.[50] He bases his claim on an analysis of Logion 11 which he believes refers to Jn 1.7; 2.9; 6.31-58; and 12.36.

Both of these articles have similar problems: do 'echoes' or deviant 'parallels' of 'Johannine ideas and vocabulary' have to suggest literary dependence of one Gospel upon another? Koester has shown us that it quite possible that both Gospels drew off a common sayings tradition instead of one another. Additionally, new methods based on the sociological and anthropological models such as Afzal's development of the notion of 'communal icons' and my concept of 'intertraditions' certainly open the door to alternative solutions.

Contrary to Sell and Marcovich, Stevan Davies thinks that the *Gospel of Thomas* originated in the same community 'that, in a later decade, produced the Gospel of John'.[51] He argues this claim by comparing wisdom motifs, eschatological sayings, and cosmological views in both Gospels:

> The Christology of Thomas shares with that of John a place of origin in the Jewish Wisdom tradition. Thomas shows familiarity with Johannine vocabulary and ideas, and uses some of the same dichotomies, such as between "world" and world, and between light and dark'.[52]

He acknowledges that 'the connection between Thomas and John is multifaceted and complex'.[53] Thus:

> Indeed, the hypothesis that the Gospel of Thomas is a sayings collection from an early state of the Johannine communities accounts for the fact that Thomas contains no quotations from the as yet unwritten Gospel and Letters of John, accounts for the use of both Johannine vocabulary and synoptic-style sayings, and to a certain extent accounts for the fact that the ideas of Thomas are less well conceptualized than the ideas of John.[54]

---

49. Sell, 'Logion 61', p. 25.

50. M. Marcovich, 'Textual Criticism on the *Gospel of Thomas*', *JTS* 20 (1969), pp. 53-74.

51. S. Davies, 'The Christology and Protology of the *Gospel of Thomas*', *JBL* 111 (1992), p. 682.

52. Davies, 'Christology', p. 116.

53. Davies, 'Christology', p. 116.

54. Davies, 'Christology', p. 116.

Davies, however, states that it would be incorrect to claim that the *Gospel of Thomas* is entirely produced by Johannine Christianity since there are striking differences in theology between the two Gospels. But, it is possible to say that the later Johannine writings are 'a developed and transformed version of Thomasine Christianity'.[55] This position is certainly difficult to maintain because it doesn't explain why there are such grave differences between these two Gospels or how the Johannine author actually may have developed Thomasine theology.

Greg Riley is the first to have published on the notion that the texts of *Thomas* and John actually allude to a debate between the two communities responsible for composing these Gospels. Even though I disagree with his hypothesis that this controversy centered on the issue of bodily resurrection, Riley publicly created a space to talk about the possible debate that engaged these communities.[56]

This can be seen with the publication of an article by Ismo Dunderberg in the proceedings volume *The Nag Hammadi Library After Fifty Years* in which he asks the question whether there is *enough* evidence to posit 'an actual controversy between Johannine and Thomas Christians'.[57] He believes that the differences between Johannine literature and the *Gospel of Thomas* are not sufficient to prove a relationship between these two communities.[58] He claims that there should be 'more specific signs of interaction' in the texts.[59] What should these signs be? In his conclusion, Dunderberg suggests that the missing signs are explicit references to other Christian groups such as we find in the *Gospel of Philip* (55.23-24; 56.15-17; 67.35-37; 73.1-3).[60]

In a later study, Dunderberg examines the I-sayings in the *Gospel of Thomas* and John. His analysis leads him to conclude that 'no certain indicators of a literary dependence between the two gospels could be found'.[61] Additionally, according to Dunderberg, the analysis of the I-

55. Davies, 'Christology', p. 116.

56. G. Riley, *Resurrection Reconsidered: Thomas and John in Controversy* (Minneapolis: Fortress Press, 1995).

57. I. Dunderberg, 'John and Thomas in Conflict?', in J.D. Turner and A. McGuire (eds.), *The Nag Hammadi Library After Fifty Years: Proceedings of the 1995 Society of Biblical Literature Commemoration* (NHMS, 44; Leiden: E.J. Brill, 1997), p. 364.

58. Dunderberg, 'John and Thomas', p. 365.

59. Dunderberg, 'John and Thomas', p. 365.

60. Dunderberg, 'John and Thomas', p. 380.

61. I. Dunderberg, '*Thomas*' I-Sayings and the Gospel of John', in R. Uro (ed.),

sayings does not suggest that the two communities had dealings with each other either on a literary level or in a reciprocal community debate because of the 'distinct ways of using similar Christian traditions and adapting Jewish Wisdom traditions in each document'.[62]

There are difficulties with these arguments. First, even if individual categories of sayings like the I-sayings may not represent the conflict between our two groups, we must leave open the possibility that other sayings and stories might. Second, to argue that more direct evidence of controversy needs to be present in the Johannine text has problems especially since professors of social models such as Wuthnow and Robbins have demonstrated that controveries between actual communities are often fictionalized and recorded as dramas in their literature rather than related in terms of verbatim dialogue. This means that stories of conflict in the Gospels (and the participating characters) can be viewed as potential dramas created as records of and responses to actual dialogues between various communities. It might also be noted that there is a difference between 'open' and 'hidden' controversy in texts. According to Marc Hirshman, ideological struggles come to the fore in the literary sources so that 'an actual historical reality' is reflected in the literary works themselves. In order to clarify the literary dimensions of polemic, Hirshman distinguishes between 'open' and 'hidden' controversy. In open controversy, 'the source explicitly mentions its ideological rival, either by name or appellation, and ascribes to him a particular stance'.[63] The hidden controversy is more difficult to demonstrate explicitly because it does not provide the above information directly. Additionally, there are various reactions to an ideology that an author dislikes. According to Hirshman, he might ignore it altogether, insist on the status quo, or conceal any material that might be helpful to his opponents.[64] We might add to this list the possibilities that the author might modify the disagreeable ideology, condemn it outright, or provide an alternative model. It is my claim that the controversy found in the Johannine Gospel is of the 'hidden' variety and that the author's response is to modify the ideology with which he disagrees.

Thomas at the Crossroads: Essays on the Gospel of Thomas (Edinburgh: T. & T. Clark, 1998), pp. 33-64 (63).

    62. Dunderberg, 'I-Sayings', p. 63.

    63. M. Hirshman, *Jewish and Christian Biblical Interpretation in Late Antiquity* (trans. B. Stein; Albany: State University of New York Press, 1996), p. 126.

    64. Hirshman, *Biblical Interpretation*, pp. 129-30.

The latest voice to enter the John and *Thomas* discussion has been that of Elaine Pagels. In her incisive article on John and *Thomas*, she compares the patterns of Genesis exegesis in both Gospels. She argues that these two respective Gospels articulate conflicting traditions about creation. She states:

> We do not know, of course, whether or not John actually read the text we call the *Gospel of Thomas*; but comparison of the Johannine prologue with the above-mentioned cluster of Thomas sayings suggest that he knew—and thoroughly disagreed with—the type of exegesis offered in Thomas. As we suggest, John's author not only was aware of this clash of traditions but actively engaged in polemic against specific patterns of Genesis exegesis he intended his prologue to refute.[65]

Pagels concludes that the Johannine author 'directs his polemic' not only against Jewish, Pagan, and Gnostic readers of Genesis, but also against the type of exegetical tradition adopted by such followers of Jesus as the author of *Thomas*.[66]

It seems that past scholarship has established that there is a connection between the Johannine and the Thomasine traditions and that the Gospels themselves allude to a literary connection and/or debate between these two communities. But the analysis of this connection or debate and surrounding issues is only in the infancy of research particularly in regard to methodological foundations. In my opinion, it remains an open question that demands more attention and careful detailed research which implements new methods like Traditio-rhetorical Criticism.

I write this monograph as a contribution to solving the mystery of the connection between these two traditions. This work will not only investigate the debate that engaged the Johannine and Thomasine communities, a debate that can be viewed in the Gospels of John and *Thomas*, but also will apply the Traditio-rhetorical model as formulated above to this discussion in hope that it will provide us with a clearer picture of the reality of the conflict behind the textualized theoretical construction of that conflict.

Not surprisingly, we will discover that these Christian communities, like so many others in the late first and early second centuries, were discoursing over the 'correct' understanding of soteriology and articu-

65. E. Pagels, 'Exegesis of Genesis 1 in the Gospels of Thomas and John', *JBL* 118 (1999), p. 479.
66. Pagels, 'Exegesis of Genesis 1', p. 491.

lating this textually in order to give authority to their own peculiar religious ideologies. It is my hope that by identifying and understanding
these communities of discourse that we will better understand the origins and implications of the ideology which the Johannine author articulated in his Gospel text. I would like to note that this monograph is
only investigating one stratum layer among many that influenced the
composition of the Gospel of John and its precussors. This investigation
offers one more piece of the complicated puzzle of Johannine origins
and should be read in addition to previous theories about John's origins
rather than as a replacement for them.

In order to accomplish this goal, Chapter 2 will be devoted to providing the scaffolding, the structure for the debate. Thus, the Religio-
historical Horizon will be defined and an overview of this horizon will
be provided. Chapter 3 will identify the Johannine community's Religious Horizon. This horizon will be found to be connected specifically
to its Opponent's Horizon, the horizon of the Thomasine community.
The Johannine author's representation of the actual debate or Point of
Discourse between his community and Thomas's will only represent his
side of the discourse and, therefore, must be understood to be a theoretical construction of the historical discourse itself. Thus his portrayal
will mirror his truth, leaving him creative space to develop the Interpretative Trajectory and the Synthetic End Point in his Gospel. In the
fourth chapter, I will attempt to reconstruct the empty side of the argument, the Thomasine discourse, based on the contemporaneous document of the Thomasine community, the *Gospel of Thomas*. In so doing,
the opponent's horizon and the Point of Discourse—in this case, the
soteriology of the Thomasine Christians—will be examined in detail.
Chapter 5 will discuss John's Interpretative Trajectory and his creative
solution to the soteriological crisis, to the discourse between his community and Thomas's. The Synthetic End Point is the creation of his
own brand of mystical soteriology, the mysticism of faith. In the final
chapter, we will turn to early Syrian literature in order to determine
whether or not this discourse continued after the composition of the
Gospel of John.

Chapter 2

VISION MYSTICISM IN THE ANCIENT WORLD:
THE RELIGIO-HISTORICAL HORIZON

What you see you shall become
(*Gospel of Philip* 61.34-35).

Past commentators on the Gospel of John have suggested that it reflects knowledge of early Jewish mysticism.[1] Verses 3.3 and 3.13 feature prominently in these discussions[2] since they address the hallmarks of

1.   On the connections between John and early Jewish mysticism, see H. Odeberg, *The Fourth Gospel Interpreted in its Relationship to Contemporaneous Religious Currents in Palestine and the Hellenistic-Oriental World* (repr. Amsterdam: B.R. Grüner, 1974 [1929]); G. Quispel, 'Nathanael und der Menschensohn (Joh 1:51)', *ZNW* 47 (1956), pp. 281-83; *idem*, 'L'Evangile de Jean et la Gnose', in M.-E. Boismard (ed.), *L'Evangile de Jean: Etudes et problèmes* (RechBib, 3, Bruges: Desclé de Brouwer, 1958), pp. 197-208; N.A. Dahl, 'The Johannine Church and History', in W. Klassen and G. Synder (eds.), *Current Issues in New Testament Interpretation* (New York: Harper, 1962), pp. 124-42; P. Borgen, *Bread From Heaven: An Exegetical Study of the Concept of Manna in the Gospel of John and the Writings of Philo* (NovTSup, 10; Leiden: E.J. Brill, 1965); Borgen, *Philo, John and Paul: New Perspectives on Judaism and Early Christianity* (BJS, 131; Atlanta: Scholars Press, 1987), pp. 103-20, 171-84; W. Meeks, *The Prophet-King: Moses Traditions and the Johannine Christology* (NovTSup, 14; Leiden: E.J. Brill, 1967); A.F. Segal, *Two Powers in Heaven: Early Rabbinic Reports About Christianity and Gnosticism* (SJLA, 25; Leiden: E.J. Brill, 1978), pp. 213-14; C. Rowland, 'John 1.51, Jewish Apocalyptic and Targumic Tradition', *NTS* 30 (1984), pp. 498-507; J. Dunn, 'Let John be John: A Gospel for Its Time', in P. Stuhlmacher (ed.), *Das Evangelium und die Evangelium: Vorträge vom Tübinger Symposium 1982* (WUNT, 28; Tübingen: J.C.B. Mohr, 1983), pp. 322-25, provides a brief summary of some of these ideas.
2.   Odeberg, *Fourth Gospel*, pp. 72-89; Dahl, 'The Johannine Church', p. 141; Borgen, *Bread From Heaven*, p. 185 n. 2; Borgen, *Philo, John and Paul*, pp. 103-20; cf. E.M. Sidebottom, *The Christ of the Fourth Gospel in the Light of First Century Thought* (London: SPCK, 1961), pp. 120-21; S. Schulz, *Untersuchungen zur*

early Jewish mysticism: ascent, vision, and transformation.[3] These verses read:

> Truly, truly, I say to you, unless one is born anew (γεννηθῇ ἄνωθεν), he cannot see (ἰδεῖν) the kingdom of God (3.3).
>
> No one has ascended into heaven (ἀναβέβηκεν εἰς τόν οὐρανόν) except//but (εἰ μὴ)[4] he who descended from heaven, the Son of Man who is in heaven (3.13).

As early as 1898, Guillaume Baldensperger recognized the polemical nature of these verses and suggested that they were targeted against mystical Jews.[5] More recently, Hugo Odeberg has argued that these statements are a polemic directed against the Jewish visionaries who sought their personal salvation by ascending into heaven and encountering the deity visually and through the acquisition of heavenly knowledge.[6] Thus he comments on 3.13 as follows:

Menschensohnchristologie im Johannesevangelium (Göttingen: Vandenhoeck & Ruprecht, 1957), p. 105; Meeks, *Prophet-King*, p. 141; cf. M. Lelyveld, *Les Logia de la Vie dans L'Evangile selon Thomas* (NHS, 34; Leiden: E.J. Brill, 1987), pp. 41-43.

3.   C. Morray-Jones, 'Transformational Mysticism in the Apocalyptic-Merkabah Tradition', *JJS* 48 (1992), pp. 1-31; M. Lieb, *The Visionary Mode: Biblical Prophecy, Hermeneutics, and Cultural Change* (Ithaca, NY: Cornell University Press, 1991); M. Himmelfarb, *Ascent to Heaven in Jewish and Christian Apocalypses* (New York: Oxford University Press, 1993), esp. pp. 47-71; A.D. DeConick, *Seek to See Him: Ascent and Vision Mysticism in the Gospel of Thomas* (VCSup, 33; Leiden: E.J. Brill, 1996), pp. 99-125.

4.   Scholars cannot agree how to render this phrase: cf. J.H. Bernard, *A Critical and Exegetical Commentary on the Gospel according to St. John* (ICC; New York: Charles Scribner's Sons, 1929), pp. 72-111; F.J. Moloney, *The Johannine Son of Man* (BSR, 14; Rome: LAS, 1976), pp. 52-60; J. Ashton, *Understanding the Fourth Gospel* (Oxford: Clarendon Press, 1991), pp. 348-56. Whether or not this phrase suggests that the Son of Man is a divine or human figure is not at issue in the present discussion: it is clear that the protatis asserts that no human has ascended into heaven. Cf. J. Fossum, 'The Son of Man's Alter Ego: John 1.51, Targumic Tradition and Jewish Mysticism', in *idem, The Image of the Invisible God: Essays on the Influence of Jewish Mysticism on Early Christology* (NTOA, 30; Freiburg: Universitätsverlag; Göttingen; Vandenhoeck & Ruprecht, 1995), pp. 149-50 n. 59.

5.   G. Baldensperger, *Der Prolog des vierten Evangeliums* (Tübingen: J.C.B. Mohr, 1898).

6.   Odeberg, *Fourth Gospel*, pp. 72-89; cf. R. Bultmann, *The Gospel of John: A Commentary* (trans. G.R. Beasley-Murray; eds. R.W.N. Hoare and J.K. Riches; Oxford: Basil Blackwell, 1971), p. 150 n. 1; Borgen, *Philo, John and Paul*, pp. 103-

> The preceding context contains two ideas connected with the ascent into
> heaven; viz. the vision of (or entrance into) the Kingdom of God, the
> highest realm of the celestial world [3^3] and the knowledge of the celes-
> tial realities [3^{12}]. Now the vision of the heavens, especially the highest
> heaven, the Divine Abode, and the knowledge concerning Divine Secrets
> of Past, Present and Future derived therefrom, are precisely the central
> features of the ideas in Jewish Apocalyptic and, at the time of Jn, also in
> some of the Merkaba-ecstatic circles.[7]

According to Odeberg, John is specifically lodging an attack on these
Jewish mystical circles.[8]

Nils Alstrup Dahl interpreted the Gospel of John in light of Jewish
mystical traditions too. He argues that the Johannine Christians were
attempting to connect their beliefs about Jesus with the Old Testament
in order to provide authority for their traditions.[9] He examines Jn 1.51
and 12.41 within what he calls the Merkavah mystical tradition. But he
also sees a 'polemical note' in Jn 1.18, 3.13, and 6.46, attacking Merkavah mysticism.[10]

Peder Borgen has continued the line of reasoning that John's Jewish
background can be located in Merkavah mysticism, particularly 6.31-
58.[11] Adopting Priess's concept of 'juridicial mysticism', he explains
Johannine theology with the idea of 'agency'. Since an agent 'is' the
one who sent him, people can be denied a direct vision of the sender
(God) while at the same time participating in that vision through the
mediation of the agent (the Son).[12]

Further analysis has led Borgen to argue that John also contains
polemics against certain Jewish ascent traditions. This conclusion
largely is based on his observations regarding Moses' theophany in
Exod. 24.16 as interpreted by the Jewish theologian Philo in *Quaest. in
Exod.* 2.4 where God called to Moses out of a cloud:

> But the calling above of the prophet is a second birth better than the first.
> For the latter is mixed with body and had corruptible parents, while the
> former is an unmixed and simple soul of the sovereign, being changed

120, 171-84; W.A. Meeks, 'The Man from Heaven in Johannine Sectarianism', *JBL*
91 (1972), pp. 144-72 (52); Moloney, *Son of Man*, p. 54.

  7.   Odeberg, *Fourth Gospel*, p. 95.
  8.   Odeberg, *Fourth Gospel*, pp. 94, 97-98.
  9.   Dahl, 'The Johannine Church', pp. 128-30.
 10.   Dahl, 'The Johannine Church', pp. 131-32.
 11.   Borgen, *Bread From Heaven*, pp. 2, 147, 177.
 12.   Borgen, *Bread From Heaven*, pp. 162-63.

from a productive to an unproductive form, which has no mother but only a father, who is (the Father) of all. Wherefore *the calling above* or, as we have said, *the divine birth* happened...on the seventh day, in this (respect) differing from the earth-born first moulded man, for the latter came into being from the earth and with a body, while the former (came) from the ether and without a body (*Quaest. in Exod.* 2.4).

In this passage, Moses was called above and was transformed from an earthly man to a heavenly man. This change was a second birth in contrast to the first. According to Borgen, Jn 3.13 probably serves as:

a polemic both against the idea of Moses' ascent and against any similar claims of or for other human beings. Jn 3.13 may thus imply a polemic against persons in the Johannine environment who maintained that they were visionaries like Moses.[13]

Borgen continues this discussion by noting that the Gospel of John 'reflects an environment in which Jewish versions of such ascent traditions existed'. The polemic in John against humans who claim that they have ascended into heaven is 'partly due to the conviction that what is to be sought in heaven, such as God's glory, is now in the Incarnate One present on earth'.[14]

The Moses traditions have been further explored by Wayne Meeks. Relying on Philo, Josephus, *Pseudo-Philo, Ezekiel the Tragedian*, the Dead Sea Scrolls, rabbinic texts, Samaritan sources, and Mandaean materials, he develops a case for the existence of Jewish mystical circles in the first centuries of the Common Era. He believes that these Jews sought heavenly knowledge and held Moses to be their hero, the great prototype mystic who ascended into heaven in order to receive the Torah, and who was made Israel's king and the mediator of secret heavenly knowledge.[15] He uncovers in John an understanding of Jesus

---

13. Borgen, *Philo, John and Paul*, p. 103. There certainly were those who maintained that Moses was divinized. See Quispel's comments on *Ezekiel the Tragedian* in 'Judaism, Judaic Christianity, and Gnosis', in A.H.B. Logan and A.J.M. Wedderburn (eds.), *The New Testament Gnosis: Essays in Honour of Robert McLachlan Wilson* (Edinburgh: T. & T. Clark, 1983), pp. 48-52.

14. P. Borgen, 'The Gospel of John and Hellenism', in R. Alan Culpepper and C. Clifton Black, *Exploring the Gospel of John: In Honor of D. Moody Smith* (Louisville, KY: Westminster/John Knox Press, 1996), p. 103.

15. Meeks, *Prophet-King*, pp. 205-206, and 215; cf. W. Meeks, 'Moses as God and King', in J. Neusner (ed.), *Religions in Antiquity: Essays in Memory of E.R. Goodenough* (NumenSup, 14; Leiden: E.J. Brill, 1968), pp. 354-71.

as this Moses 'Prophet-King'.[16] This means that John had usurped the
Moses traditions for Christian purposes. Thus, Meeks agrees with Odeberg, Dahl, and Borgen that Jn 3.3, 3.5 and 3.13 are polemical statements against the Jewish mystics whose beliefs centered around Moses
instead of Jesus.[17]

In his article on Jn 1.51, C. Rowland has noted the importance of
v. 1.18 for this discussion:

> No one has ever seen God (θεὸν οὐδεὶς ἑώρακεν πώποτε); the only
> Son, who is in the bosom of the Father, he has made him known.

He recommends that the claim in this verse that only Jesus can make
God known must be set in the context of the claims made by the Jewish
mystics that they revealed the divine secrets. The Gospel of John deliberately rebuffs those mystics who claim to know God apart from the
revelation of God in Jesus. Thus Rowland understands Jn 3.13 to refer
to the vision of the prophets of old which are invalid if they are understood without reference to Jesus. John, therefore, emphasizes that the
Jews, unlike Jesus, have never seen God's form or heard his voice: 'His
voice you have never heard, his form you have never seen (οὔτε εἶδος
αὐτοῦ ἑωράκετε)' (5.37); and 'Not that anyone has seen the Father
except him who is from God; he has seen the Father (οὐχ ὅτι τὸν
πατέρα ἑώρακεν τις εἰ μὴ ὁ ὢν παρὰ τοῦ θεοῦ, οὗτος ἑώρακεν τὸν
πατέρα)' (6.46).[18] Thus he agrees with A. Segal who argued previously
that 6.46 is a polemic against ascension and theophany themes and
amounts to a new interpretation of Exod. 33.20 in the Sinai theophany.
Specifically, since the mortal Moses was not allowed to see God's face,
John proclaims that only Jesus, the heavenly figure from God, can have
a vision of God.[19]

These previous theories have been furthered by the work of James
Dunn in which he reflects on the historical context of John. He defines
this context as a dialogue between John and mystical-apocalyptic Judaism, first-century rabbis, and other Christians.[20] He acknowledges that

16. Meeks, *Prophet-King*, pp. 286-91, 301-307.

17. Meeks, *Prophet-King*, pp. 297-301.

18. Rowland, 'John 1:51', pp. 499-500; cf. G. Quispel, 'Gnosticism and the
New Testament', in Quispel (ed.), *Gnostic Studies* (Nederlands Historisch-Archaeologisch Instituut te Istanbul, 34; 2 vols.; Leiden: E.J. Brill, 1974), I, p. 211.

19. Segal, *Two Powers*, pp. 213-14.

20. Dunn, 'Let John be John', p. 333.

in the first century there existed circles of Jews who were particularly interested in engaging in mystical ascent to God's throne such as was reported in Ezekiel 1, Isaiah 6, Daniel 7, and Genesis 1. John is in dialogue with this form of Judaism, arguing that the real goal of the mystic is to 'see' God through Jesus (Jn 1.51; 6.29-58). Thus Jn 3.3, 3.5, and 3.13 are polemical sayings, driving home the point that only Christ who is from above can bear witness to what he alone has seen above.[21]

Most recently, Jey Kanagaraj has continued this trend. In his book, he examines seven basic motifs in John that he argues 'show strong influence of the Merkabah mysticism that was familiar in the late first century'.[22] These themes are ascent, glory, king, commissioning, indwelling, light, and the Logos. Kanagaraj's interpretation is sensitive to the idea that I feel is so central to understanding John: that the Johannine author *reworks* the mystical traditions in accordance with his own theology. Thus, Kanagaraj correctly notes that ascent into heaven is limited to the end-time when Jesus' disciples will go with him into the Father's house. The Merkavah vision of God on his throne-chariot is reinterpreted by John to be Jesus on the Cross as the manifested Glory and King. Jesus, as the light of the world and the Son of Man, represents the enthroned *kābôd* surrounded by light. He concludes:

> The esoteric character of the Gospel makes it probable that John himself, having come from a priestly family, had Merkabah mystical background and that naturally he adopted the esoteric tendency to proclaim the message of Christ to his fellow-Christians as well in order to strengthen them in Christian faith in the wake of persecution.[23]

Lately, Jonathan Draper has contributed an article to this discussion, an article which he plans to develop into a monograph.[24] He is convinced that the Johannine author had connections with Merkavah mysticism which was the ground for such passages as 1.14, 47-51; 2.21-22; 2.23–3.21; 4.1-42; 7.37-39; 10.3-5, 34-36; 12.28-30, 37-41, 14.1-6; and 15.1-10. He bases this conclusion on the fact that these texts contain themes that parallel those in Merkavah mysticism such as ascent, speculations about the Divine Name and the Temple, the vision of Isaiah, and

21. Dunn, 'Let John be John', pp. 326-27.
22. J.J. Kanagaraj, *'Mysticism' in the Gospel of John: An Inquiry into its Background* (JSNTSup, 158; Sheffield: Sheffield Academic Press, 1998), p. 311.
23. Kanagaraj, *'Mysticism' in John*, p. 317.
24. J. Draper, 'Temple, Tabernacle and Mystical Experience in John', *Neot* 31 (1997), pp. 263-88.

'true vine' imagery. The major interpretative problem with Draper's piece is that he does not seem to recognize that even though the Johannine author may be aware of Merkavah mystical themes, this does not mean that he employed them in a comparable manner. In fact, I will be arguing in this monograph that the Johannine author 'corrects' many of the Jewish mystical themes such as his statement *against* heavenly ascent in 3.13. Only Jesus can move freely back and forth between earth and heaven. At the Eschaton, he will lead the believers along this vertical axis (14.2-4). But for the present, the open heaven of the Merkavah tradition has been closed by John.

It seems to me that previous research has established that verses like 1.18; 3.3, 13; 5.37 and 6.46 were written as an attack on some form of Jewish mystical ascent theology. I would like to add to this discussion that the Gospel of John also contains several statements attributed to Jesus in which he proclaims that he will *not* be able to be followed into heaven, to the place where he is going. In 7.33-34, Jesus states that he will be going to God[25] and 'you will seek me and you will not find me; where I am you cannot come'. He teaches the Jews in 8.21 that seeking him after he has gone away will *not* bring them salvation: 'I go away, and you will seek me and die in your sin; where I am going, you cannot come.' He repeats this to his own disciples in 13.33: 'Little children, yet a little while I am with you. You will seek me; and as I said to the Jews so now I say to you, "Where I am going you cannot come".' Only a few verses later (13.36), Simon Peter asks Jesus: 'Lord, where are you going?' Jesus replies: 'Where I am going you cannot follow me now; but you shall afterward.' These sayings climax in ch. 14 when Jesus explains to his disciples that he will be going to 'prepare a place for you' and only then will he 'come again and will take you to myself, that where I am you may be also' (14.3). Undisputably, the Gospel of John was discoursing against the notion of esctatic pre-eschatological ascent and vision which was a popular *topos* in the ancient Greco-Roman world.

The premise of this *topos* is summarized in an adage preserved for us in the second-century CE text from Nag Hammadi, the *Gospel of Philip*:

---

25. ὑπάγειν in 7.33, according to C.K. Barrett, *The Gospel According to St. John* (London: SPCK, 1955), p. 268, is used for the departure of Jesus from this world here and at 8.14, 21-22; 13.3, 33, 36; 14.4-5, 28; 16.5, 10, 17.

What you see you shall [become] (ⲡⲉⲧⲕⲛⲁⲩ ⲅⲁⲣ ⲉⲣⲟϥ ⲉⲕⲛⲁⲱ[ⲱⲡⲉ ⲙ̄ⲙⲟϥ]) (*Gos. Phil.* 61.34-35).[26]

For twentieth-century people, this notion makes little sense. We better understand the slogan, 'You are what you eat'. Both of these sayings, ancient and modern, reflect a fundamental experience of the mystical experience: the complete identification of one's self with the object that one encounters. It may be that the visionary experience was operative in this manner because of the ancient belief that the 'seen' image enters the seer through his eye and transforms his inner soul. For example, we find in Achilles Tatius, *Clitophon and Leucippe*:

> The pleasure which comes from vision enters by the eyes and makes it home in the breast; bearing with it ever the image...it impresses it upon the mirror of the soul and leaves there its image (ἡ δὲ τῆς θέας ἡδονὴ διὰ τῶν ὀμμάτων εἰσρέουτα τοῖς στέρνοις ἐγκάθηται ἕλκουσα δὲ τοῦ ἐρωμένου τὸ εἴδωλον ἀεί, ἐναπομάττεται τῳ τῆς ψυχῆς κατόπτρῳ, καὶ ἀναπλάττει τὴν μορφήν) (5.13).[27]

Thus, in the ancient world, the mystical encounter was usually visual. First, one would leave the physical realm behind by ascending into the sacred zone of heaven.[28] Once in this sacred place, the person would

26. B. Layton, *Nag Hammadi Codex II,2-7 together with XII,2 Brit. Lib. Or. 4926 (1), and P. Oxy. 1, 654, 655*. I. *Gospel According to Thomas, Gospel According to Philip, Hypostasis of the Archons, and Indexes* (NHS, 20; Leiden: E.J. Brill, 1989), p. 162-63.

27. S. Gaselee, *Achilles Tatius* (LCL; Cambridge, MA; Harvard University Press, 1984), pp. 262-63.

28. The more general concept of ascent has been the subject of several works: W. Bousset, 'Die Himmelsreise der Seele' (*ARW*, 4; Freiburg: J.C.B. Mohr, 1901), pp. 136-69, 229-73; G. Widengren, *The Ascension of the Apostle and the Heavenly Book* (UUÅ, 7; Uppsala: Lundeqvist, 1950); C. Colpe, 'Die "Himmelsreise der Seele" ausserhalb und innerhalb der Gnosis', in U. Bianchi (ed.), *Le Origini dello Gnosticismo, Colloquio di Messina 13–18 Aprile 1966* (Studies in the History of Religions; NumenSup, 12; Leiden: E.J. Brill, 1967), pp. 429-47; A. Segal, 'Heavenly Ascent in Hellenistic Judaism, Early Christianity, and their Environment', *ANRW*, II, pp. 1333-94; U. Mann, 'Geisthöhe und Seelentiefe: Die vertikale Achse der numinosen Bereiche', *Eranos* 50 (1981), pp. 1-50; M. Smith, 'Ascent to the Heavens and the Beginning of Christianity', *Eranos* 50 (1981), pp. 403-29; I.P. Culianu, ' "L'Ascension de l'âme" dans les mystères et hors des mystères', in U. Bianchi and M.J. Vermaseren (eds.), *La Soteriologia dei culti orientali nell' Impero romano* (Leiden: E.J. Brill, 1982), pp. 276-302; Culianu, *Psychanodia*. I. *A*

encounter the divinity who resided there. As a result of this encounter, the person would experience a complete transformation and would become like the divine entity he or she saw.

Vision mysticism, deification as a result of a *visio Dei*, is an ancient belief that criss-crossed religious boundaries in the ancient world at least as early as the ancient mystery religions. As such it represents the Religio-historical Horizon of the discourse identified in the Gospel of John.

In the following survey, I discuss references to the visionary God-experience in ancient texts which were part of living *religious* traditions. In my opinion, they do not represent literary fantasies or philosophical ponderings. Rather they are intimately connected to the type of religious experience which emphasizes the immediate and direct experience of God as represented in particular religious traditions. Having said this, however, I want to make it clear that I am not attempting to define or systematize 'mysticism' in this chapter. I only hope to describe elements which reflect the way in which the ancients imaged their religious experience.

1. *Ancient Mystery Religions*

The roots of vision mysticism certainly lay in Hellenistic piety, particularly the piety and worship praxis of the Hellenistic mystery religions. The climax of the mystery celebration was the *epopteia*, the vision of sacred objects and the god or goddess enshrouded in light.[29]

According to Walter Burkert, the most influential text by far about this visionary experience of the mysteries is preserved in Plato's

---

Survey of the Evidence Concerning the Ascension of the Soul and Its Relevance (Leiden: E.J. Brill, 1983); Culianu, *Expériences de l'extase* (Paris: Payot, 1984); M. Dean-Otting, *Heavenly Journeys: A Study of the Motif in Hellenistic Jewish Literature* (Bern: Peter Lang, 1984); J.D. Tabor, *Things Unutterable: Paul's Ascent to Paradise in its Greco-Roman, Judaic, and Early Christian Contexts* (Lanham, MD: University Press of America, 1986); Himmelfarb, *Ascent to Heaven*.

29. Cf. Hipp., *Ref. Haer.* 5.8; Plut., *frag.* 178; *Dio Chrys.* 12.33; Plut., *Mor.* 81e; G. Anrich, *Das antike Mysterienwesen in seinem Einfluss auf das christentum* (Göttingen: Vandenhoeck & Ruprecht, 1894), pp. 30, 63-65; K. De Jong, *Das antike mysterienwesen in religionsgeschichtlichen* (Leiden: E.J. Brill, 1909), pp. 15-17, 313-15; P. Boyancé, 'Sur les Mystères d'Eleusis', *REG* 75 (1962), pp. 460-82; L. Deubner, *Attische Feste* (Berlin: H. Keller, 1932), p. 87.

Phaedrus.[30] Plato creates the unforgettable image of the chariot of the soul ascending through the sky to the highest summit where the vision of heaven and the gods is possible. A dim memory of this 'sacred vision (εἶδον ἱερῶν)' lies dormant in some souls (*Phaed.* 250a).[31] This memory is to be quickened by the images of beauty in this world. Suddenly these souls remember the 'beauty' which they once saw shining (κάλλος δὲ τότ' ἦν ἰδεῖν λαμπρόν, *Phaed.* 250b).[32] They 'saw this blessed vision (μακαρίαν ὄψιν τε καὶ θέαν)' and 'were initiated into that mystery which it is right to call the most blessed of all' (*Phaed.* 250b).[33] This they celebrated as initiates (μυούμενοί), gazing in rapture (ἐποπτεύοντες) at the sacred apparitions (φάσματα) which were revealed to them (*Phaed.* 250c).[34] This was the ultimate vision according to Plato.

Thus the mystery religions stress that the true state of blessedness is not in emotional ecstasy but in the act of 'seeing' what is divine.[35] With this vision comes eternal life. This is quite blatant in the *Homeric Hymn to Demeter* where the initiated who has seen the mysteries of the goddess is said to be blessed and to now participate in eternal life:

> Blessed is he among men on earth, who has beheld this (ὄλβιος ὃς τάδ' ὄπωπεν ἐπιχθονίων ἀνθρώπων). Never will he who has not been initiated into these ceremonies, who has had no part in them, share in such things. He will be as a dead man in sultry darkness (*Homeric Hymn to Demeter* 480-82).[36]

So also Pindar exclaims: 'Blessed is he who, after seeing those things passes under the earth (ὄλβιος ὅστις ἰδὼν κεῖν' εἶσ' ὑπὸ χθόν'). He

30. W. Burkert, *Ancient Mystery Cults* (Cambridge, MA: Harvard University Press, 1987), p. 92.

31. G. Long and A.J. Macleane, *The Phaedrus of Plato* (London: Whittaker, 1868), p. 58. A. Nehamas and P. Woodruff (trans.), *Plato: Phaedrus* (Indianapolis: Hackett, 1995), p. 38, renders this phrase: 'sacred objects'. For a more literal translation, see W.C. Helmbold and W.G. Rabinowitz, *Plato's Phaedrus* (The Library of Liberal Arts, 40; Indianapolis: Bobbs–Merrill, 1968), p. 33, which I prefer here.

32. Long and Macleane, *Phaedrus*, p. 59.

33. Long and Macleane, *Phaedrus*, p. 59; Helmbold and Rabinowitz, *Phaedrus*, p. 33.

34. Long and Macleane, *Phaedrus*, p. 60.

35. Cf. K. Kerényi, *Eleusis: Archetypal Image of Mother and Daughter* (London: Routledge & Kegan Paul, 1967), pp. 95-102.

36. N.J. Richardson, *The Homeric Hymn to Demeter* (Oxford: Clarendon Press, 1974), p. 134.

knows the end of life and knows its god-given beginning (οἶδε μὲν βίον τελευτάν, οἶδεν δὲ διόσδοτον ἀρχάν)' (Frag. 121).[37] This is confirmed by Sophocles: 'Thrice blessed are those among men who, after beholding these rites, go down to Hades (ὡς τρισόλβιοι κεῖνοι Βροτῶν, οἳ ταῦτα δερχθέντες τέλη μόλω᾽ ἐς "Αιδου). Only for them is there life (τοῖσδε γὰρ μόνοις ἐκεῖ ζῆν ἔστι); all the rest will suffer an evil lot' (*Frag.* 837).[38]

Thus the goal of the initiation ceremony was to behold the deity. Although these ceremonies were secretive, we do have allusions to the initiation experience of the Isis mysteries in Apuleius' *Metamorphoses*. The initiated one, Lucius, reports:

> I came to the boundary of death and, having trodden the threshold of Proserpina, I traveled through all the elements and returned. In the middle of the night, I saw the sun flashing with bright light. I came face to face with the gods below and the gods above (*deos inferos et deos superos accessi coram*) and paid reverence to them from close at hand (Apuleius, *Met.* 11.23).[39]

This encounter with the deity brings about the transformation of Lucius from a mortal man to an immortal. This transformation is symbolized by clothing the initiated in special garments, the robes of the deity. Thus, after Lucius crosses the threshold of the realm of the dead, travels through all the elements, and enters into the presence of the gods, he emerges from the sanctuary wearing 12 garments and the halo of the god. This is deification through the *visio Dei*. So the tranformed Lucius exclaims to Isis: 'I shall store your divine visage (*divinos tuos vultus*) and sacred godhead in the secret places of my heart, forever guarding it and picturing it to myself' (Apulieus, *Met.* 11.25).[40]

2. *Hermeticism*

Such notions of deification through the vision of God can be found as a central tenet of Hermetic tradition which teaches about 'the way of im-

37. C.M. Bowra, *Pindar* (Oxford: Clarendon Press, 1964), p. 90. Cf. Clem., *Strom.* 3.17.2.

38. A.C. Pearson, *The Fragments of Sophocles*, III (Cambridge: Cambridge University Press, 1917), p. 52.

39. G.P. Goold, *Apuleius: Metamorphoses* (2 vols.; LCL; Cambridge, MA: Harvard University Press, 1989), II, pp. 340-41.

40. Goold, *Apuleius: Metamorphoses*, II, pp. 346-47.

mortality (ⲧⲟⲓⲏ ⲛ̄ⲧⲙ̄ⲛ̄ⲧⲁⲧⲙⲟⲩ)' (*Disc. 8–9* 63.10-11).[41] A quite striking passage describing the *visio Dei* in the *Corpus Hermeticum* reads: 'He who has not ignored these things can know God and even, if I may say so, he can become an eyewitness of God and behold him and he can become blessed, because he has seen him (αὐτόπτης γενόμενος θεάσασθαι καὶ θεασάμενος μακάριος γενέσθαι)' (*CH* fr. 6.18).[42]

These teachings seem to be contemporaneous to the composition of the Gospel of John now that J.-P. Mahé has demonstrated that the Hermetic sayings in the Armenian and Greek *Definitions* predate the second-century *Corpus Hermeticum*.[43] Recently, Mahé has written a preliminary article on a newly reconstructed demotic text, *The Book of Thoth*, dating from the first century BCE. He concludes that this Egyptian text is 'pre-Hermetic' since 'the literary genre, the names of the characters, the settings, the issues raised by the interlocutors are really akin to the *Hermetica*'.[44] Such a proposal would mean that the existence of Hermeticism in the late first century CE is historically plausible.

In general, the religious philosophy of Hermetic tradition teaches about the divinity within humanity, the dual nature of humankind: 'Mankind is twofold: in the body mortal but immortal (ἀθάνατος) in the essential man' (*CH* 1.15).[45] It is the quest of the human to gain knowledge of his true self or divine nature (*CH* 1.18, 19, 21; 4.4; 13.10;

---

41. P.A. Dirkse, J. Brashler, and D.M. Parrott, 'The Discourse on the Eighth and Ninth', in D.M. Parrott (ed.), *Nag Hammadi Codices V, 2-5 and VI with Papyrus Berolinensis 8502, 1 and 4* (NHS, 11; Leiden: E.J. Brill, 1979), pp. 370-71. See J.-P. Mahé's excellent comprehensive study which argues that from the diverse Hermetic literature can be drawn a synthesis of belief about this immortalization process: 'La voie d'immortalité á la lumière des *Hermetica* de Nag Hammadi et de découvertes plus récentes', *VC* 45 (1991), pp. 347-75.

42. A.-J. Festugière, *Corpus Hermeticum*. III. *Fragments, Extraits de Stobeé I–XXII* (Paris: Société d'édition les belles lettres, 1954), p. 39.

43. J.-P. Mahé, *Hermès en Haute-Egypte* (BCNH, 7; Québec: Presses de l'Université Laval, 1982).

44. J.-P. Mahé, 'Preliminary Remarks on the Demotic *Book of Thoth* and the Greek *Hermetica*', *VC* 50 (1996), pp. 353-63 (361).

45. A.D. Nock and A.-J. Festugière, *Corpus Hermeticum*. I. *Traités I–XII* (Paris: Société d'édition les belles lettres, 1945), p. 11. For a more recent translation, see B.P. Copenhaver, *Hermetica: The Greek Corpus Hermeticum and the Latin Asclepius in a New English Translation, With Notes and Introduction* (Cambridge: Cambridge University Press, 1992).

14.2).[46] Such a quest will result in shedding the bodily sheath, the journey through the heavenly spheres, and the final vision of the deity. Such a journey ends in divinization or, as the Hermetics say, 'becoming god (θεωθῆναι)' (*CH* 1.26; 13.3, 10, 14).[47] Thus, in *Corpus Hermeticum* 1, upon death, when one ascends back to the divine, the soul will cast off different vices at each planetary stage and eventually will be absorbed into God (1.24-26).

Other Hermetica maintain that such divinization can occur during the initiate's lifetime (*Disc. 8–9* 57.28–58.22; *CH* 10; 13; cf. 11.20; 12.1; *Asc. Isa.* 6.22). Thus in discourse 10 of the *Corpus Hermeticum*, Hermes teaches Tat about the *visio Dei*, the one experience that God the father wills for humans to achieve. God wishes 'for one who can see (τῷ δυναμένῳ ἰδεῖν)' for 'this seeing to happen (τοῦτο θέλει εἶναι)' (*CH* 10.4). Hermes explains that 'the vision of the Good (ἡ τοῦ ἀγαθοῦ θέα)', when it occurs 'illuminates to the extent that one capable of receiving the influence of intellectual splendor can receive it. It probes more sharply, but it does no harm, and it is full of all immortality (ἀθανασίας)' (*CH* 10.4). Not all humans are ready to behold this magnificent vision. But 'in the moment when you have nothing to say about it, you will see it (αὐτὸ ὄψει), for the knowledge of it is divine silence and suppression of all the senses' (*CH* 10.5). The person 'who has looked on it (ὁ τοῦτο θεασάμενος)' can not 'look on anything else (ἄλλο τι θεάσασθαι)' because all of his bodily senses have been forgotten (*CH* 10.6). The vision of this beauty draws the soul upward and 'changes his whole person into essence (ὅλον αὐτὸν εἰς οὐσίαν μεταβάλλει)' (*CH* 10.6). Thus the soul which 'has looked on <the> beauty of the Good (ἀποθεωθῆναι <τὸ> τοῦ ἀγαθοῦ κάλλος)' is 'deified (θεασαμένην)', having abandoned the mortal sheath and flown to God (*CH* 10.6; cf. 11.20-22).[48]

Those who have 'raised themselves (ἑαυτοὺς ὑψώσαντες)' beyond heaven and have 'seen the Good (εἶδον τὸ ἀγαθὸν)' are now 'immortal rather than mortal (ἀθάνατοι ἀντὶ θνητῶν)' and scorn this corporeal temporal world.[49] They spend their time now hastening 'toward the one

---

46. See also, H.D. Betz, 'The Delphic Maxim ΓΝΩΘΙ ΣΑΥΤΟΝ in Hermetic Interpretation', *HTR* 63 (1970), pp. 465-84.

47. Nock and Festugière, *Corpus Hermeticum* I, p. 16.

48. Nock and Festugière, *Corpus Hermeticum*, I, p. 114-16.

49. Nock and Festugière, *Corpus Hermeticum*, I, p. 51.

and only' (*CH* 4.5). Tat, therefore, is taught about the Monad, 'God's image':

> If your vision (εἰ θεάσῃ) of it [God's image] is sharp and you under-
> stand it with the eyes of your heart, believe me, child, you shall discover
> the road that leads above or, rather, the image itself will show you the
> way. For the vision (ἡ θέα) of it has a special property. It takes hold of
> those who have had the vision (θεάσασθαι) and draws them up, just as
> the magnet stone draws iron (*CH* 4.11).[50]

Such elite religious ideology bears out in the popular magical papyri
as well. In the famous 'Mithras Liturgy' (*PGM* 4.475-829),[51] the initiate
aims at gaining immortality through ascent and vision. The initiate
describes the heavenly journey which culminates in the face-to-face
encounter with the god and 'immortalization (ἀπαθανατισμός)' (*PGM*
4.741, 749).[52] The initiate cries out to be given over to 'immortal birth'
(μεταπαραδῶναί με τῇ ἀθανάτῳ γενέσει)' (*PGM* 4.501).[53] He asks to
'gaze upon the immortal beginning with the immortal spirit (ἐποπ-
τεύσω τὴν ἀθάνατον ἀρχὴν τῷ ἀθανάτῳ πνεύματι)' (*PGM* 4.504-
505).[54] The initiate claims:

> I am about to behold (μέλλω κατοπτεύειν) the immortal Aion with [my]
> immortal eyes (τοῖς ἀθανάτοις ὄμμασι)—I, born mortal from mortal
> womb, but transformed into something better by tremendous power and
> an incorruptible right hand and with immortal spirit (*PGM* 4.516-21).[55]

The initiate is told to 'gaze earnestly on the god (ἀτένιζε τῷ θεῷ)' and
'greet him thus' (*PGM* 4.712):[56]

> Lord, while being born again, I am passing away; while growing and
> having grown, I am dying; while being born from a life-generating birth,
> I am passing on, released to death—as you have founded, as you have
> decree, and have established the mystery (*PGM* 4.717-22).[57]

---

50. Nock and Festugière, *Corpus Hermeticum*, I, p. 53.
51. On this, see, A. Dieterich, *Eine Mithrasliturgie* (Stuttgart: Teubner, 1966).
52. *PGM*, I, p. 98; ET H.D. Betz, *The Greek Magical Papyri in Translation
including the Demotic Spells* (Chicago: University of Chicago Press, 1986), p. 52.
53. *PGM*, I, p. 90; Betz, *Papyri*, p. 48.
54. *PGM*, I, p. 90; Betz, *Papyri*, p. 48.
55. *PGM*, I, p. 90, my translation.
56. *PGM*, I, p. 96; my translation.
57. *PGM*, I, p. 96; Betz, *Papyri*, p. 52.

In the Hermetic literature, we are taught that the mythology of this visionary ascent is equivalent to the psychologic experience of self-encounter. A self-vision is the same as a universal God-vision. The transformation result is fixed. Thus in the *Discourse on the Eighth and the Ninth*, the mystagogue and initiate ascend and, following their self-visions, become unified with the universal mind. They pray to be given access into the eighth and ninth heavens in order to 'see the form of the image (ⲉⲧⲣⲉⲛⲛⲁⲩ [ⲉ]ⲧⲙⲟⲣⲫⲏ ⲛ̄ⲑⲓⲕⲱⲛ) that has no deficiency' (*Disc. 8–9* 57.6-7).[58]

First, the mystagogue is successful in his desires, seeing the indescribable depths of the universe, and the 'Mind', the 'one that moves me from pure forgetfulness' (*Disc. 8–9* 58.4-7). He sees himself: ϯⲛⲁⲩ ⲉⲣⲟⲉⲓ (*Disc. 8–9* 58.8)![59] As a result of this vision, he declares: 'I am Mind. I have seen! (ⲁⲛⲟⲕ ⲡⲉ ⲡⲛⲟⲩⲥ ⲁⲉⲓⲛⲁⲩ)' (*Disc. 8–9* 58.15-16).[60] Subsequently, the initiate attains his ascent and vision, stating: 'I myself see this same vision in you (ⲁⲛⲟⲕ ϯⲛⲁⲩ ⲉⲧⲉⲉⲓⲑⲉⲱⲣⲓⲁ ⲛ̄ⲟⲩⲱⲧ ⲛ̄ϩⲣⲁⲓ ⲛ̄ϩⲏⲧⲕ̄)' (*Disc. 8–9* 59.27-28).[61] He claims: 'I see myself (ϯⲛⲁⲩ ⲉⲣⲟⲉⲓ)!' (*Disc. 8–9* 60.32–61.1).[62]

Corpus Hermeticum 13 as well contains important descriptions of self-vision and its meaning. In this chapter, Tat has prayed that he might be taught about rebirth, wanting to know about the 'way to be born again' (*CH* 13.3). Hermes says that he is unable to relate anything to this end except to share a particular visionary experience when he left his human body and assumed 'an immortal body (ἀθάνατον σῶμα)' (*CH* 13.3).[63] Apparently this body is his spiritual body. He is no longer 'what I was before (εἰμι νῦν οὐχ ὁ πρίν). I have been born in Mind' (*CH* 13.3).[64] The human body that can be experienced through the senses has disintegrated. The new self does not have color or mass, nor can it be touched. This self that Hermes now is cannot be seen by anyone who uses the human eyes. Thus Hermes explains: 'Now you see me with your eyes, my child, but by gazing with bodily sight you do <not>

---

58. Dirkse, Brashler, and Parrott, 'Discourse', pp. 356-57.
59. Dirkse, Brashler, and Parrott, 'Discourse', pp. 358-59.
60. Dirkse, Brashler, and Parrott, 'Discourse', pp. 358-61.
61. Dirkse, Brashler, and Parrott, 'Discourse', pp. 362-63.
62. Dirkse, Brashler, and Parrott, 'Discourse', p. 365.
63. A.D. Nock and A.-J. Festugière, *Corpus Hermeticum*. II. *Traites XIII–XVIII, Asclépius* (Paris: Société d'édition les belles lettres, 1945), p. 201.
64. Nock and Festugière, *Corpus Hermeticum*, II, p. 201.

understand what <I am>; I am not seen with such eyes, my child' (*CH* 13.3).

Tat is frustrated and states that he feels like he is crazy because he does not share his teacher's self-vision, he complains, 'I do not see myself now (ἐμαυτὸν νῦν οὐχ ὁρῶ)' (*CH* 13.4).[65] Hermes then gives him more instruction regarding the need to cleanse one's self of the 12 evil inclinations that torment the 'inner person (τὸν ἐνδιάθετον ἄνθρωπον)', the person who resides in the bodily prison (*CH* 13.7). These vices disappear under the influence of the ten powers of God. Once this has happened, the new spiritual birth is possible and with it divinity: 'My child, you have come to know the means of rebirth. The arrival of the decad sets in order a birth of mind that expels the twelve; we have been divinized by this birth (ἐθεώθημεν τῇ γενέσει)' (*CH* 13.10).[66]

Thus Tat is finally capable of rejoicing in a self-vision: 'Father, I see the universe and I see myself in mind (τὸ πᾶν ὁρῶ καὶ ἐμαυτὸν ἐν τῷ νοΐ)' (*CH* 13.13). Hermes declares: 'This, my child, is rebirth' (*CH* 13.13). Moreover, this spiritual self can not be dissolved because, unlike the sensible body, it is 'immortal (ἀθάνατον)' (*CH* 13.14).[67]

3. *Judaism*

Although the notion that the vision of a god makes one divine was Greek in origin, early Jewish mystics seemed to have welded this idea into their traditions about celestial journeys. Thus, in the Second Temple period, they taught that when one ascended into heaven and gazed on God or his enthroned bodily manifestation, the *kābôd* or 'Glory', one was transformed. In particular, it was believed that exceptionally righteous or worthy humans would be divinely transformed or 'glorified' upon gaining a vision of God. The paradigms for such transformations were the transformations of the heroes of the heavenly ascent narratives such as Moses, Ezekiel, and Enoch as well as the Jewish tradition that the righteous would be transformed in the world to come.[68]

---

65. Nock and Festugière, *Corpus Hermeticum*, II, p. 202.
66. Nock and Festugière, *Corpus Hermeticum*, II, pp. 203-204.
67. Nock and Festugière, *Corpus Hermeticum*, II, p. 206.
68. Morray-Jones, 'Transformational Mysticism', pp. 13-14; Lieb, *The Visionary Mode*, pp. 54, 59-60, 76, and 94; Himmelfarb, *Ascent to Heaven*, pp. 47-71; cf. I. Chernus, 'Visions of God in Merkabah Mysticism', *JSJ* 13 (1983), pp. 123-46;

These mystical traditions were textualized largely in the Jewish and
Christian apocalyptic literature,[69] in the writings of the Jewish theologian, Philo of Alexandria,[70] in the Qumran literature,[71] and perhaps by

C. Rowland, 'The Visions of God in Apocalyptic Literature', *JSJ* 10 (1979),
pp. 137-54; DeConick, *Seek to See Him*, pp. 99-125.

   69. G. Scholem, *Major Trends in Jewish Mysticism* (New York: Schocken
Books, 1956), pp. 40-79; Scholem, *Jewish Gnosticism, Merkavah Mysticism and
Talmudic Tradition* (New York: Jewish Theological Seminary of America, 1960);
Scholem, *On the Kabbalah and its Symbolism* (trans. R. Manheim; New York:
Schocken Books, 1965); Scholem, *Kabbalah* (Jerusalem and New York: Merdian,
1974), pp. 8-21; Scholem, *Origins of the Kabbalah* (ed. R.J.Z. Werblowsky; trans.
A. Arkush; Princeton, NJ: Princeton University Press, 1987), pp. 18-24; Scholem,
On the Mystical Shape of the Godhead: Basic Concepts in the KABBALAH (ed.
J. Chipman; trans. J. Neugroschel; foreword by J. Dan; New York: Schocken
Books, 1991). I. Gruenwald, *Apocalyptic and Merkavah Mysticism* (AGJU, 14;
Leiden: E.J. Brill, 1980); C. Morray-Jones, *Merkabah Mysticism and Talmudic Tra-
dition* (PhD dissertation, University of Cambridge, 1988).
   A challenge to this view has been proposed by some scholars who believe that
rabbinic traditions about Ezek. 1 do not presuppose actual endeavors to ascend but
are merely exegetical and speculative developments. Moreover, the Hekhalot tradition originates in circles marginal to rabbinic Judaism during the post-Talumdic era.
See D.J. Halperin, *The Merkabah in Rabbinic Literature* (New Haven: American
Oriental Society, 1980); *idem, The Faces of the Chariot* (Tübingen: J.C.B. Mohr,
1988); P. Schäfer, 'Tradition and Redaction in Hekhalot Literature, *JSJ* 14 (1983),
pp. 172-81; *idem*, 'The Aim and Purpose of Early Jewish Mysticism', in *Hekhalot-
Studien* (Texte und Studien zum Antiken Judentum, 19; Tübingen: J.C.B. Mohr,
1988); *idem*, 'Merkavah Mysticism and Rabbinic Judaism', *JAOS* 104 (1984),
pp. 537-54; M. Himmelfarb, 'Heavenly Ascent and the Relationship of the Apocalypses and the *Hekhalot* Literature', *HUCA* 59 (1988), pp. 73-100; *idem, Ascent to
Heaven*.
   On Paul's familarity with mystical Judaism, see especially now A.F. Segal, *Paul
the Convert: The Apostolate and Apostasy of Saul the Pharisee* (New Haven: Yale
University Press, 1990), pp. 34-71; C. Morray-Jones, 'Paradise Revisited (2 Cor.
12.1-12): The Jewish Mystical Background of Paul's Apostolate. Part 1: The Jewish
Sources' and 'Part 2: Paul's Heavenly Ascent and its Significance', *HTR* 86 (1993),
pp. 177-217 and 265-92. For the Jewish mystical influence on Johannine literature,
refer to the beginning of this chapter.
   70. See the classic work by E.R. Goodenough, *By Light, By Light* (Amsterdam:
Philo Press, 1969). There is a growing opinion among scholars that Philo's mysticism should be understood as a form of early Jewish mysticism. K. Kohler first
determined that elements of Merkavah mysticism can be found in Philo: 'Merkabah', *JewEnc* VIII, p. 500. H. Chadwick has suggested that agreements between
Paul and Philo may be the result of a common background in Jewish mysticism:

the Palestinian Jewish school of Yohanan ben Zakkai.[72] Thus, there is a growing number of scholars, myself included, who contend that there was some precursor in the first century to later Merkavah and Hekhalot mysticism.[73] Subsequently, these mystical traditions were absorbed into the Pharisaic and Tannaitic trajectory,[74] some forms of Christianity,[75] Gnostic schools,[76] and later Kabbalistic materials.[77]

'St. Paul and Philo of Alexandria', *BJRL* 48 (1966), pp. 286-307.

71. Gruenwald, *Merkavah Mysticism*, p. vii; L.H. Schiffman, 'Merkavah Speculation at Qumran: The 4Q Serekh Shirot 'Olat ha-Shabbat', in J. Renharz and D. Swetschinski (eds.), *Mystics, Philosophers, and Politicians: Essays in Jewish Intellectual History in Honor of A. Altmann* (Durham, NC: Duke University Press, 1982), pp. 15-47.

72. Cf. Scholem, *Major Trends*, p. 41; E.E. Urbach, 'Ha-Masorot 'al Torat ha-Sod bi-Tequfat ha-Tannaim', in A. Altmann (ed.), *Studies in Mysticism and Religion: Presented to G.G. Scholem on his Seventieth Birthday* (Jerusalem: Magnes Press, 1967), pp. 2-11; J.W. Bowker, 'Merkavah Visions and the Visions of Paul', *JJS* 16 (1971), pp. 157-73; J. Neusner, *A Life of Yohanan ben Zakkai: Ca. 1–80 CE* (Leiden: E.J. Brill, 2nd rev. edn, 1970); A. Goldberg, 'Der Vortrag des Ma'asse Merkawa: Eine Vermutung zur frühen Merkavamystik', *Judaica* 29 (1973), pp. 9-12; C. Rowland, *The Influence of the First Chapter of Ezekiel on Jewish and Early Christian Literature* (PhD dissertation, Cambridge University, 1974); Rowland, *The Open Heaven: A Study of Apocalyptic in Judaism and Early Christianity* (London: SPCK, 1982), pp. 282-83, 303-305; Gruenwald, *Merkavah Mysticism*, pp. vii, 73-86; cf. Morray-Jones, *Merkabah Mysticism and Talmudic Tradition*; J.J. Kanagaraj, *'Mysticism' in the Gospel of John* (JSNTSup, 158; Sheffield: Sheffield Academic Press, 1998), pp. 150-58.

73. For a contrary view, see Halperin, *Merkabah*, pp. 107-40 and 179-85; P. Schäfer, 'New Testament and Hekhalot Literature: The Journey into Heaven in Paul and in Merkavah Mysticism', *JJS* 35 (1984), pp. 19-35.

74. Cf. Schiffman, 'Merkavah Speculation', p. 46.

75. Particularly refer to my *Seek to See Him.*

76. On this, see especially my recent articles, 'Heavenly Temple Traditions and Valentinian Worship: A Case for First-Century Christology in the Second Century', in C.C. Newman, J.R. Davila and G.S. Lewis (eds.), *The Jewish Roots of Christological Monotheism: Papers from the St. Andrews Conference on the Historical Origins of the Worship of Jesus* (JSJSup, 63; Leiden: E.J. Brill, 1999), pp. 308-41; 'Entering God's Presence: Sacramentalism in the Gospel of Philip', in *Seminar Papers for Society of Biblical Literature Annual Meeting 1998* (Atlanta: Scholars Press, 1998), pp. 483-523.

77. Cf. E.R. Wolfson, *Through a Speculum that Shines: Vision and Imagination in Medieval Jewish Mysticism* Princeton, NJ: Princeton University Press, 1994).

As far as the origins of the mystical traditions and the literature which speaks about them, there is an ongoing scholarly discussion. I am a strong supporter of the position that the Jews and Christians connected with mysticism in this period were part of a shared exegetical tradition. The biblical passages which were being exegeted included Exodus 24 and 33, Ezekiel 1 and 40–48, Daniel 7, Isaiah 6 and the creation stories. But I think that there were at least four religious reaons for this kind of exegesis.

1. To describe the experiences of God they believed they were having.
2. To attempt to invade heaven and achieve their own direct experience of God after the fashion of their heros.
3. To develop liturgies which vicariously allowed them to experience God.
4. To create theology which reflected their experience of God.

These exegetical traditions became the basis for the development of communal mystical practices in some groups such as the Qumran community and the Therapeutae.

The idea that Jewish and Christian apocalyptic or mystical texts are only literary or imaginative writings seems to me to be a modern idea, not acknowledging the fact that the ancient Jews and Christians were deeply religious people. I want to caution our own interpretations of this material which superimpose upon this literature the modern mourning over God's death. As postmodern thinkers, if we do not believe in the sacred ourselves, that is one thing. But in our research, I think that it is important at least to acknowledge that the ancients did. They believed that they experienced the sacred and they wrote about it. So I understand this material to be coming out of *living religious traditions*. In my judgment, these texts are filled with feelings about and hopes for religious experience as understood and imaged by the ancients.

What ideas make up this complex of *early* mystical traditions? First, these traditions are visionary in nature.[78] One of the purposes of early mysticism was to achieve a visionary experience, to enter before the throne of God and gaze upon his majesty. The purpose of this vision

---

78. The visionary nature of mysticism in Jewish literature seems to be downplayed as time proceeds, while it becomes the focus of many Gnostic and later Christian mystical traditions.

was transformative in that the person becomes 'angelic' or 'glorified'. Second, the adherent was believed to ascend through the heavenly temple and observe the activities and creatures in each of the heavens. The celestial Temple is envisioned in these texts as a series of *hêkālôt*, 'shrines or holy chambers', which occupy various heavens. Therefore, ascent through the layers of heaven is depicted as a journey through increasingly holy rooms of the Temple to the holiest of the chambers, the *dᵉbîr* or 'Holy of Holies', where the manifestation of God is enthroned on his *merkābâ* or 'chariot'. A veil is sometimes depicted surrounding the throne, concealing God from direct view. This curtain hangs between the outer sanctum and the Holy of Holies.[79] This means that the worship of God had been elevated to the celestial realms in place of the earthly Temple which was known in these circles to have been corrupted or destroyed. Therefore, great care was often taken to describe the heavenly beings (including the 'body' of God himself), their surroundings, and their worship performances.

Third, the ascent and vision journey were believed to be very dangerous for the ordinary human. So it was taught that the mystic should prepare himself or herself by practicing certain ascetic behaviors like celibacy, fasting, and other dietary restrictions. Fourth, the study of Scripture was central to their practices, particularly passages like Ezekiel 1, 8, 10, 40–48, Daniel 7, Isaiah 6, and Exodus 33. So their records of their dreams and waking visions are filled with interpretations of these particular scriptural passages. In particular, Ezekiel's vision in 1.26-27 formed the basis for their speculations.[80] Here, the prophet sees a sapphire-like throne and 'seated above the likeness of a throne was a likeness as it were of a man (דמות כמראה אדם)' which appeared like 'fire' with 'brightness round about him'. And 'such was the appearance of the likeness of the glory (כבוד) of the Lord' (1.28). Thus, God's *kābôd*, was often depicted as an anthropomorphic figure of fire or light (cf. Ezek. 1.27-28; Isa. 6.1-4) seated on the *merkābâ*, the special throne consisting of two cherubim with wings spread over the *kapporet*, the lid

79. References to a veil, curtain, or covering can be found in the following texts: Exod. 26.31-35; 35.12, 39.34; 40.21; Num. 4.5; Philo, *Vit. Mos.* 2.86, 87, 93; Josephus, *Ant.* 3.108-133; Josephus, *War* 5.212; *Targ. Ps.-J.* 26.9; *b. Ḥag.* 12b; *3 En.* 45.1-6; *b. Ber.* 18b; *Alph. R. Akiba, BH* 3.44; *b. Yom.* 77a; *Mek. on Exod.* 19.9.

80. On this, see the treatment by Lieb, *The Visionary Mode.*

of the Ark of the Covenant (cf. 1 Chron. 28.18; cf. 1 Kgs 6.23-28; 8.6-7; 2 Chron. 3.10-11; 5.7-8).[81]

a. *The Visionary Experience*

In Jewish traditon, such speculations about ascent to God's throne are at least as early as *Ezekiel the Tragedian*, written by an Alexandrian Jewish poet who lived in the second century BCE.[82] He transposes elements of Ezekiel's vision to Moses who in a dream gazes on the heavenly throne and the seated *kābôd*:

> On Sinai's peak I saw what seemed a throne so great in size it touched the clouds of heaven. Upon it sat a man of noble mien, becrowned, and with a scepter in one hand while with the other he did beckon me (*Ezek. Trag.* 68-73).

In turn, Moses' divinization is described: he is seated upon a great throne and is given a scepter and a royal crown; the stars or angels bow down to him in adoration:

> I made approach and stood before the throne. He handed over the scepter and bade me mount the throne, and gave to me the crown. Then he himself withdrew from off the throne. I gazed upon the whole earth round about; things under it, and high above the heaven. Then at my feet a multitude of stars fell down, and I their number reckoned up. They passed by me like armed ranks of men (*Ezek. Trag.* 73-81).

The pre-Maccabean *1 Enoch* 14 also relies on the visionary structure of Ezekiel's *visio Dei*.[83] In this heavenly ascent narrative, Enoch travels to heaven and gazes upon 'a lofty throne' and the 'Great Glory' sitting upon it (*1 En.* 14.18-20). Although there is no mention of a transformation of Enoch at this point, in ch. 71 composed in the first century BCE, after Enoch has a vision of God, the 'Head of Time', he states, 'my whole body mollified, and my spirit transformed' (*1 En.* 71.10-11).

---

81. See the detailed presentation of the *kābôd* by J. Fossum, 'Glory כבוד δόξα', in K. van der Toorn *et al.* (eds.), *Dictionary of Deities and Demons in the Bible* (Leiden: E.J. Brill, 1996).

82. This date is determined by R.G. Robertson in the Introduction to his English translation of *Ezekiel the Tragedian* in *OTP*, II, pp. 803-807; the most recent modern edition of this text can be found in B. Snell, *Tragicorum Graecorum Fragmenta*, I (Göttingen: Vandenhoeck & Ruprecht, 1971), pp. 288-301.

83. This date is given to the ch. 14 by E. Isaac in his Introduction to the English translation of the *Ethiopic Book of Enoch* in *OTP*, I, pp. 5-12.

He then is greeted by an angel as the divine judge, the 'Son of Man' (*1 En.* 71.14).

The transformation of Enoch is quite developed in the first-century CE writing *2 Enoch* where Enoch is brought into the tenth heaven before God.[84] He 'saw the face of the Lord' which is 'like iron made burning hot in a fire [and] brought out, and it emits sparks and is incandescent' (*2 En.* 22.1 J).[85] Immediately following this vision, God orders Michael to strip Enoch from his 'earthly clothing' and 'anoint him with my delightful oil, and put him into the clothes of my glory' (*2 En.* 22.8 J). In so doing, Enoch is transformed into an angelic being: 'And I looked at myself, and I had become like one of his glorious ones, and there was no observable difference' (*2 En.* 22.10 J and A). By the time of the compilation of *3 Enoch*, Enoch experiences a fiery transformation into the angel Metatron, the Prince of the Divine Presence (cf. *3 En.* 15) Clearly the mechanism of vision mysticism has informed these narrative cycles.

That these ideas were a current in other first-century Judaisms, is most vivid in the Philonic corpus. This is not too surprising since Philo attempted to rewrite Jewish tradition in light of Hellenistic mysteriosophy.[86] So W. Bousset has observed that 'no mysticism reached the height of Philo's desire for union with the living, all-highest God'.[87]

---

84. F.I. Anderson in the Introduction to *2 Enoch* in *OTP*, I, pp. 91-97, suggest the late first century CE as a date for this text. This may be too late since we find the pre-70 command in 51.4 to pray to the Temple three times daily. For this Jewish custom, see Dan. 6.11 and Acts 3.1.

85. 22.1 A simply states: 'I saw the Lord. His face was strong and very glorious and terrible.'

86. It has been suggested that Philo was influenced by Hermeticism. On this subject, see R. Reitzenstein, *Poimandres* (Leipzig: Teubner, 1906); C.H. Dodd, *The Interpretation of the Fourth Gospel*, pp. 54-73, discusses possible thematic connections between Hermeticism and Philo; H.D. Betz, 'The Delphic Maxim', pp. 477-82, notes the striking similarity of the interpretation of the Delphic maxim in Philo and Hermeticism. Now that J.-P. Mahé in *Hermès en Haute-Égypte*, II, has discovered the Armenian and Greek *Definitions* which prove that the Hermetic sayings are older than the treatises that comprise the *Corpus Hermeticum*, it is quite plausible that Philo could have been influenced by Hermeticism. Lately, Mahé has even argued that the *Book of Thoth* from the first century BCE is a 'pre-Hermetic' writing: see his '*Book of Thoth*', pp. 353-63. See also the work of G. Quispel, 'Hermes Trismegistus and the Origins of Gnosticism', *VC* 46 (1992), pp. 1-19.

87. W. Bousset, *Die Religion des Judentums in späthellenistischen Zeitalter* (ed. H. Gressman; HNT, 21; Tübingen: J.C.B. Mohr, 1966), p. 452. Cf. Goodenough, *By*

This desire for union and immortality hinged upon abandonment of the body and ascent into the heavens. Thus, for Philo, the life-long aim of the human was to 'see' God.

Sight was the most excellent and divine of the senses for Philo because it alone was able to 'raise its head' and 'look up' to the heavens and God (*Abr.* 164). Thus the name 'Israel' was extraordinary, designating the special race of humans who see God (cf. *Rer. Div. Her.* 35–36, 76; *Plant.* 46; *Leg. Gai.* 4–5; *Migr. Abr.* 18; *Fug.* 140). Philo states: 'This race is called in the Hebrew tongue Israel, but expressed in our tongue, the word is "he that sees God (ὁρῶν θεόν)" and to see him seems to me of all possessions, public or private, the most precious' (*Leg. Gai.* 4).[88] This special race which has 'the faculty of seeing' strives 'to press upwards to heaven (φθάνειν πρὸς οὐρανὸν ἀναγκαῖον)'.[89]

Once there, this race of visionaries 'may banquet on incorruption and remain unscathed forever (τῆς ἀφθαρσίας ἑστιαθεῖσα τὸν ἀεὶ χρόνον ἀπήμων διαμένῃ)' (*Rer. Div. Her.* 35-36).[90] 'The good man alone sees (μόνος βλέπει ὁ ἀστεῖος)' (*Rer. Div. Her.* 78).[91] Advancing to God, the good man sees him and partakes of the divine manna, the 'heavenly, incorruptible food of the soul—the soul which is fond of the visionary experience (τὴν οὐράνιον ψυχῆς φιλοθεάμονος ἄφθαρτον τροφήν)' (*Rer. Div. Her.* 78–79).[92] Those people who have arrived at such a state of knowledge 'have passed over to the immortal and most perfect race of beings (τὸ ἄφθαρτον καὶ τελεώτατον γένος)' (*Sacr.* 7).[93] Philo emphasizes that the immortality of the mind is proven by the fact that 'there are some persons whom God…has enabled to soar above all species and genera' and has brought before him to stand next to him in heaven (*Sacr.* 8). They have become angels!

Light; D. Winston, 'Was Philo a Mystic?', in J. Dan and F. Talmadge (eds.), *Studies in Jewish Mysticism* (Cambridge, MA: Association for Jewish Studies, 1982), pp. 15-41.

88. F.H. Colson, *Philo*, X (Cambridge, MA: Harvard University Press, 1943), pp. 4-5.

89. F.H. Colson and G.H. Whitaker, *Philo*, IV (LCL; London: Harvard University Press, 1932), pp. 300-301.

90. Colson and Whitaker, *Philo*, IV, pp. 300-301.

91. Colson and Whitaker, *Philo*, IV, pp. 320-21.

92. Colson and Whitaker, *Philo*, IV, p. 320; my translation.

93. F.H. Colson and G.H. Whitaker, *Philo*, II (LCL; London: Harvard University Press, 1942), pp. 98-99.

The paradigm hero of this philosophy for Philo is Moses. Philo relates in *De posteritate Caini* that Moses yearned 'to see (ὁρᾶν) God and to be seen (ὁρᾶσθαι) by him' (*Poster. C.* 13).[94] So Moses ascended to God by entering into 'the thick darkness where God was' (Exod. 20.21) (*Poster. C.* 14). Philo frequently describes Moses' attempts to 'see' God after he has ascended to heaven as related in Exodus 33. In *De mutatione nominum*, Moses is 'the explorer of nature which lies beyond our vision (ὁ τῆς ἀειδοῦς φύσεως θεατὴς [καὶ θεόπτης])' (*Mut. Nom.* 7), the man who tells us that 'the Lord of all was seen (ὀφθῆναι τὸν τῶν ὅλων κύριον)' (*Mut. Nom.* 2). This vision is assumed by Philo because in Exod. 33.23 it is stated that Moses entered 'into the darkness'. This expression, 'the darkness', means figuratively 'the invisible and incorporeal essence (τὴν ἀόρατον καὶ ἀσώματον οὐσίαν)' (*Mut. Nom.* 7).[95] Thus, Moses, by entering the darkness, has achieved vision and union with God.

Philo, however, insists that God 'by his very nature cannot be seen (ὁρᾶσθαι)' (*Mut. Nom.* 9; cf. *Fug.* 101)[96] because 'the man that wishes to set his gaze upon the Supreme Essence, before he sees (ἰδεῖν) him will be blinded by the rays that beam forth all around him' (*Fug.* 165).[97] Thus Philo cites that Moses 'turned away his face' (Exod. 3.6) and saw only God's backside (Exod. 33.23; cf. *Fug.* 165; *Poster. C.* 169; *Mut. Nom.* 6). So Moses is the great 'hierophant' whose soul embarked on the mission of the *visio Dei* even though he knew that to comprehend God's essence is impossible and that God's essence is invisible. Regardless, the hero Moses entreated God 'to be his own interpreter and reveal his own nature to him, for he says, "Show me yourself" ' (Exod. 33.12). This demonstrated that Moses knew that no human, by relying on human faculties and physical senses including the eyes, is competent to learn the nature of God in his essence. So he must call upon God for assistance and gaze upon him with the eyes of his soul (*Poster. C.* 15–16).

The ideal humans, according to Philo, were a group of first-century Jewish mystics who lived near the lake Mareotic in Egypt. They sought to ascend and secure a vision of God, as Philo relates: 'But it is well

94. Colson and Whitaker, *Philo*, II, pp. 334-35.
95. F.H. Colson and G.H. Whitaker, *Philo*, V (LCL; London: Harvard University Press, 1934), pp. 142-45.
96. Colson and Whitaker, *Philo*, V, pp. 146-47.
97. Colson and Whitaker, *Philo*, V, pp. 100-101.

that the Therapeutae, a people always taught from the first to use their sight (βλέπειν), should desire the vision of the Existent (τῆς τοῦ ὄντος θέας) and soar above the sun of our senses' (*Vit. Cont.* 11).[98] They accomplished these vision quests by living a life of austerity, contemplating holy texts, praying, and singing hymns. We are told that because they adhere to such an austere program, they are fit to live 'in the soul alone' and are called 'citizens of Heaven' (οὐρανοῦ πολιτῶν)' (*Vit. Cont.* 90).[99] Thus they believed themselves to be transformed into angelic beings as the result of their contemplative lives and visionary experiences. Philo tells us that once they had soared to heaven and gazed upon God, they 'never leave their place in this company which carries them on to perfect happiness' (*Vit. Cont.* 11). Such is their 'deathless and blessed life' which has replaced their mortal one (*Vit. Cont.* 13).

b. *The Journey through the Celestial Temple*
Unlike Hellenism, within Judaism the visionary experience was intricately linked to the heavenly journey through the Temple. Therefore, it is difficult, if not inconceivable, to study the visionary experience apart from the celestial Temple traditions. In Judaism, the visionary experience is the culmination of the practioner's journey through the holy rooms or *hêkālôt* of the Temple. Gazing on God's manifestation in the heavenly Holy of Holies was part of the worship program as well as the transformative process.

It has been shown by Rachel Elior that, in the aftermath of the destruction of the Temple in 70 CE, Jews within mystical circles were perpetuating Temple worship by fostering the idea of a surrogate heavenly Temple,[100] developed largely from the visions of Ezekiel that were written following the destruction of the first Temple.[101] Refusing to

98. F.H. Colson, *Philo*, IX (LCL; Cambridge, MA: Harvard University Press, 1941), pp. 118-19.

99. Colson, *Philo*, IX, pp. 168-69.

100. See R. Elior, 'From Earthly Temple to Heavenly Shrines: Prayer and Sacred Song in the Hekhalot Literature and its Relations to Temple Traditions', *JSQ* 4 (1997), pp. 217-67. Cf. J. Maier, *Vom Kultus zur Gnosis* (Salzburg: Mueller, 1964), pp. 133-35; C. Newsom, *Songs of the Sabbath Sacrifice* (HSS, 27; Atlanta: Scholars Press, 1985); Newsom, '"He Has Established for Himself Priests"', in L. Schiffman (ed.), *Archaeology and History in the Dead Sea Scrolls* (JSPSup, 8; Sheffield: JSOT Press, 1990), pp. 114-15.

101. For the biblical background of this imagery, refer to J.D. Levenson, 'The

accept the end of their religious worship in the wake of the destruction of their cult center, they focused on the notion of a spiritual world whose cultic practices now operated on a mystical-ritual praxis. The structure of the earthly Temple was projected into the heavens as a series of three or seven *hêkālôt* or shrines, *merkābôt* or chariots, *dᵉbîrîm* or Holy of Holies.[102] According to Elior, the priestly and Levitical traditions of Temple worship were elevated and transferred to these supernal regions in the form of angelic duties and liturgical practices. The priestly ritual was understood to be performed by the angels in the heavenly sanctuary. As the primary liturgical performers, the angels were responsible for the ceremonies associated with the priestly blessing, the use of Divine Names, the pronunciation of the unutterable Name of God, the recitation of prayers, and the performance of music.

Because of the linkage between visionary experience and these celestial Temple traditions, a survey of these traditions in Second Temple Jewish literature is in order. This survey should help to inform us about the nature of the heavenly Temple and journeys that climax in beholding, serving, or worshiping the enthroned deity in the Holy of Holies. The vision in *1 En.* 14.8-25,[103] based on Ezekiel 1, represents one of the

Temple and the World', *JR* 64 (1984), pp. 275-98; Levenson, *Sinai and Zion: An Entry into the Jewish Bible* (Minneapolis: Winston, 1985); Levenson, 'The Jerusalem Temple in Devotional and Visionary Experience', in A. Green, *Jewish Spirituality From the Bible Through the Middle Ages* (World Spirituality, 13; New York: Crossroad, 1986); E. Theodore Mullen, *The Divine Council in Canaanite and Early Hebrew Literature* (HSM, 24; Chico, CA: Scholars Press, 1980), pp. 147-69; Himmelfarb, *Ascent to Heaven*; C. Morray-Jones, 'The Temple Within: The Embodied Divine Image and its Worship in the Dead Sea Scrolls and Other Early Jewish and Christian Sources', in *Seminar Papers 1998 for Society of Biblical Literature Annual Convention* (Atlanta: Scholars Press, 1998), pp. 400-31; Morray-Jones, *A Transparent Illusion: The Dangerous Vision of Water in Hekhalot Mysticism. A Source-Critical and Tradition-Historical Inquiry* (forthcoming).

102. Cf. the three heavens, see Morray-Jones, 'Paradise Revisited', pp. 203-205. These are replaced by a seven-tier system. On this, refer to A.Y. Collins, 'The Seven Heavens in Jewish and Christian Apocalypses', in J.J. Collins and M. Fishbane (eds.), *Death, Ecstasy and Other Worldly Journeys* (Albany: SUNY, 1995), pp. 62-87.

103. For translation see E. Isaac, *OTP*, I, pp. 13-89. Cf. M. Black, *Apocalypsis Henochi Graece* (PVTG, 3.1; Leiden: E.J. Brill, 1970); Black, *The Book of Enoch or 1 Enoch: A New English Edition* (SVTP, 7; Leiden: E.J. Brill, 1985); J.T. Milik and M. Black, *The Books of Enoch: Aramaic Fragments from Qumran Cave 4* (Oxford: Claredon Press, 1976); M.A. Knibb and E. Ullendorf, *The Ethiopic Book*

earliest accounts of a person ascending through a heavenly shrine of fire (*1 En.* 14.10-14) to a holier shrine within (*1 En.* 14.15-17) where the 'Great Glory' is enthroned (*1 En.* 14.19-20).[104] His throne, like the one in Ezekiel's vision, has 'wheels like the shining sun' (*1 En.* 14.18; cf. Ezek. 1.15-21).

In this passage, we have a reference to the outer sanctuary or *hêkāl* of the Jerusalem Temple and the interior room, the Holy of Holies, ele-vated and transferred to the celestial realms. As he entered the first heavenly shrine, Enoch states that he passed through a wall of hail-stones and fire (*1 En.* 14.9). It is plausible that this refers to the rear wall of the Temple's *'ûlām* or porch through which the priest entered the outer sanctuary.[105] These three structures seem to reflect a cos-mology of three heavens where the wall and shrines occupy the three layers of heaven.[106]

Enoch remarks that 'a flaming fire' surrounded and stood before the Glory so that even the angels could not come too close to him (*1 En.* 14.23). Ten thousand times ten thousand angels stand before the Glory in praise (*1 En.* 14.22-23). These angels are the priests of the supernal Temple who in God's holy chamber 'draw near' to him 'by night or by day', never leaving his presence (*1 En.* 14.22-23).[107] Such a picture of the heavens is similarly recounted by Philo of Alexandria when he states in his tract, *De specialibus legibus*, that 'the highest and truest temple of God' has as its most holy place 'the heaven', as its votive offerings 'the stars', and as its priests 'the angels' who are the ministers of his power (*Spec. Leg.* 1.66).

The *Testament of Levi*[108] recounts an ascent into the heavenly Temple comparable to *1 Enoch*. Researchers have argued that earlier versions of this text rely on a cosmology of three heavens through which Levi

of Enoch: A New Edition in the Light of the Aramaic Dead Sea Fragments (2 vols.; Oxford: Claredon Press, 1978).

104. Himmelfarb, *Ascent to Heaven*, pp. 9-31.

105. Himmelfarb, *Ascent to Heaven*, p. 14.

106. Morray-Jones, 'Paradise Revisited', pp. 203-205; Cf. Himmelfarb, *Ascent to Heaven*, pp. 9-31, who assumes that this is a single heaven.

107. Himmelfarb, *Ascent to Heaven*, pp. 20-23.

108. For translation, see H.C. Kee, *OTP*, I, pp. 788-95; cf. R.H. Charles, *The Tes-taments of the Twelve Patriarchs* (London: A. & C. Black, 1908); H.W. Hollander, H.J. de Jonge, and Th. Korteweg, *The Testaments of the Twelve Patriarchs: A Criti-cal Edition of the Greek Text* (PVTG, 1.2; Leiden: E.J. Brill, 1978).

journeys. Later versions have expanded the heavens to seven.[109] In any case, the uppermost heaven is clearly associated with the celestial Temple. Levi states that 'in the uppermost heaven of all dwells the Great Glory in the Holy of Holies superior to all holiness' (*T. Levi* 3.4). The upper realms are populated with multiple thrones and angels who offer praise to God eternally (*T. Levi* 3.8). Priestly duties are performed by the angels in the *Testament of Levi*. In the upper heavens, bloodless sacrifice on behalf of the sins of the people is made by the angels, the heavenly priests. In Levi's second vision, he ascends again and is put through a priestly consecration ceremony. He is anointed, washed, and fed bread and wine by the angels. Afterwards, he is dressed in priestly garments, indicating his transformation (*T. Levi* 8).

The same is true of the second-century account of Enoch's ascent through seven heavens and his investiture in *2 Enoch*.[110] The sixth and seventh heavens represent the scene of Temple worship where the angelic liturgy is performed at its best (*2 En.* 8–9). Like the Holy of Holies, the seventh heaven is the dwelling place of God's presence upon his throne (*2 En.* 9.9-11). Enoch is brought before God's throne and prostrates himself twice before the deity (*2 En.* 9.8; 9.12-14). Reminiscent of priestly consecration, he is anointed and dressed in 'glorious garments' (*2 En.* 19.17). As we saw earlier, when Enoch sees himself, he reports that he had been transformed into an angel (*2 En.* 9.19).

Although the *Apocalypse of Abraham* does not explicitly equate its seven heavens with chambers of the celestial Temple, it alludes to this. This is particularly clear in the fact that just as priests make sacrifices on the altar outside the Jerusalem Temple, Abraham must perform sacrifices before ascending into the heavens (*Apoc. Abr.* 9–16). In addition, he must recite the proper liturgy before he is allowed access to the highest heaven (*Apoc. Abr.* 17). Once admitted into the seventh heaven, the scene described belongs to speculations about Ezekiel's visions of God's throne:

109. R.H. Charles, *The Greek Versions of the Testaments of the Twelve Patriarchs* (repr.; Oxford: Oxford University Press, 1960), p. xxviii; Kee, *OTP*, I, pp. 775-80 and 788-89 nn. 2d and 3a; Rowland, *Open Heaven*, p. 81; Collins, 'Seven Heavens', pp. 62-66; Morray-Jones, 'Paradise Revisited', pp. 202-203; Morray-Jones, 'The Temple Within'.

110. For translation, see F.I. Anderson's, *OTP*, I, pp. 102-221. Cf. A. Vaillant, *Le livre des secrets d'Hénoch: Texte slave et traduction française* (Paris: Institut d'études slaves, 1976).

> And as the fire rose up, soaring to the highest point, I saw under the fire a throne of fire and the many-eyed ones round about, reciting song, under the throne four fiery living creatures, singing. And the appearance of each of them was the same, each having four faces. And this (was) the aspect of their faces: of a lion, of a man, of an ox, and of an eagle. Each one had four heads on its body so that the four living creatures had sixteen faces... And while I was still standing and watching, I saw behind the living creatures a chariot with fiery wheels... (*Apoc. Abr.* 18.3-12).

There is no doubt that Abraham has entered the Holy of Holies, the highest of the heavens.

The fragments of the *Apocalypse of Zephaniah*[111] also recount a journey through various heavens. According to a reference from this text preserved by Clement of Alexandria, the angels who lived in these heavens were enthroned in Temple shrines and participating in heavenly liturgy:

> And a spirit took me and brought me up into the fifth heaven. And I saw angels who are called 'lords', and the diadem was set upon them in the Holy Spirit, and the throne of each of them was sevenfold more (brilliant) than the light of the rising sun. (And they were) dwelling in the temples of salvation and singing hymns to the ineffable most high God (*Stromata* 5.11.77).

The Qumran literature suggests that these ideas were not merely imaginative stories in texts.[112] In this first-century community, these ideas were communal beliefs connected with living liturgical practices. Because the Qumranites believed that the Jerusalem Temple was defiled and its priesthood corrupt, they seem to have turned their attention to developing a cult of the celestial Temple. This is quite vivid in the liturgical text, *Songs of the Sabbath Sacrifice*, which describes the throne-room of God as a heavenly Temple and the angels as God's priests.[113]

---

111. Translated by O.S. Wintermute in *OTP*, I, pp. 508-15. Cf. G. Steindorff, *Das Apokalypse des Elias, eine unbekannte Apokalypse und Bruchstücke der Sophonias-Apokalypse* (TU, 17; Berlin: Akademic Verlag, 1899); H.P. Houghton, 'The Coptic Apocalypse', *Aegyptus* 39 (1959), pp. 43-67, 177-210.

112. Cf. Himmelfarb, *Ascent to Heaven*, pp. 3-8, 95-114. For other contrasting studies, see Halperin, *The Merkabah*; Halperin, *Faces of the Chariot*; Schäfer, 'Tradition and Redaction'; Schäfer, 'Aim and Purpose'; Schäfer, 'Merkavah Mysticis', pp. 537-54.

113. Newsom, *Songs*; *idem*, 'Merkavah Exegesis in the Qumran Sabbath Shirot', *JSJ* 38 (1987), pp. 11-30; J. Strugnell, 'The Angelic Liturgy at Qumran' (VTSup, 7; Leiden: E.J. Brill, 1960), pp. 318-45; Schiffman, 'Merkavah Speculation', pp. 14-47;

The text itself consists of thirteen songs to be performed on the first thirteen Sabbaths of each year. The intent of the Qumranites was to establish and maintain a state of purity so that, through these songs, they could engage in the heavenly worship service before God's *mer-kābâ*, communing with the angels and sharing in their priestly duties. The songs begin by praising God and addressing the angels. Several of the songs provide a liturgical journey through the lower sanctuaries of the Temple and its courts. Through the performance of this liturgy, the participant is taken into the Holy of Holies in order to join the angelic worship before God's throne.

Thus, our first certain reference to a Merkavah vision occurs in the Qumran literature, a literature that may represent a community of Jewish mystics who liturgically built the heavenly Temple in their midst each Sabbath and entered it to worship alongside the angels before God's throne-chariot (cf. 4Q400-407, 11Q17, 4Q286-87 and 4Q491). It was probably the intent of the Qumranites to establish and maintain a state of purity so that, through the singing of the liturgical songs, they could engage in heavenly worship and gaze mystically on God on his throne-chariot. In various texts found at the Dead Sea (1QH XIV 13-14; 1QH XIX 20-23; 1QH XIX 10-14; 1QH XXIII 10; 1QS XI 5-10), the Qumranites insist that they actually belong to the congregation of angels. In a fragmentary poem, the author claims to have ascended into heaven and taken a seat there, 'reckoned with gods and established in the holy congregation'.[114] Even though the Qumran texts do not explicitly state that the goal of the journey into the celestial Temple is visionary, this certainly is implied since their liturgical songs describe the heavens in great detail, making it possible for the practioner to visualize his movement through the *hêkālôt* into the Holy of Holies where he can view God and worship him appropriately. The evidence

J. Baumgarten, 'The Qumran Sabbath Shirot and Rabbinic Merkabah Traditions', *RQ* 13 (1988), pp. 199-213; S. Segert, 'Observations on Poetic Structures in the Songs of the Sabbath Sacrifice', *RQ* 13 (1988), p. 215-23; B. Nitzan, *Qumran Prayer and Religious Poetry* (STDJ, 12; Leiden: E.J. Brill, 1994), pp. 273-311; Morray-Jones, 'The Temple Within'; C. Fletcher-Louis, 'Ascent to Heaven and the Embodiment of Heaven: A Revisionist Reading of the Songs of the Sabbath Sacrifice' (SBLSP; Atlanta: Scholars Press, 1998), pp. 367-99.

114. M. Smith, 'Two Ascended to Heaven: Jesus and the Author of 4Q491', in J.H. Charlesworth (ed.), *Jesus and the Dead Sea Scrolls* (New York: Doubleday, 1992), pp. 290-301.

seems to support the conclusion that the Qumranites actually were practicing ascent through the esoteric Temple by means of liturgy.[115] According to Christopher Morray-Jones, they may even have been ritually constructing the ideal Temple through liturgical performance and intensive visualization.[116]

4. *Conclusion*

One of the objects of this work is to expand our knowledge of vision mysticism in early first-century Christianity by viewing the Gospel of John as a product of this horizon.[117] It is not a new observation that early Christianity was characterized by a variety of soteriological systems. The vision mystical form has often been overlooked, perhaps because research on soteriology largely has focused on New Testament literature which does not develop a mystical scheme of salvation to any great extent.

This does not mean that the New Testament literature is unaware of this salvific pattern. It is certainly alluded to in 2 Cor. 3.18 where Paul states that the vision of the Glory initiates a metamorphosis into the divine likeness:

> And we all, with unveiled face, beholding in a mirror the Glory of the Lord, are being changed into his likeness from one degree of Glory to another for this comes from the lord, who is the Spirit (ἡμεῖς δὲ πάντες

---

115. M. Smith, *Clement of Alexandria and a Secret Gospel of Mark* (Cambridge, MA: Harvard University Press, 1973), pp. 239-40; Smith, 'Ascent to the Heavens', pp. 411-12; Smith, 'Two Ascended to Heaven', pp. 290-301; see also, Strugnell, 'Angelic Liturgy', pp. 318-45; Scholem, *Jewish Gnosticism*, pp. 29, 128; Schiffman, 'Merkavah Speculation', pp. 14-47; Newsom, *Songs*; Newsom, 'Merkavah Exegesis', pp. 11-30.

116. Morray-Jones, 'The Temple Within'.

117. For previous work on the subject of mysticism in early Christianity, see Rowland, *Open Heaven*; J. Fossum, *The Name of God and the Angel of the Lord* (WUNT, 36; Tüingen: J.C.B. Mohr, 1985); Fossum, 'Jewish–Christian Christology and Jewish Mysticism', *VC* 37 (1983), pp. 260-87, Fossum, 'The Magharians: A Pre-Christian Jewish Sect and its Significance for the Study of Gnosticism and Christianity', *Henoch* 9 (1987), pp. 303-44; Fossum, 'Colossians 1.15-18a in the Light of Jewish Mysticism and Gnosticism', *NTS* 35 (1989), pp. 183-201; G. Stroumsa, 'Form(s) of God: Some Notes on Metatron and Christ', *HTR* 76 (1985), pp. 269-88; Segal, *Paul the Convert*, pp. 34-71; Morray-Jones, 'Paradise Revisited', pp. 177-217, 265-92.

ἀνακεκαλυμμένῳ προσώπῳ τὴν δόξαν κυρίου κατοπριζόμενοι τὴν αὐτὴν εἰκόνα μεταμορφούμεθα ἀπὸ δόξης εἰς δόξαν καθάπερ ἀπὸ κυρίου πνεύματος).[118]

Even though this passage has received an enormous amount of scholarly energy, I wish to draw attention solely to the motif that those who see the Glory are transformed into the Glory.[119] It is arguable that Paul speaks here of the face-to-face encounter with one's self by implementing the middle form of the verb κατοπτρίζω which means 'to produce one's own image in a mirror' or 'to behold oneself in a mirror'.[120] This rendering suggests that the vision is a vision of one's divine self. When one sees oneself in a mirror, one is viewing the Lord's Glory. This vision creates change, transforming the person, degree by degree, *into* the divine Glory which is seen in the mirror.[121] It is obvious that this

118. For a fuller discussion of this passage, refer to DeConick, *Seek to See Him*, pp. 170-71.

119. Recently, Segal, *Paul the Convert*, p. 60, noted that 'Paul's use of the language of transformation often goes unappreciated' as is the case in 2 Cor. 3.18 where the Christian beholds the *kābôd* as 'in a mirror and are transformed into his image'. On possible connections with bowl divination, see Segal, *Paul the Convert*, pp. 323-24 n. 94. It has been argued that the mystical beholding in 2 Cor. 3.18 has been divested by Paul of its authentic mystical sense since the moment of beholding, for Paul, is primarily Christian worship. On this, see R. Bultmann, *The Second Letter to the Corinthians* (ed. E. Dinkler; trans. R.A. Harrisville, Minneapolis, 1985), p. 96.

120. LSJ, 'κατοπρίζω'; cf. J. Dupont, 'Le chrétien, miroir de la gloire divine d'après 2 Cor. III,18', *RB* 56 (1949), pp. 394-95; P. Corssen, 'Paulus und Porphyrios (Zur Erklärung von 2 Kor 3,18)', *ZNW* 19 (1920), pp. 2-10; N. Hugedé, *La métaphore du miroir dans les Epitres de saint Paul aux Corinthians* (Neuchâtel and Paris, 1957), pp. 52-62; Bultmann, *Second Corinthians*, pp. 90-96. For the translation 'to behold as in a mirror', refer to L.L. Belleville, *Reflections of Glory: Paul's Polemical Use of the Moses-Doxa Tradition in 2 Corinthians 3.1-18* (JSNTSup, 52; Sheffield: JSOT Press, 1991), p. 279 n. 3. For the translation 'to reflect', see Belleville, *Reflections of Glory*, pp. 280-81 and n. 1 on both pages where the classic work by W.C. van Unnik, '"With Unveiled Face", an Exegesis of 2 Corinthians iii 12-18', *NovT* 6 (1963), pp. 153-69, is noted.

121. See R. Reitzenstein, *Historia Monachorum und Historia Lausiaca: Eine Studie zur Geschichte des Mönchtums und der frühchristlichen Begriffe Gnostiker und Pneumatiker* (FRLANT, 24; Göttingen: Vandenhoeck & Ruprecht, 1916) pp. 242-55; I. Hermann, *Kyrios und Pneuma* (Munich: Kösel, 1961), p. 55; H. Windisch, *Der zweite Korintherbrief* (Göttingen: Vandenhoeck & Ruprecht, 1924), p. 128; C. Wagner, 'Gotteserkenntnis im Spiegel und Gottesliebe in den beiden Korintherbriefen', *Bijdragen* 19 (1958), pp. 380-81. Bultmann, *Second*

text belongs to one of the oldest strata of vision mysticism of early Christianity. Other Pauline passages that speak of being transformed into Christ or his image should probably be understood as echoes of this type of mytical soteriology (cf. Gal. 4.19; Rom. 8.29; 12.2; Phil. 2.5; 3.20-21; 1 Cor. 15.49; 2 Cor. 5.17; Col. 3.9-10).

Similarly in 1 Jn 3.2, we find a reference to transformation into the divine as the result of a *visio Dei*:[122]

> Beloved, we are God's children now; it does not yet appear what we shall be, but we know that when he appears we shall be like him, because we shall see him as he is (οἴδαμεν ὅτι ἐὰν φανερωθῇ, ὅμοιοι αὐτῷ ἐσόμεθα, ὅτι ὀψόμεθα αὐτὸν καθώς ἐστιν).

It appears that here we find that the visionary experience and the transformation has been postponed from the present moment to the indefinite future (cf. Col. 3.4). This transposes the experience from the realm of mysticism to the realm of eschatology. This combination of Greek mysteriosophy (transformation by gaze) and Jewish eschatology (transformation of the righteous in the eschaton) has not been sufficiently pointed out by previous exegetes.[123] As we shall see later, it is significant that we find this happening in the Johannine corpus.

We might also mention the Christian–Jewish apocalypse from the late first or early second century, the *Ascension of Isaiah*.[124] It seems to belong to this vision mystical trajectory as well. According to the text, Isaiah ascends through the first five heavens. He sees in each celestial realm an enthroned angel with other angels flanking him and offering his praise. The praise of the angels is directed toward God who resides far above in the seventh heaven (*Asc. Isa.* 7.17). As Isaiah ascends, he is progressively transformed, until he reaches the seventh heaven. In

---

Corinthians, p. 95, notes that 'the meaning is not that we are changed into a "likeness" of the Kyrios, but rather that we are made like his essence, thus also become δόξα...we are changed into that which we behold'. Cf. Rom. 8.29; Phil. 3.21. Thus, Bultmann understands the vision to be that of the 'essence' not the 'form'.

122. Cf. R. Bultmann, *The Johannine Epistles*, (ed. R.W. Funk; trans. R.P. O'Hara, L.C. McGaughy, and R.W. Funk; Hermeneia; Philadelphia: Fortress Press, 1973), pp. 48-49.

123. The best commentary on this is by R. Schnackenburg, *The Johannine Epistles* (New York: Crossroad, 1992), although the religio-historical derivations are not sufficiently distinguished.

124. For translation, see M.A. Knibb, *OTP*, II, pp. 156-76; cf. R.H. Charles, *The Ascension of Isaiah* (London: A. & C. Black, 1900).

this heaven, Isaiah sees the souls of the righteous dead gazing 'intently upon the Glory'. Isaiah and the angels make quick glances at God (*Asc. Isa.* 9.37-38). It is in this heaven that Isaiah is completely transformed into an angel (*Asc. Isa.* 9.30).

As we have seen, broadly speaking, the tenets of vision mysticism in the ancient Greco-Roman world at the time of the composition of the Johannine Gospel taught that in order to have life, one could ascend to heaven and view the deity. This *visio Dei* transformed the person into the divine. Such is the Religio-historical Horizon that informed the discourses about heavenly ascent and visionary experience in the Gospel of John.

It is to this horizon that John is reacting when he makes the statements that no one has ascended into heaven except Jesus nor has anyone ever seen the Father except the Son. Moreover, it is from this horizon that John will draw meaningful images in order to create his own peculiar soteriology. By so doing, he keeps this soteriology relevant to his audience. At the same time that he articulates with the Religio-historical Horizon, he disarticulates from it in order to remain faithful to his community's experiences and teachings.

Chapter 3

JOHANNINE POLEMIC AGAINST VISION MYSTICISM: THE TRADITIO-
RELIGIOUS HORIZON AND THE POINT OF DISCOURSE[1]

> You will seek me and you will not find me;
> where I am you cannot come
>
> (John 7.34).

It seems that the Gospel of John was in discourse with some variety of
mystical ascent theology popular in first-century Jewish and Christian
esoteric circles. The Johannine discourse certainly intersects with the
Religio-historical Horizon of vision mysticism as discussed in the previous chapter. The time has arrived, however, to focus on a more specific target. That is, can we determine the Traditio-religious Horizon of
the Johannine community and its Point of Discourse?

In order to answer this question, we must first proceed by determin-
ing more exactly the Point of Discourse that John has identified. I suggest that analysis of three major passages, Jn 14.3-7; 14.20-23; and
20.24-29, will identify more precisely the Point of Discourse according
to John. In this identification, John's Traditio-religious Horizon will be
mirrored. It must be recognized that this horizon will only be reflective
of Johannine space and thus will only bear a relative relationship to the
historical event of the discourse itself.

---

1.   A short version of this chapter was presented to the faculty and students of
the Department of Philosophy and Religion at Colgate University under the title,
'Faith Mysticism in the Gospel of John: The Johannine Response to Ascent and
Vision Mysticism' (13 December 1993, Hamilton, New York), and to the Thomas
Christianity Consultation at the annual SBL convention in Philadelphia, 1995,
under the title: '"Blessed are those who have not seen" (Jn 20.29): Johannine Polemic Against the Mystical Thomas Tradition.' Since then, an earlier version of this
chapter was published as, ''Blessed are those who have not seen' (Jn 20.29): Johan-
nine Dramatization of an Early Christian Discourse', in J.D. Turner and A. McGuire,
*The Nag Hammadi Library After Fifty Years: Proceedings of the 1995 Society of
Biblical Literature Commemoration* (Leiden: E.J. Brill, 1997), pp. 381-98.

1. *John 14.3-7*

The dialogue in the first of these passages, Jn 14.3-7, centers around the crucial term 'the way (ἡ ὁδός)':

> 'And when I go and prepare a place for you, I will come again and will take you to myself, that where I am you may be also. And you know the way (τὴν ὁδόν) where I am going'. Thomas said to him, 'Lord, we do not know where you are going; how can we know the way (τὴν ὁδόν)?' Jesus said to him, 'I am the way (ἡ ὁδός), and the truth, and the life; no one comes to the Father, but by me. If you had known me, you would have known my Father also; henceforth you know him and have seen him'.

According to R. Bultmann, 'the way' is a reference to the mythology that, when the soul separates from the body, it journeys to the sacred realm often guided by a superior being.[2] In other words, it is the route to heaven and divinity.

A vivid instance of this in Christian literature is seen in the Syrian *Odes of Solomon* 39.9-13,[3] where the Lord's footsteps to heaven create a path for his own to follow and, in this manner, 'the Way has been appointed for those who cross over after him, and for those who adhere

2. R. Bultmann, *The Gospel of John: A Commentary* (trans. G.R. Beasley-Murray; eds. R.W.N. Hoare and J.K. Riches; Oxford: Basil Blackwell, 1971), pp. 603ff. where he refers to Hipp., *El.* 5.10.2, 5.16.1, 5.26.23; *Exc. Theo.* 38, 74; Iren., *Adv. Haer.* 1.13.6; 1.21.5; Epiph., *Pan.* 36.3.2-5; Origen *c. Celsus* 6.31; *Acts Thom.* 148, 167; *Odes Sol.* 39.9ff. [cp. 7.3, 13f.; 11.3; 22.7, 11; 24.13; 33.7ff.; 41.11]; *Mand. Lit.* 38, 77, 97f., 101, 132f., 134f.; *Joh.-B.* 198.20f., 199.3f., 239.14; *Ginza* 95.15, 247.16ff., 271.26f., 395.3ff., 429.17ff., 439.14ff., 487.8ff., 523.23ff., 550.1ff; *CH* 1.26, 1.29, 4.11, 7.2, 9.10, 10.21. He states that the parabolic usage of the way in the Old Testament (e.g. Ps. 143.10; Isa. 63.14) is of little revelance here, p. 604 n. 5. Furthermore, he notes that 'the way' belongs together with 'the door' in 10.7 which mythologically represents the entrance into life or the world of light, 377-78 n. 7, 604 n. 5. Cf. Bultmann, 'Die Bedeutung der neuerschlossenen mandäischen und manichäischen Quellen für das Verständnis des Johannesevangeliums', *ZNW* 24 (1925), pp. 100-146, esp. p. 135. Odeberg, *Fourth Gospel*, pp. 319-27, convincingly argues that the expression 'door' in Jn 10.9 refers to the door or gate of heaven being opened and is the same spiritual reality as described in Jn 1.51.

3. J.H. Bernard, *The Odes of Solomon* (Texts and Studies, 8.3; Cambridge: Cambridge University Press, 1912); J.H. Charlesworth, *The Odes of Solomon* (Oxford: Clarendon Press, 1973).

to the path of his faith; and who adore his name' (*Odes Sol.* 39.13). In *Ode* 11, the hymnist tells us that 'I ran in the Way in his peace, in the Way of truth' (*Odes Sol.* 11.3). This verse functions as the beginning of a song about the hymnist's ascent to Paradise (*Odes Sol.* 11.16), his vision of the Lord (*Odes Sol.* 11.13), and his transformation into a light-being (*Odes Sol.* 11.11). The Lord caused the mystic odist to 'ascend from the regions below' (*Odes Sol.* 22.1) and this is the Lord's 'Way' which is 'incorruptible' (*Odes Sol.* 22.11).

This use of the concept 'the way' as the heavenly route is already present in Judaism as evidenced in Philo. In *De migratione Abrahami* 168-75, Philo explains that Exod. 24.1, 'Come up to thy Lord, thou and Aaron and Nadab and Abihu and seventy of the Senate of Israel', means that the soul must 'come up' to 'behold the Existent One' (*Migr. Abr.* 169). Furthermore, Aaron who symbolizes combining understanding and speech, Nadab who symbolizes voluntarily honoring the deity, and Abihu who symbolizes having need of God, are 'the powers that form the bodyguard of the mind' (*Migr. Abr.* 170). These 'bodyguards' are necessary because 'the soul has reason to fear ascending in its own strength to the sight of Him that IS, ignorant as it is of *the way* (τὴν ὁδόν)' (*Migr. Abr.* 170).[4] So Moses, Philo's paradigm mystic, in Exod. 33.15 'prays that he may have God Himself, to guide him to *the way* that leads to Him (τὴν πρὸς αὐτὸν ἄγουσαν ὁδόν)' (*Migr. Abr.* 171).[5] Philo warns unprepared mystics, however, that it is better to forego mystic ascent and roam through mortal life, than to ascend without 'divine direction' and become shipwrecked along *the way* (*Migr. Abr.* 171).

The study of J. Pascher indicates that Philo interprets the 'royal way (βασιλικὴ ὁδός)' of Num. 20.17 as the way to the knowledge and vision of God.[6] Philo describes the 'royal way' as the road of 'wisdom' by which the 'souls can make their escape to the Uncreated. For we may well believe that he who walks unimpeded along the King's way

4. F.H. Colson and G.H. Whitaker, *Philo*, IV (LCL; Cambridge, MA: Harvard University Press, 1932 and reprints), pp. 230-31; my emphasis.

5. Colson and Whitaker, *Philo*, IV, pp. 230-31.

6. J. Pascher, *Η ΒΑΣΙΛΙΚΗ ΟΔΟΣ: Der Königsweg zu Wiedergeburt und Vergottung bei Philon von Alexandreia* (Studien zur Geschichte und Kultur des Altertums, 17.3-4; Paderbuorn: F. Schöningh, 1931). Cf. E.R. Goodenough, *By Light* (Amsterdam: Philo Press, 1969), who understands the 'way' to be the Mystic Road to God (pp. 14, 136, 145, 214, 219, 244, 280, 316, 355-56).

(ὁδοῦ τῆς βασιλικῆς) will never flag or faint, till he comes into the presence of the King' (*Deus Imm.* 159-61).[7] Philo explains that the 'royal way' is the eternal and indestructible way described in Gen. 6.12 which leads to the recognition and knowledge of God; those who are endowed with 'vision', that is Israel, are able to journey along this road although they will be tempted to swerve off course by the earthly senses (*Deus Imm.* 142-44, cf. 162; *Gig.* 64; *Migr. Abr.* 146).

Philo's employment of ὁδός in the technical sense as the road to heavenly ascent and vision is similar to the manner in which Hermeticism uses ὁδός. In *CH* 4.11, Hermes tells Tat that 'if your vision of it [God's image] is sharp and you understand it with the eyes of your heart, believe me, child, you shall discover *the way* that leads above (τὴν πρὸς τὰ ἄνω ὁδόν) or, rather, the image itself will show you *the way* (ὁδηγήσει)'. He continues by informing Tat that vision has a special drawing power, taking hold of the mystic and drawing him up to God like a 'magnet stone draws iron' (cf. *CH* 1.26-27). In the *Excerpts of Stobaeus* 6.18, Hermes explains that the one who has seen God is blessed but this visionary experience is not possible while one is in the body. One 'must train his soul in this life, in order that, when it has entered the other world, where it is permitted to see God, it may not miss *the way* (ὁδοῦ) <which leads to Him>'.

Since the goal of the ascent and vision is to become divinized like Hermes, *the way* of Hermes is '*the way* of immortality (ⲉⲟⲓⲏ ⲛⲧⲙⲛⲧⲁⲧⲙⲟⲩ)', the ascent to the ninth heavenly sphere (*Disc. 8–9* 63.10-14; cf. *CH* 10.7; 13.3).[8] As we saw in Chapter 1, this immortalization is the result of vision of God. So the Hermetics speak of the experience of becoming God (*CH* 13.3, 10, 14) by casting off materiality, ascending to heaven, and being absorbed into God (*CH* 1.24-26; 10.13; *Disc. 8–9* 57.28–58.22; cf. *CH* 11.20; 12.1; *Asc.* 6.22). Thus, they explain: 'If you ask about god, you ask also about the beautiful. Only one *way* (ὁδὸς) travels from here to the beautiful—reverence combined with knowledge' (*CH* 6.5; cf. 11.22).[9]

---

7.   F.H. Colson and G.H. Whitaker, *Philo*, III (LCL; Cambridge, MA, 1930 and reprints), pp. 90-91.

8.   For an excellent summary of the Hermetic immortalization process, see J.-P. Mahé, 'La voie d'immortalité á la lumière des *Hermetica* de Nag Hammadi et de découvertes plus récentes', *VC* 45 (1991), pp. 347-75.

9.   A.D. Nock and A.-J. Festugière, *Corpus Hermeticum*. I. *Traités I–XII* (Paris: Société d'édition les belles lettres, 1945), p. 75.

A passage from the *Excerpts of Stobaeus* 2B.3-8 contains a synthesis of this theology. Tat is taught about 'the only *way* that leads to Reality (ἡ πρὸς ἀλήθειαν ὁδός)' (2B.5).[10] This way is a 'holy and divine way (ὁδός)' which is difficult to travel while the soul 'is in the body' (2B.5).[11] The soul must feud against the vices and strive toward the Good (2B.6-7). Once the soul has won this contest, it is able to 'mount upward' and begin the 'journey to the world above' (2B.8). The soul yearns for the Good and must learn to know the Father so that the soul is freed and will not fail 'to know whither it must wing its upward flight' (2B.3-4).

Connected to this is the discussion in *Corpus Hermeticum* 13 where Tat inquires about the way to be 'born again' (*CH* 13.3). Hermes explains that he is incapable of relating anything about this except to share a specific visionary experience when he left his human body and assumed 'an immortal body (ἀθάνατον σῶμα)' (*CH* 13.3).[12] He goes on to describe a vision of his spiritual Self. He tells Tat that the Self must be cleansed of the twelve vices under the influence of the ten powers of God. Hermes, of course, is refering to the way of ascent through the planetary spheres, the removal of particular vices at each sphere, and the final absorption into the divine (cf. *CH* 1.24-26).[13] Once this has happened, the new spiritual birth is possible and with it, divinity (*CH* 13.10). Thus the road of ascent and vision is the way of rebirth.[14]

It is significant that all these texts, whether describing pre- or post-mortem ascent, agree that ὁδός means the path that the soul will journey when it goes to heaven. It is quite certain that the Johannine author employs the terminology 'the way' in this technical sense. Thus

---

10. A.-J. Festugière, *Corpus Hermeticum. III. Fragments extraits de Stobée I–XXII* (Paris: Société d'édition les belles lettres, 1954), p. 14.

11. Festugière, *Corpus Hermeticum*, III, p. 14.

12. A.D. Nock and A.-J. Festugière, *Corpus Hermeticum*, II, *Traités XIII–XVIII, Asclépius* (Paris: Société d'édition les belles lettres, 1945), p. 201.

13. Refer to A.D. DeConick, *Seek to See Him: Ascent and Vision Mysticism in the Gospel of Thomas* (VCSup, 33; Leiden: E.J. Brill, 1996), pp. 136-47, for a discussion of the role of the vices and virtues in ascent patterns.

14. C.H. Dodd, *The Interpretation of the Fourth Gospel* (Cambridge: Cambridge University Press, 1953), pp. 44-53, discusses *CH* 13 and notes 'expressions which recall the language of the Fourth Gospel and the First Epistle of John' including the notion of rebirth. He argues that there lie 'real similarities in thought' behind these verbal parallels (p. 49). He provides a useful chart which compares passages from *CH* 13 and John (pp. 50-51).

Thomas's reply makes sense: 'Lord, we do not know where you are going; how can we know the way?' (14.5). It appears that Thomas's answer reflects the popular association of ὁδός with proleptic heavenly ascents.

At the same time, the disciple Thomas is portrayed by the Johannine author as the fool in this discourse because of this ignorant statement.[15] Clearly, in this passage, the Johannine author attributes to Thomas the confession that he *and* others with him are ignorant of the true way or route to heaven.

It is probable that here we see evidence of the textualization of discourse from the point of view of the Johannine community. The author, by deliberately characterizing Thomas as a fool in this passage, condemns the hero of the Thomasine Christians. Moreover, his articulation of the discourse points to a particular feature of the dispute: the journey or ascent to heaven. John tells us that such ascent is not necessary, that Jesus himself is the only 'way' into heaven. This is stated in contradistinction to the Thomasine belief which, from Thomas's answer in 14.5, appears to have encouraged proleptic heavenly ascents.

2. *John 14.20-23*

The next pericope that requires attention is Jn 14.20-23 where a certain Judas who is distinguished from Judas Iscariot ('Ιούδας οὐχ ὁ Ἰσκαριώτης)[16] is given the dunce cap:

> In that day you will know that I am in my Father, and you in me, and I in you. He who has my commandments and keeps them, he it is who loves me; and he who loves me will be loved by my Father, and I will love him and manifest (ἐμφανίσω) myself to him'. Judas (not Iscariot) ('Ιούδας οὐχ ὁ Ἰσκαριώτης) said to him, 'Lord, how is it that you will manifest (ἐμφανίζειν) yourself to us, and not to the world?' Jesus answered him, 'If a man loves me, he will keep my word, and my Father will love him, and we will come to him and make our home with him'.

Judas is concerned about the method by which the followers of Jesus will be able to have a vision of Jesus when he is not in the 'world'

---

15. Cf. J.H. Charlesworth, *The Beloved Disciple: Whose Witness Validates the Gospel of John?* (Valley Forge, PA: Trinity Press International, 1995), esp. pp. 261-64.

16. The gloss, 'not Iscariot', was probably added to this passage by the Johannine redactor since Judas Iscariot had left the scene earlier.

anymore. Judas has interpreted the phrase 'manifest myself to him (ἐμφανίσω αὐτῷ ἐμαυτόν)' to refer to a theophany since he demands to know how the followers of Jesus will be able to behold the manifestation while others in the world will not see it.

The word ἐμφανίζειν is used only in the New Testament in Jn 14.21-22 in this sense, but it is a word that is associated with the theophany in Exod. 33.13, 18 which is quoted by Philo in *Leg. All.* 3.101. He states that Moses represents the 'mind more perfect and more thoroughly cleansed, which has undergone initiation into the great mysteries' and which lifts its eyes 'above and beyond creation' and 'obtains a clear vision (ἔμφασιν) of the uncreated One' (*Leg. All.* 3.100). Thus Moses says in Exod. 33.13: 'Manifest Thyself to me (Ἐμφάνισόν μοι σαυτόν), let me see Thee that I may know Thee (γνωστῶς ἴδω σε)' (*Leg. All.* 3.101). Philo exegetes this passage, stating that Moses meant that he did not want God to 'be manifested (ἐμφανισθείης)' to him 'by means of heaven or earth or water or air or any created thing at all' (*Leg. All.* 3.101). He believed that one can only receive 'the clear vision (ἔμφασιν) of God directly from the First Cause Himself' (*Leg. All.* 3.102).[17] Thus Philo employs the term ἐμφανίζειν to describe the vision of God himself.

According to the Johannine author, it is actually a misunderstanding that Judas expects Jesus' manifestation to be a theophany. When Jesus speaks of manifesting himself in the future to his followers, according to John, he intends to do this through a manifestation of divine love, not through a mystical visionary encounter such as that which Judas is anticipating.

The identity of this 'Judas' is arguably linked with the Syrian Thomas tradition where the apostle Thomas has the unique appellation 'Judas Thomas'.[18] The author of the *Gospel of Thomas* is named, 'Didymos Judas Thomas (ⲆⲓⲆⲨⲘⲞⲤ ⲒⲞⲨⲆⲀⲤ ⲐⲰⲘⲀⲤ)' (Prologue) while the *Book of Thomas the Athlete* is said to be the writing of Matthaias as

17. F.H. Colson and G.H. Whitaker, *Philo*, I (LCL; Cambridge, MA: Harvard University Press, 1929 and reprints), pp. 368-69.

18. H.-Ch. Puech, 'The Gospel of Thomas', in E. Hennecke and W. Schneemelcher (eds.), *New Testament Apocrypha* (trans. R.McL. Wilson; Philadelphia: Westminster Press, 1963), pp. 278-307; followed by H. Koester, 'GNOMAI DIAPHOROI: The Origin and Nature of Diversification in the History of Early Christianity', in J.M. Robinson and H. Koestler (eds.), *Trajectories through Early Christianity* (Philadephia: Fortress Press, 1971), pp. 127-28.

it was spoken to 'Judas Thomas (ιογΔΔC ΘωΜΔC)' (*Thom. Cont.* 138.2).[19] The Greek *Acts of Thomas* introduce him as 'Judas Thomas who is also Didymos (Ἰούδα Θῶμας τῷ καὶ Δίδυμῳ)',[20] while generally the Syriac reads 'Judas Thomas the Apostle'.[21] In the oldest extant Syriac version of the *Acts of Thomas*, however, the principle character is simply called 'Judas'.[22] When Eusebius quotes the text of the Abgar Edessian legend, he uses 'Judas who is also Thomas' (Ἰούδας ὁ καὶ Θωμᾶς),[23] but in his own summary, he only writes 'Thomas' (Θωμᾶς) (1.13.4; 2.1.6).[24] In all these instances, however, in the Syriac translation of Eusebius, 'Judas Thomas' is supplied.[25] In the *Doctrine of Addai*, the apostle is known as 'Judas Thomas'.[26] Significantly, according to the Syrian tradition, the apostle in Jn 14.22 is known as 'Judas Thomas' or 'Thomas' in the Curetonian Syriac version of Jn 14.22, 'Judas, not Iscariot' reads 'Judas Thomas' while Codex Syrus Sinaiticus reads simply, 'Thomas'.

What these traditions suggest is that in addition to Judas Iscariot, there was a disciple of Jesus whose actual name was 'Judas'. At some point in time, Judas received the nickname 'the Twin': Δίδυμος ('twin') is a Greek rendition of the Aramaic אמאת ('twin') which has

---

19. J.D. Turner, *The Book of Thomas the Contender from Codex II of the Cairo Gnostic Library from Nag Hammadi (CG II,7): The Coptic Text with Translation, Introduction, and Commentary* (SBLDS, 23; Missoula, MT: Scholars Press, 1975), pp. 8-9.

20. A.F.J. Klijn, *The Acts of Thomas: Introduction, Text, Commentary* (NovTSup, 5; Leiden: E.J. Brill, 1962), p. 158.

21. Klijn, *Acts of Thomas*, p. 5.

22. In the fifth- or sixth-century fragmentary manuscript, *Acta Mythologica Apostolorum* (ed. A. Smith Lewis; Horae Semiticae, 3 and 4; London, 1904); in the complete tenth-century Syriac manuscript, the name 'Judas' is found, but this has afterwards been changed into 'Thomas'; for a complete discussion, refer to A.F.J. Klijn, 'John XIV 22 and the Name Judas Thomas', in *Studies in John presented to Professor Dr. J.N. Sevenster on the occasion of his Seventieth Birthday* (NovTSup, 24; Leiden: E.J. Brill, 1970), p. 92.

23. K. Lake, *Eusebius: The Ecclesiastical History*, I (2 vols.; LCL; Cambridge, MA: Harvard University Press, 1926), pp. 90-91.

24. Lake, *Eusebius: The Ecclesiastical History*, I, pp. 86-87, 106-107 respectively.

25. Klijn, *Acts of Thomas*, p. 158.

26. G. Howard, *The Teaching of Addai* (Texts and Translations, 16; Early Christian Literature Series, 4; Chico, CA: Scholars Press, 1981), pp. 10-11.

been transliterated into Greek letters as θωμᾶ(ς).[27] Thus the Syrian Thomas tradition preserves the primitive name of their hero 'Judas' along with the honorific title the 'Twin'. Other traditions such as those found in Matthew, Mark, Luke, and John remember this apostle as simply 'Thomas'.

These traditions point to the probability that there was a disciple who was known as 'Judas' in the earliest traditions. In order to differentiate him from Judas Iscariot, the nickname 'Thomas' or 'Twin' was appended to Judas probably at an early date: thus, 'Judas Thomas' is preserved in the Syrian traditions. Eventually the name 'Judas' fell out of favor because it was so closely linked to the man who betrayed Jesus. As the name 'Judas' became unfavorable, 'Judas' was dropped in some traditions and the disciple was addressed by his nickname 'Thomas' or 'Twin'.[28]

That John was aware of the fact that 'Thomas' was only a title meaning 'Twin' and not the actual name is evidenced in John's phrase ὁ λεγόμενος Δίδυμος which is added to the name Thomas in Jn 11.16, 20.24, and 21.2 (cf. 14.5d).[29] Moreover, the presence of the disciple's actual name 'Judas' in Jn 14.22 probably suggests that the Johannine author or redactor was familiar with the very early tradition that there was an apostle named Judas. It is plausible that Jn 14.22 represents a very early layer of tradition belonging to the Johannine community

27. See Klijn, 'Judas Thomas', pp. 89-91; and Turner, *The Book of Thomas*, p. 114. Koester suggests that this Judas is to be identified with Judas the brother of James in Jude 1 and was probably a brother of Jesus according to primitive traditions, 'GNOMAI DIAPHOROI', pp. 134-35.

28. Cf. Klijn, 'Judas Thomas', pp. 88-96. The author of Lk. 6.15-16 and Acts 1.13b shows how confusing the traditions surrounding the name 'Judas Thomas' were by the late first century. He has recorded both a 'Thomas' *and* a 'Judas son of James' in his list of the disciples, thereby seemingly representing this single disciple twice in his lists. The Gospels of Matthew and Mark, however, only record this disciple once under the name 'Thomas' and present the twelfth disciple as 'Thaddaeus' (Mt. 10.3; Mk 3.18). The tradition that Judas was the son of James rather than the brother of James and Jesus is likely to also be a later confusion. On the tendency to soften the stress on the sibling relationship between Judas Thomas and Jesus, see Koester, 'GNOMAI DIAPHOROI', pp. 134-35. Refer as well to J. Dart's treatment of the name Judas in his article, 'Jesus and His Brothers', in R. Joseph Hoffman and G.A. Larue (eds.), *Jesus in History and Myth* (Buffalo, NY: Prometheus Books, 1986), pp. 181-90.

29. Klijn, *Acts of Thomas*, p. 158; Klijn, 'Judas Thomas', p. 89; cf. Barrett, *The Gospel According to St John*, p. 327.

about the disciple 'Judas Thomas'. It is highly significant that the Johannine author has assigned the same role to Judas in Jn 14.22 as he does to Thomas in Jn 14.5 and, as we will see, Jn 20.25: that of a fool who misunderstands salvation as ascent and vision mysticism.[30]

Thus it would seem that, in the Gospel of John, there are preserved two of the stages in the development of the name 'Thomas': the earliest stage where this disciple was known by his actual name 'Judas', and the later stage where the disciple was beginning to be known by his epiphet 'Twin' or 'Thomas'. This seems to signal that the Johannine author was familiar with early Syrian Thomasine traditions and had some type of contact with the Thomasine community.[31]

In this story we see remnants of the discourse between these two communities. The Point of Discourse, as articulated by the Johannine author, focuses on the question of visionary experience. Fragments of this discourse recovered from its textual environment tell us that the Thomasine tradition expected theophany experiences whereas the Johannine Christians did not. In textualizing the Point of Discourse, the Johannine author has painted the hero of the Thomasine Christians as an ignoramus, a fool who repeatedly misunderstands salvation.[32]

3. *John 20.24-29*

The third passage that merits analysis is Jn 20.24-29 which reads:

> Now Thomas, one of the twelve, called the Twin (ὁ λεγόμενος Δίδυ-μος), was not with them when Jesus came. So the other disciples told

---

30. Of interest as well is the foolish statement made by Thomas in Jn 11.16 where he misunderstands Jesus' role as Life-giver. When Jesus hears of Lazarus's death, he decides to go to Bethany to raise him from the dead. Thomas, however, contends that their journey to Bethany will only end in death apparently because, in John's narrative, the Jews were seeking to stone Jesus for blasphemy (Jn 11.8; cf. 10.22-39). Thus Thomas says: 'Let us also go, that we may die with him' (Jn 11.16). Thomas does not seem to understand that life is imparted through belief in Jesus as God's Glory on earth and that Jesus' journey to Lazarus's tomb was intended to witness to this (Jn 11.15). Clearly Thomas's role in Jn 11.16, 14.5, and 20.25, as Judas's role in Jn 14.22, is that of the disciple who was foolish when it came to the topic of soteriology.

31. R. Schnackenburg, *The Gospel According to St. John*, I (New York: Crossroad, 1982), p. 152, concludes that 'the Johannine tradition, originating in Palestine, was subjected to Syrian influences before it reached Asia Minor (Ephesus), where it was fixed and edited'.

32. Cf. Charlesworth, *Beloved Disciple*, esp. p. 267.

him, 'We have seen the Lord ('Εωράκαμεν τὸν κύριον)'. But he said to
them, 'Unless I see in his hands the print of the nails, and place my
finger in the mark of the nails, and place my hand in his side, I will not
believe'. Eight days later, his disciples were again in the house, and
Thomas was with them. The doors were shut, but Jesus came and stood
among them, and said, 'Peace be with you'. Then he said to Thomas,
'Put your finger here, and see my hands; and put out your hand, and
place it in my side; do not be faithless, but believing (μὴ γίνου ἄπιστος
ἀλλὰ πιστός)'. Thomas answered, 'My Lord and my God!' Jesus said to
him, 'Have you believed because you have seen me? Blessed are those
who have not seen and yet believe ("Οτι ἑώρακάς με πεπίστευκας
μακάριοι οἱ μὴ ἰδόντες καὶ πιστεύσαντες)'.

To interpret this story outside its context is a gross injustice to the
integrity of the Gospel's narrative and results in a misunderstanding of
the author's point. This story must be read as the third and climactic
story about Jesus' appearances after his death. As we shall see, the issue
in all three of these episodes is one of *identity* not Jesus' corporeality as
some have suggested.[33]

The sequence of stories begins in Jn 20.14-18, where Mary Magdalene encounters Jesus outside his tomb. The text is very clear that the
point of the story is one of Jesus' identity: 'She turned around and saw
Jesus standing, but she did not know that it was Jesus (καὶ οὐκ ᾔδει ὅτι
Ἰησοῦς ἐστιν)' (20.14). Jesus even talks to her and she still does not
recognize him. In fact, the reader can only be amused by the subsequent
narrative when it is says that Mary even confided in him, considering
him to be the gardener who had stolen Jesus' body. She pleads with him
to take her to the missing body. It is not until he addresses her by name
that she finally recognizes the man as Jesus. This point of recognition is
driven home at the end of this pericope when Mary meets with the other
disciples and announces: 'I have seen the Lord ('Εώρακα τὸν κύριον)'
(20.18).

This resurrection story, as presented by John, bears the hallmark
structure of traditional folktale. According to the Russian Formalist,
Vladimir Propp, any individual folktale is a combination of a concrete
set of elements or 'functions' which are gathered into spheres of action.
According to Propp, the characters or actors are defined by the spheres
of action in which they participate. These are classified as seven actants

33. Most recently, G. Riley, *Resurrection Reconsidered: Thomas and John in
Controversy* (Minneapolis: Fortress Press, 1995).

and include such figures as the hero and the false hero. Each of the spheres of action consists of clusters of functions that are attributed to the actors. Thus a tale is characterized by an inventory of 31 functions and their sequential order.[34]

This model was later revised and condensed by Algirdas Greimas.[35] He specifically reduces the number of Propp's functions to 20 concrete elements by coupling several of them because of their binary character. Moveover, he emphasizes the transformational nature of the folktale, particularly in regard to the sequential order. Thus he defines narrative as 'a discursive manifestation, unfolding, by means of the consecution of its functions, an implicit transformational model'.[36]

In both of these models, we find at the finale of the sequences of functions, and thus at the conclusion of the narrative, a cluster of elements that are particularly significant for the present analysis of John 20. Greimas articulates them in the following manner:

16.   unrecognized arrival of the hero
17.   difficult trial versus success
18.   recognition of the hero
19.   exposure of the false hero versus revelation of the hero

In the episode where Mary encounters Jesus, we discover the actant, the hero, playing out his proper function at this point in the narrative: his arrival *incognito*. Function 17, the victory, has been ingeniously hinged by the author on element 18, the recognition of the hero. Jesus, by overcoming his death, is successful in his trial. This victory is revealed through Mary's exclamations, 'Rabboni!' (20.16) and 'I have seen the Lord!' (20.18). Thus, Mary, by recognizing Jesus, acknowledges his victory over death.

This cluster of functions is duplicated, and therefore emphasized and reinforced in the second episode when Jesus appears to the disciples who are in hiding. He shows them his hands and his side. Through this visionary experience, the disciples are able to recognize Jesus. The text reiterates the theme of vision: 'The disciples were glad when they *saw*

34. V. Propp, *Morphologie du Conte* (Paris: Seuil, 1928, repr. 1970).
35. A. Greimas, *Sémantique structurale: Recherche d e méthode* (Paris: Larousse, 1966); see now, *Structural Semantics: An Attempt at a Method* (trans. D. McDowell, R. Schleifer, and A. Velie; Lincoln: University of Nebraska Press, 1983).
36. A. Greimas, *Structural Semantics*, p. 225.

the Lord (ἐχάρησαν οὖν οἱ μαθηταὶ ἰδόντες τὸν κύριον)' (19.20). Here again the emphasis is on identification, through vision, of the hero Jesus who has arrived *incognito*. This identification is a celebration of Jesus' victory.

A common *topos* in ancient Greek literature is the identification of a character through the exposure of his wounds and the touching of his body. Nowhere is this more evident than in the *Odyssey* when the disguised hero, Odysseus arrives at his home.[37] Eurykleia is asked to wash Odysseus' feet after his long journey (*Od*. 19.357-60). Odysseus withdraws into the shadows in order to keep his identity secret (*Od*. 19.388-89). But alas, as she takes his feet into her hands, she notices a scar that a boar had inflicted on him years ago (*Od*. 19.392-94). Thus lines 467-75 read:

> The old woman, holding him in the palms of her hands, recognized this scar as she handled it. She let his foot go, so that his leg, which was in the basin, fell free, and the bronze echoed... Pain and joy seized her at once, and both eyes filled with tears, and the springing voice was held within her. She took the beard of Odysseus in her hands and spoke to him: 'Then, dear child, you are really Odysseus. I did not know you before; not until I had touched my lord all over'.[38]

The special connection between identifying the hero and touching him is brought out here and goes a long way to explain Jn 20.17 where Mary touches Jesus and exclaims, 'Rabboni', as she recognizes him.

This generic *topos* spilled over into literature about the dead so that quite often the dead are found displaying their wounds to the living.[39] For instance, when the murdered Clytemnestra appears in the famous

---

37. My thanks to Dennis MacDonald who reminded me of this story following my presentation of this thesis at the 1995 SBL Convention in Philadelphia.

38. See R. Lattimore (trans.), *The Odyssey of Homer* (New York: Harper & Row, 1967), p. 294.

39. Cf. the warriors in Homer, *Iliad* 11.41; Clytemnestra in Aeschylus, *Eumenides* 103; Eurydice in Ovid, *Met*. 10.48-49; Sychaeus in Virgil, *Aeneid* 1.355; Eriphyle in *Aeneid* 6.445-46; Dido in *Aeneid* 6.450; Deiphobus in *Aeneid* 6.494-97; Plato, *Gorgias* 524-25; Tibullus 1.10.37; 2.6.38-40; Propertius 4.7.7; Statius, *Silvae* 2.1.154-56; Silius Italicus 12.547-50; Apuleius, *Met*. 8.8. For a discussion of these texts, see J. Bremmer, *The Early Greek Concept of the Soul* (Princeton, NJ: Princeton University Press, 1983), pp. 70-84; Riley, *Resurrection Reconsidered*, pp. 50-51. The dead are often depicted on vases with their wounds. Refer to J. Chamay, 'Des défunts portant bandages', *Bulletin Antieke Beschaving* 52–53 (1977–78), pp. 247-51.

scene in *Eumenides*, she cries out, 'Do you see these wounds (ὁρᾶτε πληγὰς τάσδε)?!' (*Eumenides* 103) as a way to identify herself and her violent death, and to elicit pity for her dreadful fate.[40] There are several scenes in Virgil's *Aeneid* that speak to this end, scenes in which Aeneas is able to identify several of the dead by their death wounds.[41] For example, the Trojan hero stops by the side of the woman Dido. He sees 'her wound still fresh', 'recognizing her dim form in the darkness'. In that instant he wept and spoke softly to her, 'So the news they brought me was true, unhappy Dido? They told me you were dead and had ended your life with the sword' (*Aeneid* 6.450-58). Following this, he sees Deiphobus standing there 'his whole body mutilated and his face cruelly torn. The face and both hands were in shreds. The ears had been ripped from the head. He was noseless and hideous' (*Aeneid* 6.450-58)! Perhaps the most vivid example is Aeneas' vision of the dead Hector found in *Aeneid* 2.272-73, 277-79:

> In a dream, behold, before my eyes most sorrowful Hector seemed to be present and be weeping copiously, as of old dragged by [Achilles'] chariot, black with gory dust, and pierced in his swollen feet with thongs...wearing a squalid beard and hair clotted with blood, and those many wounds he received around the walls of his fatherland.[42]

Since this seems to be a common theme in ancient literature, the readers of the Gospel of John would have understood the display of the death marks in the second pericope to be his badge of identification. So the story emphasizes that Jesus showed them his hands and side. This display revealed his true identity and celebrated his victory over death. Thus the story builds on the premise that the disciples identified Jesus by seeing him.

Finally, in the crucial third episode, the climax of the narrative, we find Thomas 'the Twin', the one who is reported to have missed the resurrection appearance of Jesus to his disciples (Jn 20.24), singled out. The reader expects Thomas to receive the third vision in a row and identify Jesus on this basis, following the pattern set up in the two previous encounters. The reader may even be waiting for Thomas finally to

---

40. A.J. Podlecki, *Aeschylus: Eumenides* (Warminster: Aris & Phillips, 1989), pp. 68-69.

41. See especially, D. West, *Virgil: The Aeneid* (New York: Penguin Books, 1990), pp. 146-48.

42. West, *Virgil: The Aeneid*, p. 148.

be absolved from his past misunderstandings since he has been chosen
for his own special vision of Jesus.

Thus the narrative functions of the first two episodes are triplicated
here. They are amplified to the extreme. Thomas does not believe the
reports of the others that they have seen the Lord (Jn 20.25). He must
see for himself Jesus and the death wounds. Therefore, Thomas's
statement in Jn 20.25, 'Unless I see in his hands the print of the nails,
and place my finger in the mark of the nails, and place my hand in his
side, I will not believe', is a rhetorical intensification of the storyline
begun in Jn 20.20 when Jesus showed his death wounds to the other
disciples in order to reveal his identity to them. Like Eurykleia in the
Odyssey who did not recognize Odysseus until she had touched his scar,
Thomas must handle the death wounds before he recognizes Jesus and
is able to proclaim his identity.

So the story may surprise the reader when Jesus appears to Thomas
and rebukes him, 'Do not be faithless, but believing' (Jn 20.27),
because Thomas confesses his belief that Jesus is God on the basis of
his vision of Jesus (Jn 20.28). The effect of this rebuke has a dyadic
function in the narrative. First, the Johannine author has written
Thomas into the role of the actant, the false hero, and has forwarded the
movement of the narrative so that we find function 19 being articulated:
the false hero is exposed through the revelation of the hero's identity.
By identifying the specific actor, Thomas, with the actant, the false
hero, the Johannine author is driving home his point that the hero of the
Thomasine Christians is really no hero at all.[43]

Second, the Johannine author has created space for his own message,
for his critique of the visionary experience and his praise of the faith
experience. The exposure of the false hero erupts in the climactic
saying in v. 29 where Thomas is admonished by Jesus that visions of
him are not necessary for belief: 'Have you believed because you have
seen me (ὅτι ἑώρακάς με πεπίστευκας)? Blessed are those who have
not seen and yet believe (μακάριοι οἱ μὴ ἰδόντες καὶ πιστεύσαντες)'
(Jn 20.29). Clearly, a conflict is set up here between the false hero,
Thomas, who insists that a *visio Dei* is necessary, and John's hero,
Jesus, who rebutts this in favor of faith.

The Johannine story, therefore, should not be confused with the
Lukan post-resurrection narratives. It was not meant to be understood

43. Cf. Charlesworth, *Beloved Disciple*, pp. 226-33, 274-85.

as Lk. 24.37-43: as a demonstration of the corporeality of Jesus' resurrection. It should be noted that ancient readers were familar with the notion that the dead soul could interact with the living. It could be touched, and even made love to.[44] So for the dead Jesus to appear and be touched was not *necessarily* a demonstration of his corporeality. Even Luke has to *inform* his readers that Jesus' appearance was not that of his spirit *as they supposed*, but of 'flesh and bones': 'See my hands and my feet, that it is I myself; handle me, and see; for a spirit has not flesh and bones as you see that I have' (Lk. 24.36). How different from John's statement in 20.25 where Luke's definitive qualification, 'for a spirit has not flesh and bones as you see that I have', does not appear!

The Johannine scholar, John Ashton, in his balanced monograph on the Gospel of John, warns us about plunging into a morass when interpreting this story, of reading beyond the intent of the author as, unfortunately, Barnabas Lindars has done in his statement: 'According to the Jewish idea of bodily resurrection presupposed by John, Jesus is touchable, and perfectly able to invite Thomas to handle him.'[45] Ashton reminds us to keep the *author's* point of the story foremost in mind: 'If John invented this story, as there is every reason to believe, it was not, surely, to stimulate his readers to reflect upon the tangibility of risen bodies, but to impress upon them the need for faith.'[46]

Based on this reading of the Gospel, I therefore disagree with Greg Riley's suggestion that Jn 20.24-29 represents a dispute between the Johannine community and the Thomasine Christians over the issue of bodily resurrection.[47] Aside from the fact that the intent of Jn 20.24-29 is not to confirm a fleshly resurrection but to criticize visionary experience in favor of faith, it must be noted that nowhere does the *Gospel of Thomas* mention resurrection as a *spiritual* raising.

In Logion 51, it is said that the 'rest of the dead' has already happened, but the nature of this resurrection is not discussed. It is clear that many early Christians including Paul held that the resurrection had already started with Jesus' own resurrection (cf. 1 Cor. 15.20). Some of

---

44. For a summary of the ancient texts, see Riley, *Resurrection Reconsidered*, pp. 51-58. In this discussion, he makes obvious the dispute among the ancient Greeks over the palpability of the soul.

45. B. Lindars, *Behind the Fourth Gospel* (London: SPCK, 1971), p. 607.

46. J. Ashton, *Understanding the Fourth Gospel* (Oxford: Clarendon Press, 1991), p. 514.

47. Riley, *Resurrection Reconsidered*.

these Christians, especially those who espoused an encratite lifestyle like the Thomasites, interpreted Lk. 20.34-36 as evidence for the fact that their life *on earth now* was part of this new era, the age of the resurrection. They believed that they had to imitate the angels in the way that they conducted their lives (Clement of Alexandria, *Strom.* 3.12.87).[48] But nothing is delineated regarding the nature of this resurrection.

Very recently Ron Cameron has written an extensive critique of Riley's position. He states that 'while an intertextual conversation between *Thomas* and John is certainly not implausible', Riley did not establish in his book that the story of Jesus' appearance to Thomas in Jn 20.24-29 was 'designed to correct a theological position actually held by the *Gospel of Thomas*'. Even though, according to Cameron, the notion that Thomas's role in this story was created literarily to represent the views of his community 'is interesting and worthy of consideration', the 'simple drama about touching the resurrected body of Jesus' does not demand that the story was designed to convince the Thomasine community of the physical reality of the resurrection. Rather:

> the entire story has been revised to bring the gospel to a conclusion with a saying that is addressed to future generations of Johannine Christians, to assure those persons who were not eyewitnesses that they are the ones to be blessed with faith.[49]

Thus I continue to maintain that this story is not about bodily resurrection and must be distinguished from Lk. 24.36. Rather the impetus of this story for the Johannine writer is encapsulated in the climactic saying attributed to Jesus which blesses those who have faith in Jesus even though they have not had a visionary encounter (Jn 20.29). Behind this articulation we can reconstruct the Point of Discourse. For Johannine Christians, faith in Jesus was the basis of their salvation, whereas for the Thomasine Christians, the mystical visionary encounter was paramount. The discourse between these communitites on this subject is preserved here from the perspective of the Johannine community which

48. On this, see U. Bianchi, 'The Religio-Historical Relevance of Lk 20:34-36', in van den Broek and Vermaseren (eds.), *Studies in Gnosticism and Hellenistic Religions*, pp. 31-37.

49. R. Cameron, 'Ancient Myths and Modern Theories of the Gospel of Thomas and Christian Origins', *Method and Theory in the Study of Religion* 11 (1999), pp. 236-57 (241).

presents its 'correct' version of soteriology that developed as a result of the discourse.

4. *Conclusion*

Clearly, in each of these three scenarios, Thomas is the actant, the false hero, a fool who misunderstands the path of salvation. In the words of Charles Kingsley Barrett: 'Thomas...appears in John as a loyal but dull disciple, whose misapprehensions serve to bring out the truth.'[50] According to John, Thomas's misunderstanding is that he believes that in order to achieve life, one must seek the 'way' to Jesus, the route of ascent into heaven, and a *visio Dei*.

Traditio-rhetorical Criticism when applied to the Gospel of John has borne results. It has revealed a discourse between the Thomasine and Johannine communities.[51] The Point of Discourse has emerged as a dispute over soteriology, specifically over the validity of proleptic visionary flights to heaven. The assumption of this methodology is that the Johannine author is not painting an arbitrary picture of the apostle Thomas, the hero of Syrian Christianity, when he portrays him as a false hero whose mystical soteriology is corrected by Jesus. Thus he created his discourse by dramatizing actual features of his Traditio-religious Horizon and incorporating them at the textual level. The articulation certainly mirrors Johannine space and perspective, reflecting only partially the historical discourse itself.

The true test of verification for these results is to turn to the contemporaneous *Gospel of Thomas* and attempt to reconstruct the empty space in this discourse: the Traditio-religious perspective represented by *Thomas*. Should Thomasine soteriology parallel that alluded to by John, the results derived from our application of Traditio-rhetorical Criticism will be verified.

50. C.K. Barrett, *The Gospel According to St. John*, p. 382.
51. The implications for dating the Thomas tradition and perhaps even the *Gospel of Thomas* are paramount. Since John's geographical origin is Asia Minor or Syria, it is quite possible that the author was familiar with the Syrian *Gospel of Thomas*. If John is writing in response to the *Gospel of Thomas* itself rather than traditions associated with it, this would suggest a first-century date for the composition of the *Gospel of Thomas* probably around 70–80 CE. This lends support to S. Patterson's convincing arguments for a 70–80 CE date for *Thomas*; refer to his discussion in *The Gospel of Thomas and Jesus* (Somona, CA: Polebridge Press, 1993), pp. 113-20.

Chapter 4

THOMASINE SUPPORT FOR VISION MYSTICISM:
THE TRADITIO-RELIGIOUS HORIZON OF JOHN'S OPPONENTS*

> Look for the Living One while you are alive,
> lest you die and then seek to see him
> and you will be unable to see him
> (*Gospel of Thomas* 59).

The Johannine author has identified the Thomasine community as the horizon of his opponents, the particular early Christian community whose religious system has provided the opportunity for dialogue and the identification of the Point of Discourse. He has accomplished this by textualizing the community and its beliefs in the character of Thomas and his statements, and by articulating the Johannine discourse in the pronouncements of Jesus. Such literary devices provided the Johannine author with creative space for his platform on which he laid out the Point of Discourse: the conflict between a soteriology based on vision mysticism and one based on faith.

Such conclusions as these are certainly provocative. But can they be substantiated from a source external to John's Gospel? Moreover, can we reconstruct the empty space in the discourse and provide a more

---

* The following chapter is a summary of my previous works on the *Gospel of Thomas*. Because of its brevity, this presentation does not contain detailed references or arguments. For the comprehensive analyses that have led me to the conclusions presented here in sections 1 and 2, refer to DeConick, *Seek to See Him: Ascent and Vision Mysticism in the Gospel of Thomas* (VCSup, 33; Leiden: E.J. Brill, 1996). In addition to *Seek to See Him*, section 3 of this chapter is a summary of my previous works, 'Fasting From the World: Encratite Soteriology in the Gospel of Thomas', in U. Bianchi (ed.), *The Notion of 'Religion' in Comparative Research: Selected Proceedings of the XVI IAHR Congress* (Rome: 'L'Erma' di Bretschneider, 1994), pp. 425-40, and the article that I coauthored with J. Fossum, 'Stripped Before God: A New Interpretation of Logion 37', *VC* 45 (1991), pp. 123-50.

balanced picture of the discourse before it became textualized in the theoretical constructions of John?

In order to determine plausible answers to these questions, I suggest that we attempt to reconstruct the soteriology of the early Thomasine Christians by analyzing relevant Logia in the contemporaneous Syrian *Gospel of Thomas*. Unlike the Gospel of John which portrays Thomas as the false hero, the *Gospel of Thomas* preserves traditions that praise Thomas as Jesus' equal, the only disciple who truly understands who Jesus is. Thus in Logion 13, Thomas delivers the correct answer to Jesus' question, 'Compare me to someone and tell me whom I am like?' Thomas replies where the other disciples have failed: 'Teacher, my mouth is utterly incapable of saying whom you are like.' This answer demonstrates to Jesus that Thomas has gained a full understanding of Jesus' identity because Jesus tells Thomas that he is no longer Thomas's teacher. It appears that such an understanding of Jesus' identity has been informed by the Jewish tradition of the unutterable and unpronounceable Name of God, the שם המפורש.[1]

This laudatory affiliation with Jesus becomes developed in Syrian Christianity to the point that Thomas is portrayed as Jesus' twin. So in the *Acts of Thomas* 31, Thomas is called the 'Twin of Christ' while in ch. 39, he is addressed as 'Twin of the Messiah, and Apostle of the Most High, and sharer of the hidden word of the Life-giver, and receiver of the secret mysteries of the Son of God'. Moreover, not only is such a title given to him, but he is even said to appear in the form of Jesus and be mistaken for him (chs. 11, 57, 151). This identification is also reversed so that Thomas appears in the form of Jesus! Thus, in ch. 34, a boy says to Judas: 'You are a man that has two forms (δύο μορφάς).'[2] These dual forms can only be those of himself and Jesus. Moreover, the devil tells Thomas that he is 'like God your Lord who concealed his majesty and appeared in the flesh'.[3]

1. H. Bietenhard, 'ὄνομα', *TDNT*, V, pp. 268-69; cf. B. Gärtner, *The Theology of the Gospel According to Thomas* (trans. E. Sharpe; New York: Harper & Bros., 1961), p. 123.

2. R.A. Lipsius and M. Bonnet, *Acta Apostolorum Apocrypha*. II/2. *Acta Philippi et Acta Thomae accedunt Acta Barnabae* (Leipzig: Hermannum Mendelssohn, 1903).

3. This 'twinship' is to be associated with the polymorphic Christology according to Klijn where Jesus uses different forms to appear to different people, 'Judas Thomas', pp. 94-96; see also his discussion in *Acts of Thomas*, pp. 228-29.

In addition to the articulation that Thomas is the only disciple who knows Jesus' true identity, the text also indicates that Thomas is the disciple who knows the correct interpretation of Jesus' words and the soteriological impact of this interpretation. So the text informs the reader that Thomas wrote down these sayings and 'whoever finds the interpretation of these sayings will not experience death' (L. 1). This statement, the thesis of the *Gospel of Thomas*, clearly focuses on the subject of soteriology, the lens through which one is to read the following collection of sayings. It can be said that the disciple Thomas, the representative of the early Thomasine community, declared a monopoly on 'correctly' interpreting the Christian soteriological paradigm.

I have already written a monograph on the subject of visionary mysticism as a tradition which has found its way into the *Gospel of Thomas*.[4] In this chapter, I am only *summarizing* some of the main points of that discussion. I would also like to clarify here something which seems to have been misinterpreted from my previous work. I have never taken the position that the Jewish mystical tradition is the primary basis for the creation of the *Gospel of Thomas*. Rather I understand it to be one tradition, one layer among several which are woven together into the text as we now have it. Furthermore, I understand the *Gospel of Thomas* to be a cumulative collection or rolling corpus which grew over time in response to the problems and concerns of its community. My analysis of this process will have to wait for future studies in which I will try to answer the question, 'When and why did the visionary material enter the collection?' In the meantime, I am providing an interpretation of *Thomas*' soteriology from the perspective of a completed document. So the understanding of soteriology which I am discussing in this chapter is one that I believe the last editors of *Thomas* intended.

1. *The visio Dei*

As can be seen in Logion 59, this 'correct' soteriology centers on the visionary experience:

For a survey of past research, refer also to Klijn, 'Judas Thomas', p. 96 n. 1. It would appear that the subject of twinship in the Thomasine tradition needs more work.

4.   According to S. Patterson, *The Gospel of Thomas and Jesus* (Somona, CA: Polebridge Press, 1993), p. 206, this statement indicates that Thomas has been elevated to an equal status with Jesus.

Jesus said, 'Look for the Living One while you are alive, lest you die and then seek to see him and you will be unable to see (him)' (ϬⲱϢⲧ ⲛ̄ⲥⲁ ⲡⲉⲧⲟⲛ2 2ⲱⲥ ⲉⲧⲉⲧⲛ̄ⲟⲛ2 2ⲓⲛⲁ ϫⲉ ⲛⲉⲧⲙ̄ⲙⲟⲩ ⲁⲩⲱ ⲛ̄ⲧⲉⲧⲛ̄Ϣⲓⲛⲉ ⲉⲛⲁⲩ ⲉⲣⲟϥ ⲁⲩⲱ ⲧⲉⲧⲛⲁϢϬⲙ̄ Ϭⲟⲙ ⲁⲛ ⲉⲛⲁⲩ).[5]

The vision quest in this Logion is a pre-mortem experience, something that must be achieved during the believer's lifetime, not after death. In the words of Wilhelm Bousset, such a soul journey is characterized as an ecstatic journey that occurs during the life of the performer rather than an eschatological journey that occurs only after the body's death. Such a journey certainly can *anticipate* the eschatological moment, but it must be performed in the present if it is to bear the hallmark of mysticism.[6] Thus in Logion 59 we find the commandment from Jesus to 'look for (ϬⲱϢⲧ ⲛ̄ⲥⲁ)' God while still alive.

Moreover, the soteriological concern of the vision quest is brought forward by the qualification that, if the believers wait for the eschatological vision after death, they will have waited too long. If they 'seek to see' God after they have died, they will not be able to have the desired vision. It follows logically from this that they will not achieve their salvation but will experience death instead. Only by seeking the ecstatic vision can they be guaranteed immortality.

The etiquette of such ecstatic visions is prescribed in Logion 15:

Jesus said, 'When you see the one who was not born of woman, prostrate yourselves on your faces and worship him (2ⲟⲧⲁⲛ ⲉⲧⲉⲛ̄Ϣⲁⲛⲛⲁⲩ ⲉⲡⲉⲧⲉ ⲙ̄ⲡⲟⲩ ϫⲡⲟϥ ⲉⲃⲟⲗ 2ⲛ̄ ⲧⲥ2ⲓⲙⲉ ⲡⲉ2ⲧ ⲑⲏⲩⲧⲛ̄ ⲉϫⲙ̄ ⲡⲉⲧⲛ̄2ⲟ ⲛ̄ⲧⲉⲧⲛ̄ⲟⲩⲱϢⲧ ⲛⲁϥ). That one is your Father'.[7]

This description is indicative of Jewish mystical portrayals of God's celestial throneroom, the Holy of Holies. God's manifestation is seated on the Merkavah while the angels of his court surround him and worship him in song. It is common for the mystic upon entering the heavenly throneroom to prostrate before the divine King and enter into his worship. For example, in *1 En.* 14.24, when Enoch comes before the enthroned Glory who is surrounded by his heavenly court of angels, he

5. B. Layton, *Nag Hammadi Codex II,2-7 together with XII,2 Brit. Lib. Or. 4926 (1), and P. Oxy. 1, 654, 655.* I. *Gospel According to Thomas, Gospel According to Philip, Hypostasis of the Archons, and Indexes* (NHS, 20; Leiden: E.J. Brill, 1989), p. 74; my translation.

6. W. Bousset, 'Die Himmelsreise der Seele', *ARW* 4 (Freiburg: J.C.B. Mohr, 1901), pp. 136-69.

7. Layton, *Nag Hammadi Codex II,2-7*, p. 60.

falls prostrate on the ground before him. Similarly, *2 En.* 22.4 records
that when Enoch sees God's face of light, he falls down flat on his face
and worships him. Thus, this saying suggests that the goal of the
practitioner includes more than the vision itself. As we commonly find
in other early Jewish and Christian mystical texts, the mystic joins in
the heavenly liturgy and angelic worship before God's throne. Logion
15, I argue, belongs to this context of mystic flights to God's Merkavah
and his angelic court.

The visual experience of the God is also detailed in the *Gospel of
Thomas*. In Logion 83, we are told that the light of the Father 'will
become manifest' but the Father's 'image will remain concealed by his
light'. Thus the mystic could expect to see a light phenomenon surrounding God's image, his manifestation or *kābôd*. This notion is a
development of the Jewish tradition that taught that one could not
directly see God himself. This tradition, of course, is rooted in Exod.
33.20 where Moses is told that no one can see God face to face.

Because of this belief, there developed the phenomenon of the Glory
or *kābôd* of God, the manifestation that concealed God while simultaneously revealing him. The Glory is associated with both a pillar of
cloud and fire that enshrouded Yahweh (cf. Exod. 16.10b; 24.16-17, 43-
44; 40.34-35, 38; Num. 17.7; 1 Kgs 8.10-11; Lev. 9.23-24; 1 Sam. 3.3;
4.21) and a bodily form in the appearance of a human being (i.e. Exod.
33.18–34.8).[8] This is already found in Ezekiel's heavenly vision of an
enthroned 'likeness as the appearance of a man (דמות כמראה אדם)'
(1.26). This anthropomorphic deity is the 'Glory (כבוד) of Yahweh'
(1.28; cf. 8.2; 9.3-4; 10.4; 11.22-23; 43.1-5; 44.1-2; 47.1) and appeared
as if it were 'gleaming bronze' like a 'fire' enclosed it (1.27). Further,
'there was brightness round about him' (1.27).

So there developed a tradition in Judaism that the mystic, upon his
ascent, would gaze upon an anthropomorphic figure enshrouded by
radiant light. This light would act as a barrier concealing the image of
God from direct view. The development of this imagery is very early
and can be traced back to the second century BCE to *1 Enoch* 14 where
the seer Enoch describes his vision of the 'Great Glory'. Enoch relates
that the *kābôd* was robed in a gown 'which was shining more brightly
than the sun'. This light served to conceal God from direct view as
Enoch states: 'None of the angels was able to come in and see the face

8.   J. Fossum, 'Glory כבוד δόξα', in K. van der Toorn *et al.* (eds.), *Dictionary
of Deities and Demons in the Bible* (Leiden: E.J. Brill, 1995), pp. 1486-98.

of the Excellent and the Glorious One; and no one of the flesh can see him.' The reason for this, in Enoch's words, is that 'the flaming fire was round about him, and a great fire stood before him'.

Enoch's vision in *2 Enoch* 22 is comparable. Here Michael brings Enoch 'in front of the face of the Lord' and Enoch says that he 'saw the appearance of the face of the Lord' (*2 En.* 22.1).[9] What he describes, however, indicates that he did not see God's face directly but through a light screen. Thus the text records that the face of God which Enoch beheld was 'like iron made burning hot in a fire [and] brought out, and it emits sparks and is incandescent'.

Philo attests to this tradition as well. As we saw in Chapter 2, in the *De mutatione nominum* 7 Philo relates Moses' vision of God in Exodus 33 where he 'entered into the darkness'. Even though Moses searched to see God, Philo insists that God Himself 'by His very nature cannot be seen (ὁρᾶσθαι)' (*Mut. Nom.* 9).[10] The reason for this is explained by Philo in *De fuga et inventione* 165: 'the man that wishes to set his gaze upon the Supreme Essence, before he sees (ἰδεῖν) Him will be blinded by the rays that beam forth all around Him'.[11] Consequently, Philo concludes that God said to Moses, 'What is behind Me thou shalt see, but My face thou shalt by no means see (Exod. 33.23)'. Obviously, Philo is transmitting here the Jewish tradition that God's essence is encompassed by his light. Moreover, seeing God's face directly would place the mystic in mortal danger: the vision would consume him by fire.

These traditions, I believe, provide the best context for interpreting Logion 82: 'He who is near me is near the fire, and he who is far from me is far from the Kingdom.' The reader familiar with contemporaneous mystical traditions, probably would have identified Jesus with God's Glory surrounded by fire. Thus the person who approaches Jesus, approaches the fire of the *kābôd*. The final clause suggests that Jesus could be found in the 'Kingdom'. This is a telling variation of this Jesus saying which, in other texts, reads 'life' instead of 'Kingdom' (cf. Origen, *hom. in Jer.* 20.3; Didymus the Blind, *PG*, 39 1488D). Clearly the Thomasine author wished to identify the location of Jesus as the heavenly Kingdom where he resides as God's fiery manifestation. It is telling, I think, that this understanding of Logion 82 is so similar to the

9.   *APOT*, II, p. 442.
10.   F.H. Colson and G.H. Whitaker, *Philo*, V (LCL; London: Harvard University Press, 1934), pp. 146-47.
11.   Colson and Whitaker, *Philo*, V, pp. 100-101.

interpretation which the writer of the *Gospel of the Savior* makes of his version of this saying. In the context of a vision of the glorified Jesus, John is told not to touch Jesus because 'if one is [near] to me, he will [burn]. I am the [fire that] blazes; the one who [is near to me, is] near to [the fire]; the one who is far from me, is far from life (*Gos. Sav.* 107: 39-48).'

2. *Ascent and Transformation*

Logion 83, however, contrasts the description of the *kābôd* with that of the human: 'the images are manifest to man, but the light in them remains concealed in the image of the light of the Father'. The divine condition where the image is concealed by the light is said to be the opposite of the human where the image or body is visible while the light, divine image, or spiritual body is concealed within it. This is similar to the teaching in Logion 24 that 'there is light within a person from the light' (cf. L. 29).

As might be expected, salvation must involve contact with this divine inner element. This is quite explicit in Logion 70a. Jesus says, 'If you bring forth what is within you (ΠΗ 2Ν ΤΗΥΤΝ), what you have will save you'.[12] This salvific experience is described using two sets of language in the *Thomas* gospel: a psychologic language that describes this encounter as an internal personal experience, and a mythological language that describes this encounter as a journey into the divine realm in order to experience the Transcendent there.

The psychologic language operates in the *Thomas* text in those instances where Jesus speaks of encountering the divine element within. As we have seen, according to Logia 83 and 24 (cf. 29), the Transcendent has taken up residence within the human body. Now this divinity must be encountered through self-knowledge, the knowledge of one's divine origin and nature as related in Logion 3b (cf. L. 56, 67, 80, and 111):

> When you come to know yourselves, then you will become known, and you will realize that it is you who are the sons of the living Father. But if you will not know yourselves, you dwell in poverty and it is you who are that poverty (2ΟΤΑΝ ΕΤΕΤΝωΑΝϹΟΥωΝ ΤΗΥΤΝ ΤΟΤΕ ϹΕΝΑϹΟΥω(Ν)

12. Layton, *Nag Hammadi Codex II,2-7*, p. 80; Eng. trans. M. Meyer, *The Gospel of Thomas: The Hidden Sayings of Jesus* (San Francisco: HarperSanFrancisco, 1992), p. 53.

ⲦⲎⲚⲈ ⲀⲨⲰ ⲦⲈⲦⲚⲀⲈⲒⲘⲈ ⲬⲈ Ⲛ̄ⲦⲰⲦⲚ̄ ⲡⲈ Ⲛ̄ϢⲎⲢⲈ Ⲙ̄ⲡⲈⲒⲰⲦ ⲈⲦⲞⲚⲌ ⲈϢⲰⲡⲈ
ⲆⲈ ⲦⲈⲦⲚⲀⲤⲞⲨⲰⲚ ⲦⲎⲨⲦⲚ̄ ⲀⲚ ⲈⲈⲒⲈ ⲦⲈⲦⲚ̄ϢⲞⲞⲡ ⲌⲚ̄ ⲞⲨⲘⲚ̄ⲦⲌⲎⲔⲈ ⲀⲨⲰ
Ⲛ̄ⲦⲰⲦⲚ̄ ⲡⲈ ⲦⲘ̄Ⲛ̄ⲦⲌⲎⲔⲈ).[13]

This encounter is not only revelatory but also redemptive since it is only by 'knowing' one's spiritual self, which is the inner light or soul, that one will be known by God (L. 3b) and not see death (L. 111).

This same encounter with the Transcendent, however, is also described in *Thomas* in the garb of religious mythology rather than psychology. Thus in Logion 50, we have a fragment of ascent lore where Jesus states:

> 'If they say to you,
> "Where did you come from?",
> say to them,
> "We came from the light",

(the place where the light came into being on its own accord and established [itself] and became manifest through their image).

> If they say to you, "Is it you?", say
> "We are its children,
> and we are the elect of the Living Father".

> If they ask you,
> "What is the sign of your Father in you?",
> say to them,
> "It is movement and repose" '[14]

The *Sitz im Leben* in which these questions and answers make the *most* sense is that of the ascent of the soul through the heavenly spheres and the interrogation of the soul as it journeys to God. We find such interrogations at death to be characteristic of Egyptian, Orphic, and some Gnostic traditions. Since Logion 50 gives us no indication that the context is death, we can assume a pre-mortem context based on the fact that *Thomas* advocated mystical ascent before death in Logion 59. For this idea, there is ample evidence in Jewish sources where we discover that the mystic could expect the angelic guards to be hostile and question his right and worthiness to be in heaven (cf. *Asc. Isa.* 10.28-29; *3 En.* 2, 4 and 5; *Apoc. Abr.* 13.6; *b. Ḥagigah* 15b; *b. Šab.* 88b-89a; *Shem. R.* 42.4; *Pes. R.* 96b-98a; *Gedullat Mosheh* 273; *History of the Rechabites* 5.1-2). Moreover, he could anticipate life-or-death tests to

---

13. Layton, *Nag Hammadi Codex II,2-7*, pp. 54, 55.
14. B. Layton, *Nag Hammadi Codex II,2-7*, pp. 72-73; punctuation my own.

be administered by the angels. He had to memorize passwords and hymns in order to appease the guards of heaven and insure his safe passage to the foot of God's throne (*Apoc. Abr.* 17-18; *Hekhalot Rabbati* 81, 94-106, 204-68; *Hekhalot Zuṭarti* 413-15; *b. Ḥagigah* 14b; *M. Merk.* 558, 560-62, 567-68).[15] It may even be that these words of Jesus should be understood as magical ritual words used to bring about ascent as we find in early Jewish mysticism generally.[16]

The garb of religious mythology is especially vivid in Logion 84 which reads as follows:

> When you see your likeness, you rejoice. But when you see your images which came into being before you, and which neither die nor become manifest, how much you will have to bear (ⲛ̄ϩⲟⲟⲩ ⲉⲧⲉⲧⲛ̄ⲛⲁⲩ ⲉⲡⲉⲧ-ⲛ̄ⲉⲓⲛⲉ ϣⲁⲣⲉⲧⲛ̄ⲣⲁϣⲉ ϩⲟⲧⲁⲛ ⲇⲉ ⲉⲧⲉⲧⲛ̄ϣⲁⲛⲛⲁⲩ ⲁⲛⲉⲧⲛ̄ϩⲓⲕⲱⲛ ⲛ̄ⲧⲁϩⲩ-ⲱⲡⲉ ϩⲓ ⲧⲉⲧⲛⲉϩⲏ ⲟⲩⲧⲉ ⲙⲁⲩⲙⲟⲩ ⲟⲩⲧⲉ ⲙⲁⲩⲟⲩⲱⲛϩ ⲉⲃⲟⲗ ⲧⲉⲧⲛⲁϥⲓ ϩⲁ ⲟⲩⲏⲣ)![17]

This Logion speaks of the visionary experience of self-encounter. It contrasts the act of gazing at one's corporeal likeness with the vision of one's heavenly self, image or angelic counterpart. It suggests that this visionary experience of meeting one's divine double face to face will be a traumatic experience.

Based on the transformational aspects of mystical visionary encounter with the divine self in other early Jewish, Hermetic, and Christian literature where the visionary, upon seeing his reflection is divinized,[18]

---

15. On this subject refer to the classic work by P. Schäfer, *Rivalitat zwischen Engeln und Menschen* (Berlin: W. de Gruyter, 1975); D.J. Halperin, 'Ascension or Invasion: Implications of the Heavenly Journey in Ancient Judaism', *Religion* 18 (1988), pp. 47-67; and most recently, the balanced work of R. Elior, 'Mysticism, Magic, and Angelology—The Perception of Angels in Hekhalot Literature', *JSQ* 1 (1993/94), pp. 3-53. I only had access to this latter work after the production of my analysis in *Seek to See Him*.

16. Refer to M. Swartz, *Scholastic Magic: Ritual and Revelation in Early Jewish Mysticism* (Princeton: Princeton University Press, 1996).

17. Layton, *Nag Hammadi Codex II,2-7*, pp. 84-85.

18. See, e.g., *Disc. 8–9* 57.29–58.22; *CH* 13.3, 13; *PGM* 4.154-285; *Jos. Asen.* 18; *Ps.-Clem. Hom.* 13.16; *Odes Sol.* 13; *Acts Thom.* 112.76; Ps.-Cyprian, *De mont.* 13; Clem. Alex., *Quis Div. Salv.* 21.7; 1 Cor. 13.23; 2 Cor. 3.18; *Gos. Phil.* 61.20-35). Regarding such magical practices, see T. Hopfner, *Griechisch-aegyptischer Offenbarungszauber* (2 vols.; Leipzig: W. Haessel, 1921–24), and his article, 'Mageia', PW, XIV, pp. 301-93; R. Ganszyniec, 'Lekanomanteiva', PW, XII, pp. 1879-89; A. Delatte, *La catoptromancie grecque et ses derives* (Paris: E. Droz,

we can solidly assume that the experience related in Logion 84 was understood to be a transforming one as well. Thus, I believe that it is within this context that Logion 22 becomes sensible. According to Logion 22, a person will only enter the heavenly Kingdom when he has made the two into one, when his human image has been replaced with his heavenly image of light:

> When you make the two one, and when you make the inside like the outside and the outside like the inside, and the above like the below, and when you make the male and the female one and the same, so that the male not be male nor the female female, and you fashion eyes in place of an eye, and a hand in place of a hand, and a foot in place of a foot (ϩⲟⲧⲁⲛ ⲉⲧⲉⲧⲛ̄ϣⲁⲉⲓⲣⲉ ⲛ̄ϩ̄ⲃⲁⲗ ⲉⲡⲙⲁ ⲛ̄ⲟⲩⲃⲁⲗ ⲁⲩⲱ ⲟⲩϭⲓⲝ ⲉⲡⲙⲁ ⲛ̄ⲛⲟⲩϭⲓⲝ ⲁⲩⲱ ⲟⲩⲉⲣⲏⲧⲉ ⲉⲡⲙⲁ ⲛ̄ⲟⲩⲉⲣⲏⲧⲉ), and an image in place of an image, then you will enter the Kingdom (ⲟⲩϩⲓⲕⲱⲛ ⲉⲡⲙⲁ ⲛ̄ⲟⲩϩⲓⲕⲱ(ⲛ) ⲧⲟⲧⲉ ⲧⲉⲧⲛⲁⲃⲱⲕ ⲉϩⲟⲩⲛ ⲉ[ⲧ]ⲙⲛ̄[ⲧⲉⲣ]ⲟ).[19]

Salvation is granted only to those who have encountered and been transformed into their divine image, when they have made 'an image in place of an image', fashioning 'eyes in place of an eye, and a hand in place of a hand, and a foot in place of a foot' (cf. L. 106). In so doing, the mystic is admitted to the citizenship of the Kingdom and life everlasting.

Such a mythology is most comparable to that depicted in the Syrian allegory, the *Hymn of the Pearl*. In this allegory, the Prince (the soul) is separated from his heavenly robe (his image) when he enters Egypt (fell into the world) and donned the Egyptian dress (the human body). He fell asleep but was awakened by a letter from the King (God). He stripped off the 'unclean dress') and left Egypt. When he returned to the Kingdom (ascended to heaven), he received his garment (his divine counterpart): 'When I received it, the garment seemed to me to become a mirror to myself' (*Acts Thom.* 112.76) and 'the image of the King of Kings was embroidered and depicted in full all over it' (*Acts Thom.*

1932); F. Cumont, *L'Egypte des astrologues* (Bruxelles: Edité par la fondation égyptologique reine Élisabeth, 1937), p. 161; J. Capart, 'Les anciens Egyptiens pratiquaient-ils déjà la lécanomancie?', *Chronique d'Egypte* 19 (1944), p. 263; F. Cunen, 'Lampe et coupe magiques', *Symbolae Osloensis* 36 (1960), pp. 65-71.

19. Layton, *Nag Hammadi II,2-7*, p. 62; my translation. For another interpretation of this saying, refer to T. Baarda, '2 Clement 12 and the Sayings of Jesus', in *Early Transmission of Words of Jesus* (Amsterdam: VU-Uitgeverij, 1983), pp. 261-88.

112.86). So he put on his 'bright robe' and thus the prince was reunited with his lost image. He had experienced mystic transformation.

Such mystic transformation can also be described in the language of drink. The metaphor of drink[20] in Jewish literature was connected with the phenomenon of ascent, indicating the revelation of hidden wisdom during the ascent. In *1 En.* 48.1-2, for instance, Enoch sees in heaven 'the fountain of righteousness' and 'around it were many fountains of wisdom, and all the thirsty drank, and were filled with wisdom'. After drinking from these fountains, 'their dwelling places become with the holy, righteous, and elect ones' (cf. *1 En.* 49.1; *4 Ezra* 1.47; *2 Bar.* 59.7; *Memar Marqa* 2.1; Hipp., *Ref. Haer.* 5.27.2-3; Philo, *Leg. All.* 1.82-84; *Odes Sol.* 11.6-13).

A most remarkable example of the transformational aspect of drink is located in *4 Ezra* 14.38-41 which describes one of Ezra's visions:

> a voice called me saying: 'Ezra, open your mouth and drink what I give you to drink'. Then I opened my mouth, and behold, a full cup was offered to me; it was full of something like water, but its color was like fire. And I took it and drank; and when I had drunk it, my heart poured forth understanding, and wisdom increased in my breast, for my spirit retained its memory; and my mouth was opened, and was no longer closed.

Ezra is given a cup of fire-water to drink. Upon drinking it, he acquires knowledge that formerly was hidden from him. The language used to describe his experience reflects his transformation: his heart and spirit are changed; his mouth is opened.

Logion 108 represents the heart of this language of transformational mysticism:

> He who will drink from my mouth will become like me. I myself shall become he, and the things that are hidden will be revealed to him (ⲡⲉⲧⲁⲥⲱ ⲉⲃⲟⲗ ϨⲚ ⲦⲀⲦⲀⲡⲣⲟ ϥⲚⲀϢⲱⲡⲉ ⲚⲦⲀϨⲈ ⲀⲚⲞⲔ Ϩⲱ ϮⲚⲀϢⲱⲡⲉ ⲉⲚⲦⲞϥ ⲡⲉ ⲀⲨⲱ ⲚⲉⲐⲎⲡ ⲚⲀ ⲞⲨⲱⲚϨ ⲉⲣⲟϥ).[21]

When the mystic encounters Jesus and imbibes the heavenly drink, he shall gain all the hidden knowledge and experience a mystical metamorphosis into the divine.

The process of immortalization is also characterized mythologically in Logion 19b where we find the reference to one's return to Paradise, a

---

20. H. Lewy, *Sobria Ebrietas* (BZNW, 9; Berlin: Alfred Töpelmann, 1929).
21. Layton, *Nag Hammadi Codex II,2-7*, pp. 90-91.

garden that exists cosmologically as a realm in heaven. By ascending to this garden and encountering the unmoving and undying trees, one achieves immortality:

> For there are five trees for you in Paradise which are unmoving summer and winter and whose leaves do not fall. Whoever will know them will not experience death (ογΝ̄ΤΗΤΝ̄ ΓΑΡ Μ̄ΜΑΥ Ν̄ΤΟΥ Ν̄ϢΗΝ 2Μ̄ ΠΑΡΑΔΙΣΟΣ ΕΣΕΚΙΜ ΑΝ Ν̄ϢΩΜ Μ̄ΠΡΩ ΑΥΩ ΜΑΡΕ ΝΟΥϬΩΒΕ 2Ε ΕΒΟΛ ΠΕΤΝΑΣΟΥ- ΩΝΟΥ ϤΝΑΧΙ †ΠΕ ΑΝ Μ̄ΜΟΥ).[22]

This notion of ascent and the encounter with the five trees in order to overcome death is connected with the Hermetic astrological perspective that a specific number of vices form the material person, while a like number of virtues form the spiritual person.[23] The only way for rebirth to occur is to withdraw from the vices, discarding them as one ascends past the various planets, and to arrive at the virtues (*CH* 13.7, 10; 1.24-26). Thus as *Corpus Hermeticum* 13.10 relates: 'the arrival of the decad [of virtues] sets in order a birth of mind that expels the twelve [vices]; we have been divinized by this birth'. The number of virtues and vices varies in different texts, but they are all based on two numerical systems: the twelve divisions of the zodiac and the five planetary spheres (excluding the sun and the moon) and the list of elements (breeze, wind, earth, water, and fire).[24]

This pentadantic system is quite primitive as evidenced in Col. 3.5-15 where the Christian is commanded to 'put to death (νεκρώσατε)' the earthly parts of the human (τὰ μέλη τὰ ἐπὶ τῆς γῆς) (Col. 3.5).[25] What follows are two lists of five vices that make up this 'earthly' self: forni-

22. Layton, *Nag Hammadi Codex II,2-7*, p. 60; my translation.

23. On this see especially R. Reitzenstein, 'Appendix XIII: Virtues and Vices as Members', in his *Hellenistic Mystery-Religions: Their Basic Ideas and Significance* (PTMS, 15; trans. J.E. Steely; Pittsburg: Pickwick Press, 1978), pp. 47-51, 209-212, and 338-51; G. Mussies, 'Catalogues of Sins and Virtues Personified (NHC II,5)', in van den Broek and Vermaseren, *Studies in Gnosticism and Hellenistic Religions*, pp. 315-35. For lists of vices in Jewish-Christianity and Judaism, refer to J. Zandee, ' "The Teachings of Silvanus" (NHC VII,4) and Jewish Christianity', in R. van den Broek and M.J. Vermaseren, *Studies in Gnosticism and Hellenistic Religion presented to Gilles Quispel on the Occasion of his 65th Birthday* (Leiden: E.J. Brill, 1981), pp. 502-503.

24. On these lists, see Reitzenstein, *Hellenistic Mystery-Religions*, pp. 279-82.

25. P.W. van der Horst, 'Observations on a Pauline Expression', *NTS* 19 (1973), pp. 181-87, discusses the Pauline expression, 'putting off the old man', in light of Skeptic philosophy.

cation, impurity, passion, evil desire, and covetousness (Col. 3.5); anger, wrath, malice, slander, and foul speech (Col. 3.8). A 'new nature' must be 'put on' which is a renewal of God's Image (ἐνδυσά-μενοι τὸν νέον τὸν ἀνακαινούμενον εἰς ἐπίγνωσιν κατ᾽ εἰκόνα τοῦ κτίσαντος αὐτόν) (Col. 3.10). This 'new nature' is described as con-sisting of two sets of five virtues: compassion, kindness, lowliness, meekness, patience (Col. 3.12); forbearance, forgiveness, love, peace, thankfulness (Col. 3.13-15).

Philo had already adapted such a theme to the Jewish mythology of Paradise. According to Philo's allegory, the trees of Paradise are virtues that God planted for the nourishment of the soul and the acquistion of immortality (*Leg. All.* 1.97-98; *Conf. Ling.* 61; *Migr. Abr.* 36-37; *Quaest. in Gen.* 1.6, 1.56; *Agr.* 8.19). It is not surprising that Philo lists the trees in the garden to be five: 'Life, Immortality, Knowledge, Apprehension, and Understanding of the conception of good and evil (ζωῆς, ἀθανασίας, εἰδήσεως, καταλήψεως, συνέσεως καλοῦ καὶ πονηροῦ φαντασίας)'.[26] This 'garden of virtues' brings 'the soul to per-fect happiness' and 'immortality'. Contrary to this is the 'path accord-ing to evil' which can only end 'in death'.

Certainly Logion 19b reflects this type of interpretative tradition. The five trees refer to the five virtues to which the person surrenders after his ascent. In so doing, he achieves divinity and immortality. This soteriological scheme of ascent implicit in Logion 19b is explicit in the Syrian *Odes of Solomon*. In *Ode* 11, we are told about a mystic who, upon ascending to Paradise, dons a garment of light. Then the Odist says:

> And he took me to his Paradise, wherein is the wealth of the Lord's pleasure.
>
> I contemplated blooming and fruit-bearing trees,
> and self-grown was their crown.
>
> Their branches were flourishing
> and their fruits were shining;
> their roots (were) from an immortal land.
>
> And a river of gladness was irrigating them,
> and the region round about them in the land of eternal life
> (*Odes Sol.* 11.16-16c).

---

26. F.H. Colson and G.H. Whitaker, *Philo*, III (LCL; Cambridge, MA: Harvard University Press, 1930), pp. 230-31; I understand the final genitive clause 'καλοῦ καὶ πονηροῦ φαντασίας' as qualifying 'συνέσεως'.

The trees are then interpreted in a following stanza to refer to the righteous or virtuous people who have been 'planted' in God's immortal land and who have taken their place in 'Paradise' (*Odes Sol.* 11.18). Thus they 'grow in the growth of the trees' and are therefore 'blessed' and 'have passed from darkness into light' (*Odes Sol.* 11.19). Even though this text does not interpret the trees as 'virtues', this *Ode* does allegorize the trees as the righteous people and sets forth the contemplation of these trees within the framework of ascent to Paradise and a vision of several trees.

3. *Ascent Preparations*

Such ascent and encounter with the divine can only occur, however, after certain preparations are made according to the Thomasine Christians. For example, in Logion 27, in order to prepare oneself for the journey into the Kingdom and the vision of the Father, one must first purify oneself by withdrawing from the world and by observing the sanctity of the Sabbath:

> If you do not fast from the world, you will not find the Kingdom (ἐὰν μὴ νηστεύσηται τὸν κόσμον οὐ μὴ εὕρηται τὴν βασιλείαν τοῦ θεοῦ // ετε<τῆ> τῆρνηςτεγε επκοςμος τετναϩε αν ετμῆτερο). If you do not observe the Sabbath as Sabbath, you will not see the Father (καὶ ἐὰν μὴ σαββατίσητε τὸ σάββατον οὐκ ὄψεσθε τὸν πατέρα // ετετῆτμειρε ῆπςαμβατον ῆςαββατον ῆτετναναγ αν επειωτ).[27]

The emphasis in Logion 27 on world renunciation is quite developed elsewhere in the *Gospel of Thomas* and reflects the regime of encratism, the elevation of the state of singlehood and celibacy and the degradation of the state of marriage and sexuality.[28] In addition to praising

27. For the Greek fragment see, Layton, *Nag Hammadi Codex II,2-7*, p. 118, where H. Attridge has reconstructed the Greek fragment; see also the prior work of B. Grenfell and A. Hunt, ΛΟΓΙΑ ΙΗΣΟΥ: *Sayings of Our Lord from an Early Greek Papyrus* (London: published for the Egypt exploration fund by H. Frowde, 1897), p. 10. For the coptic text, see, Layton, *Nag Hammadi Codex II,2-7*, p. 64; my translation.

28. G. Blonde understands encratism to be both a sect and a tendency within the early church at large: 'Encratisme', in M. Viller, F. Cavallera, and J. De Guibert (eds.), *Dictionnaire de Spiritualité*, IV (Paris: G. Beauchesne & Sons, 1960), pp. 628-42. It is clear from Clement's review of early Christian marriage practices in *Stromata* 3, however, that encratism was not a sect but rather a *lifestyle* that was adopted by many Christian groups which had a negative world-view. Clement con-

the *monachos* or bachelor (L. 16, 49, 75),[29] like the encratites described by Clement of Alexandria, *Thomas* defends the position that the resurrection of the dead has already occurred (cf. L. 51 to *Strom.* 3.6.48; 3.12.87; 3.14.95).[30] Several Logia are based on an encratite exegesis of the creation story which reflects the idea that the sin of Adam should be equated with the act of intercourse initiated by the separation of the sexes into two genders (L. 4, 11, 22, 23, 37, 46, 49, 75, 114). Salvation requires the movement from two into one, reunifying the genders into the androgynous prelapsarian Man (cf. L. 11, 22, and 114 to *Strom.* 3.13.92). Adam is seen as unworthy because of his sin, thus death came into existence through him (cf. L. 86 to *Strom.* 3.14.95; 3.16.100; 3.17.102). To be a Thomasite meant to be voluntarily destitute, homeless, and without family probably in imitation of Jesus (L. 33, 36, 42, 54, 63, 64, 78, and 95; cf. L. 16, 55, 99, 101 to *Strom.* 3.6.49; 3.14.97).[31] Dietary regulations that discouraged the consumption of

sidered this lifestyle to be a form of asceticism that was unacceptable because it was too extreme. G. Quispel reviews encratism and the history of scholarship about this topic in 'The Study of Encratism: A Historical Survey', in U. Bianchi (ed.), *La Tradizione dell'Enkrateia, Atti del Colloquio Internazionale—Milano 20–23 Aprile 1982* (Rome: Edizioni Dell'Ateneo, 1985), pp. 35-81; for a treatment of asceticism and sexual renunciation in early Christianity, see P. Brown, *The Body and Society: Men, Women, and Sexual Renunciation in Early Christianity* (Lectures on the History of Religions, 13; New York: Columbia University Press, 1988). See now my own contribution to this in *Seek to See Him*. For a contrary view, see now R. Uro, 'Is *Thomas* an encratite gospel?', in Uro (ed.), *Thomas at the Crossroads*, pp. 140-62.

29. For discussion of this word, see the following works: M. Harl, 'A propos des *Logia* de Jésus: Le sens du mot *monachos*', *REG* 73 (1960), pp. 464-74; F.-E. Morard, 'Monachos moine, historie du terme grec jusqu'au 4e siècle', *Freiburger Zeitschrift für Philosophie und Theologie* 20 (1973), pp. 332-411; and Morard, 'Encore quelques réflexions sur monachos', *VC* 34 (1980), pp. 395-401.

30. *Stromata* 3.12.87 refers to a version of Lk. 20.34-36. On the encratite implications of this passage, refer to Bianchi, 'The Religio-Historical Relevance of Lk 20:34-36', pp. 31-37.

31. See the recent treatment of the social history of *Thomas* in Patterson, *The Gospel of Thomas*. He uses a social model developed by G. Theissen to illuminate Thomas Christianity; the works of Theissen include: *The Sociology of Early Palestinian Christianity* (trans. J. Bowden; Philadelphia: Fortress Press, 1978); *The Social Setting of Pauline Christianity* (trans. J. Schütz; Philadelphia: Fortress Press, 1982); *Studien zur Soziologie des Urchristentums* (WUNT, 19; Tübingen: J.C.B. Mohr, 1979).

wine and meat and procedures for proper fasting are at issue in several Logia as well (cf. L. 14, 28, 60, 104 to *Strom.* 3.6.53; 3.7.58; 3.7.60; 3.12.85). The 'world', therefore, is associated with death (L. 56) and material existence (L. 80) and so must be renounced completely (L. 27, 110). Such is the meaning of the phrase ἐὰν μὴ νηστεύσηται τὸν κόσμον in Logion 27. Such an austere program of world renunciation through celibacy and dietary regulations is clearly grounded in Jewish tradition as a way to make the vision-seeker worthy to have a successful vision quest.[32]

These notions are reinforced by the imagery in Logion 37 which reads:[33]

> His disciples said, 'When will you become revealed to us and when shall we see you (ⲁϣ ⲛ̄2ⲟⲟⲩ ⲉⲕⲛⲁⲟⲩⲱⲛ2 ⲉⲃⲟⲗ ⲛⲁⲛ ⲁⲩⲱ ⲁϣ ⲛ̄2ⲟⲟⲩ ⲉⲛⲁⲛⲁⲩ ⲉⲣⲟⲕ)?'
>
> Jesus said, 'When you disrobe without being ashamed (2ⲟⲧⲁⲛ ⲉⲧⲉⲧⲛ̄ϣⲁⲕⲉⲕ ⲧⲏⲩⲧⲛ̄ ⲉ2ⲏⲩ ⲙ̄ⲡⲉⲧⲛ̄ϣⲓⲡⲉ)
>
> and take up your garments and place them under your feet like little children and tread on them (ⲁⲩⲱ ⲛ̄ⲧⲉⲧⲛ̄ϥⲓ ⲛ̄ⲛⲉⲧⲛ̄ϣⲧⲏⲛ ⲛ̄ⲧⲉⲧⲛ̄ⲕⲁⲁⲩ 2ⲁ ⲡⲉⲥⲏⲧ ⲛ̄ⲛⲉⲧⲛ̄ⲟⲩⲉⲣⲏⲧⲉ ⲛ̄ⲑⲉ ⲛ̄ⲛⲓⲕⲟⲩⲉⲓ ⲛ̄ϣⲏⲣⲉ ϣⲏⲙ ⲛ̄ⲧⲉⲧⲛ̄ϫⲟⲡϫ̄ⲡ̄ ⲙ̄ⲙⲟⲟⲩ),
> then [you will see] the Son of the Living One, and you will not be afraid (ⲧⲟⲧⲉ [ⲧⲉⲧ]ⲛ̣ⲁ̣ⲛ̣ⲁⲩ ⲉⲡϣⲏⲣⲉ ⲙ̄ⲡⲉⲧⲟⲛ2 ⲁⲩⲱ ⲧⲉⲧⲛⲁⲣ̄ 2ⲟⲧⲉ ⲁⲛ)'.[34]

This saying contains three distinct motifs: stripping off the garments without shame; treading upon them like children; and gaining the capacity to see the deity without fear.

---

32. Dan. 10.3; *4 Ezra* 5.2, 13; 6.31, 35; 9.24-25; 12.50; *Asc. Isa.* 2.9-11; *2 Bar.* 5.7; 9.2; 12.5; 21.1; 47.2; *Apoc. Abr.* 9.7-8; Philo, *Vit. Cont.* 11, 34-37, 68-89, 73-74, 90; *Cher.* 49–52; *Quaest. in Gen.* 2.19-49, 56; *Mut. Nom.* 207-209; *Rer. Div. Her.* 192; *Sacr.* 63; *Migr. Abr.* 25; *Conf. Ling.* 70, 95-97; *Ebr.* 111; *Leg. All.* 3.15-27; *b. Yom.* 4a; *Merkavah Rabbah* 678-87; *Hekhalot Rabbati* 172, 225, 288; *M. Merk.* 560, 561, 562.

33. The development of this analysis was in reaction to the article by J.Z. Smith, 'The Garments of Shame', *HR* 5 (1966), pp. 217-38.

34. Layton, *Nag Hammadi Codex II,2-7*, pp. 68-69. *P. Oxy.* 655 preserves the first part of the Greek version of this Logion; J. Fitzmyer attempts to reconstruct the fragmentary Greek from the Coptic in 'The Oxyrhynchus *Logoi* and the Coptic Gospel According to Thomas', in Fitzmyer, *Essays on the Semitic Background of the New Testament* (London: Geoffrey Chapman, 1971), pp. 408-10.

Lately, there has been some discussion about whether or not the lacunae in the last clause of this verse should be reconstructed as it has been traditionally—ⲧⲟⲧⲉ [ⲧⲉⲧ]ⲛⲁⲛⲁⲩ, 'then you will see'—or as Greg Riley has proposed—ⲧⲟⲧ[ⲉ ⲧⲉⲧ]ⲛ[ⲛ]ⲏⲩ, 'then you will come'.[35] The *Facsimile Edition* shows four letters missing following ⲧⲟⲧ and subsequent traces of 3 or 4 letters.[36] It is the second to last letter of line 34 which has become the disputed character. Riley has argued against the traditional reconstruction 'ⲁ' because he saw, in the *Facsimile Edition*, a black horizonal line that seems to link the visible vertical ink strokes. Thus he renders it 'ⲏ'.

There are serious problems with this reconstruction as Marvin Meyer has pointed out in his response to Riley's article. First, in the other photographs, negatives, and microfilm of Plate 49, there is absolutely no evidence for this horizonal stroke. Second, when Meyer examined the actual papyrus housed in Old Cairo's Coptic Museum, he was unable to detect any evidence for the stroke. Meyer explains this discrepancy as an error in the process of 'painting out' the black background of the photograph as it was prepared for the *Facsimile Edition*. According to Meyer, 'The black horizontal line Riley saw on Plate 49 of the *Facsimile Edition*, then, is not ink at all but rather an unretouched portion of the black background of the photograph'.[37] Meyer concludes that the reading ⲛⲁⲩ is the more probable reading.

For this reason, I maintain this as my reconstruction of the text. Riley's reading, however, would be very interesting if it could be maintained, since it would combine the notion of ascent or 'coming' to Jesus with the visionary experience alluded to in the disciples' question to Jesus, 'When will you become revealed to us and when will we see you?'

The first motif is rooted in speculation concerning Gen. 3.21. According to this passage, as a consequence of Adam and Eve's sin, God made them 'garments of skins, and clothed them'. These skin garments, according to the Jewish and Christian literature, are identical to the human body of flesh and need to be shed. This literature also points

35. G. Riley, 'A Note on the Text of the *Gospel of Thomas* 37', *HTR* 88 (1995), pp. 179-81; M. Meyer, 'Seeing or Coming to the Child of the Living One? More on *Gospel of Thomas* Saying 37', *HTR* 91 (1998), pp. 413-16.

36. J. Robinson (ed.), *The Facsimile Edition of the Nag Hammadi Codices: Codex II* (Leiden: E.J. Brill, 1974), Plate 49.

37. Meyer, 'Seeing or Coming', p. 415.

to the fact that the removal of the material body was a motif intimately connected with ascent experiences (*Odes Sol.* 11.10-12; 21.3-4 and 6-7; 25.8; *Leg. All.* 2.55-56; 3.46-47; *Somn.* 1.36, 43; *Poster. C.* 136-37; *Gig.* 54; *Dial. Sav.* 84-85). The qualification that one must be 'shameless' in this stripping, alludes to Gen. 2.25 which states that the primordial condition of Adam was a condition in which Adam and Eve were naked and not ashamed. Only after the Fall, were their eyes opened and they knew that they were naked (Gen. 3.7). Thus, the first motif should be understood as follows: when a person strips off the human body of flesh, he or she is regaining Adam's pre-Fall state and returning to the primordial experience of shamelessness.

The analysis of the second motif suggests that the action of treading is a metaphor for renunciation (Jos., *Ant.* 2.9.7; *Val. Exp.* 40.11-17; *Hyp. Arch.* 97.2-10; *Man. Psalm-Book* 278.26-27).[38] *Thomas* seems to employ the garment metaphor in much the same manner as the encratite leader Cassianus in his interpretation of a saying found in the *Gospel of the Egyptians* (*Strom.* 3.13.92). The saying reads:

> When Salome asked when what she had inquired about would be known, the Lord said, 'When you have trampled on the garment of shame and when the two become one and the male with the female (is) neither male nor female'.[39]

Cassianus explains that since sexual intercourse is the original sin, sexual tendencies must be renounced. Thus the person must trample on the garment of shame by becoming asexual. Rather than using gender language as the *Gospel of the Egyptians*, *Thomas* expresses the notion of asexuality by employing the imagery of 'little children'.[40] The image *paidion* is used by Ireneaus (*Adv. Haer.* 3.22.4; *Demo.* 12), Theophilius

---

38. To this discussion, I add that there is the notion that 'trampling' on the object also refers to 'mastery' over the object. This is the case in *T. Levi* 18.12, *T. Sim.* 6.6, and *T. Zeb.* 9.8 (cf. Lk. 10.19). This notion seems to be present in *Val. Exp.* 40.11-17 and *Hyp. Arch.* 97.2-10 too.

39. O. Stählin, *Clemens Alexandrinus, Werke II* (Die Griechischen christlichen Schriftsteller der ersten drei Jahrhunderte, 15; Berlin: Akademie-Verlag, 1962), p. 238.

40. *Thomas* employs the image of little children in Logia 21 and 22 too where this image represents the asexual encratite ideal. E. Peterson has collocated these two Logia with Christian texts where Adam is said to be a *paidion* or a *nēpios*, 'Einige Bemerkungen zum Hamburger Papyrusfragment der "Acta Pauli"', in *Frühkirche, Judentum, und Gnosis* (Freiburg: Herder, 1959), p. 195.

of Antioch (*Ad Auto.* 2.25), and Clement of Alexandria (*Prot.* 11.111.1) to describe Adam, in Paradise, before the Fall. Only when he succumbs to lust, is Adam no longer a child but a man. According to the second motif, the person who renounces the body is the person who has become a little child. He has renounced sex and thereby has become a celibate. In so doing he has returned to the pre-Fall state of Adam who was the child innocent of concupiscence.[41]

This renunciation of sexuality is connected in the third motif with gaining the ability to have a vision of the deity, to 'see' God without fear. It is quite common in Jewish literature for the notion of stripping off the material body to be connected with ascent and vision (especially *2 En.* 22 and *Asc. Isa.* 7 and 9). That the mystical vision is to be experienced without fear alludes to Gen. 3.10 when Adam is 'afraid' of his nakedness after the Fall and hides himself from the sight of God. Thus to return to fearlessness in God's presence indicates that the person has returned to the primordial Adamic condition, that is before Adam had a garment of skin but was naked and unafraid to see God and converse with him.

Thus, Logion 37 describes the soteriological scheme in the *Gospel of Thomas* as follows: it is necessary to renounce the body and become a celibate by mimicking Adam when he was still a child innocent of sex. In so doing, the person has achieved a new state, a Paradisiac state that allows him or her to ascend into heaven and gaze at God without fear and unencumbered by the shame of Adam's sin. Such a vision would result in immortalization.

Thus, the process by which the Thomasine Christians attempted to achieve the visionary God-experience seems to have included ascetic preparatory behaviors. In addition, as Logion 1 suggests, it is plausible that such practices involved the common meditative praxis of mystics. They were reading and contemplating the sayings of Jesus in their gospel in order to experience their hidden truth. This experience was not an intellectual or philosophical one. Rather they were attempting to encounter God himself and overcome death in the process.

41. H. Kee, ' "Becoming a Child" in the Gospel of Thomas', *JBL* 82 (1963), pp. 307-14, is not aware of the tradition that Adam was an innocent child before the Fall, although he links the idea of being a child and being a single one (L. 22), which A.F.J. Klijn, 'The "Single One" in the Gospel of Thomas', *JBL* 81 (1962), pp. 271-78, derives from Jewish speculation concerning the pre-Fall Adam where 'singleness' included asexuality.

4. *Celestial Temple Traditions*

In the *Gospel of Thomas*, we find a curious saying: 'I shall destroy this temple (ϯⲛⲁϣⲟⲣ[ϣⲣ̄ ⲙ̄ⲡⲉⲉ]ⲓⲏⲉⲓ), and no one will be able to build it [...] (ⲁⲩⲱ ⲙ̄ⲛ̄ ⲗⲁⲁⲩ ⲛⲁϣⲕⲟⲧϥ̄. [...]' (L. 71). There are a couple of issues with this saying. First, the saying is fragmentary in that following ⲛⲁϣⲕⲟⲧϥ̄ there is a lacuna which could be filled with approximately 8 letters. So we do not know exactly how the sentence ended. This makes any interpretation tentative. Second, there has been some dispute among scholars over the proper translation of ⲏⲉⲓ. Some have understood it to refer to the material world,[42] the 'conflict between the houses of the world and the people who enter the new world',[43] the metaphor of the Temple as Jesus's body,[44] and the Temple in Jerusalem itself.[45] Ron Cameron points out that this term can refer to 'several different human habitations and social relations'. He lists the following possibilities:

1. The heavenly dwelling place of the soul (e.g. *Exeg. Soul* 128.36; 129.5; 132.21; 137.11).
2. The created world (e.g. *Bar.* 3.24).
3. The abode of wisdom (e.g. Prov. 9.1; Sir. 14.24).
4. The body (e.g. 2 Cor. 5.1).
5. The self (e.g. *Gos. Truth* 25.23).

---

42. E. Haenchen, *Die Botschaft des Thomas-Evangeliums* (Theologische Bibliothek Töpelmann, 6; Berlin: Alfred Töpelmann, 1961), pp. 64 and 66; R. Kasser, *L'Evangile selon Thomas: Présentation et commentaire théologique* (Neuchâtel: Delachaux & Niestlé, 1961), p. 95; J. Leipoldt, *Das Evangelium nach Thomas: Koptisch und Deutsch* (TU, 101; Berlin: Akademie Verlag, 1967), p. 69; J. Ménard, *L'Evangile selon Thomas* (NHS, 5; Leiden: E.J. Brill, 1975), pp. 172-73; M. Fieger, *Das Thomasevangelium: Einleitung, Kommentar und Sytematik* (Neutestamentliche Abhandlungen NS, 22, Münster: Aschendorff, 1991), pp. 202-203; and R. Kuntzmann, 'Le temple dans le corpus copte de Nag Hammadi', *RSR* 67 (1993), pp. 28-29.

43. R. Valantasis, *The Gospel of Thomas* (London: Routledge, 1997), p. 150.

44. Riley, *Resurrection Reconsidered*, pp. 133-56.

45. R. McL. Wilson, *Studies in the Gospel of Thomas* (London: Mowbray, 1960), pp. 114-15; Gärtner, *Theology*, pp. 172-74; J. Crossan, *In Fragments: The Aphorisms of Jesus* (San Francisco: Harper & Row, 1983), pp. 307-12; and G. Quispel, 'The Gospel of Thomas and the Trial of Jesus', in T. Baarda, A. Hilhorst, G.P. Luttikhuizen, and A.S. van der Woude (eds.), *Text and Testimony: Essays on New Testament and Apocryphal Literature in Honour of A.F.J. Klijn* (Kampen: Kok, 1988), pp. 197-99.

6.   A people (e.g. Mt. 10.6; 15.24).
7.   The structure of the family (e.g. *Gos. Thom.* 16, 48).
8.   One's household goods (e.g. Jos., *War* 6.5.2 section 282).
9.   A building (e.g. *Cologne Mani Codex* 92.15).
10.   A royal palace (e.g. Mt. 11.8).
11.   One's ancestral lineage (e.g. Lk. 1.27, 69).
12.   A scribal school (e.g. Sir. 51.23).
13.   The church (e.g. Herm., *Sim.* 9.14.1).
14.   The city of Jerusalem (e.g. Q 13.35).
15.   The Temple in Jerusalem (e.g. Jn 2.16).[46]

So how do we proceed? It is best that the term be understood in the context of the saying itself. Since we have several variants of this saying in the canonical Gospels, it is most probable that this Logion is about the Temple in Jerusalem. It should also be noted that the Coptic ηει is associated in Greek with σκηνή (temple or house), οἶκος (temple or house of god), οἴκημα (chamber, temple, or chapel), μυχός (the innermost room), and δίαιτα (room).[47] Consider the following:

> L. 71: I shall destroy this temple, and no one will be able to build it…

> Mk 14.58; Mt. 26.61: I will destroy this temple that is made with hands, and in three days I will build another, not made with hands.

> Mk 15.29; Mt. 27.40: You who would destroy the temple and build it in three days…

> Jn 2.19: Destroy this temple, and in three days I will raise it up.

Although it is about the Temple, this Logion has substantial differences compared to its variants. Jesus talks about destroying the Jerusalem Temple in all variants, but only in Logion 71, does he state that the earthly Temple will not be rebuilt.[48] In the canonical parallels, he will rebuild or raise up the Temple in three days. Clearly, in the Gospel of John at least, this is interpreted to be a metaphor for Jesus' resurrected body (2.21): 'But he spoke of the temple of his body.'

But this is not the interpretation found in the *Gospel of Thomas*. Logion 71 does not mention rebuilding at all. Based on this, Greg Riley

---

46.   Cameron, 'Myths and Theories', p. 242.
47.   On this refer to Crum, 66a.
48.   It should be noted, however, that a lacunae is found at the end of ηλϣκοτϒ. It is theoretically possible that it might have contained the words 'except for me', using a construction with ⲛⲥⲁⲃⲏⲗ.

has contended that Logion 71 'was composed to contradict the promise of rebuilding interpreted as bodily resurrection' for 'polemical reasons'.[49] While the Gospel of John used the Temple saying to defend 'the physical nature' of the resurrection, *Thomas* employs the saying to affirm that Jesus' body would not be raised.[50] This interpretation is problematic because it must assume that the author of the *Gospel of Thomas* knew the canonical, or at least the Johannine interpretation of this saying and was responding to it. Does this mean that *Thomas* has literary connections with the canonical Gospels? The answer is unclear in Riley's presentation.

One has to wonder if there is another possible explanation. If we remember the visionary ascent traditions in *Thomas*, it is quite possible that the destruction of the Temple and its continued absence on earth was perceived by the Thomasine community as a positive historical development because they believed that God was really present in the celestial Temple where one must now journey in order to worship him. So rebuilding another physical Temple would not be advocated by this community. Therefore it would make sense that they would include this variant in their Gospel.

5. *Conclusion*

This brief summary of the soteriology of the *Gospel of Thomas* verifies the Point of Discourse, as identified by the Johannine author, to be a dispute over a soteriology built on the premises of vision mysticism. Clearly the Johannine textualization of the Thomasine position reflects knowledge of the doctrine laid out in the Thomasine Gospel: the Thomasine Christians were mystics seeking visions of God for the purpose of immortalization. John's portrayal of this, however, is done on a symbolic level where the actual features of the discourse are embedded in the Gospel narrative as words and actions exchanged between Jesus and Thomas. This dramatization of the real opposition leaves the reader with a negative view of Thomas and only sketchy references to Thomasine beliefs.

The opponent's Traditio-religious Horizon, however, can be reconstructed with a fair amount of accuracy by relying directly on the Thomasine Gospel. According to this text, the believers are supposed to

49. Riley, *Resurrection Reconsidered*, p. 142 with n. 39; cf. pp. 147, 155-56.
50. Riley, *Resurrection Reconsidered*, pp. 68, 142, 148, 149, 154.

maintain an encratite lifestyle as the way to be in a state of continual purification and sinlessness, a state of readiness for the dangerous ascent to God. Like the Therapeutae, they believed that this condition was essential for successful vision quests that would bring about their immortalization. So they lived like the angels and thought themselves to be citizens of heaven even while dwelling on earth.

Chapter 5

FAITH MYSTICISM IN THE GOSPEL OF JOHN:
THE INTERPRETATIVE TRAJECTORY AND SYNTHETIC END POINT

Blessed are those who have not seen
and yet believe

(John 20.29).

In 1953, C.H. Dodd published his now classic monograph on the Gospel of John, *The Interpretation of the Fourth Gospel*. In this book, he briefly discusses the central position of 'faith' to Johannine theology.[1] He focuses almost exclusively on 20.23-29, the episode where Thomas recognizes the risen Jesus through a vision and where Jesus tells him to have faith (μὴ γίνου ἄπιστος ἀλλὰ πιστός) (20.27).

Dodd discerned here a relationship between faith and vision. He notes that throughout the Gospel in general, the emphasis is on visions of Jesus accompanied by faith in him. Such conditions brought eternal life. But the Thomas episode, Dodd contends, is a 'transition'. Thomas

---

1. C.H. Dodd, *The Interpretation of the Fourth Gospel* (Cambridge: Cambridge University Press, 1953), pp. 179-86. For other discussion of the concept of 'faith' in the Gospel of John refer to O. Cullmann, *'Eiden kai episteusen': Aux sources de la tradition chrétienne* (Paris: Mélanges Goguel, 1950), pp. 52-61; M. Bonningues, *La foi dans l'Evangile de Saint Jean* (Brussels: Pensée Catholique, 1955); G. Philips, 'Faith and Vision in the Fourth Gospel', in F.M. Cross (ed.), *Studies in the Fourth Gospel* (London: Mowbray, 1957), pp. 83-96; T. Barrosse, 'The Relationship of Love to Faith in St. John', *TS* 18 (1957), pp. 538-59; A. Decourtray, 'La conception johannique de la foi', *NRT* 81 (1959), pp. 561-76; I. de la Potterie, *'Oida* et *ginosko*, les deux modes de la connaissance dans le quatrième évangile', *Bib* 40 (1959), pp. 709-25; G.F. Hawthorne, 'The Concept of Faith in the Fourth Gospel', *BibSac* 116 (1959), pp. 117-26; W. Grundmann, 'Verständnis und Bewegung des Glaubens im Johannes-Evangelium', *KD* 6 (1960), pp. 131-54; P. Grelot, 'Le problème de la foi dans le quatrième évangile', *BVC* 52 (1963), pp. 61-71; J. Gaffney, 'Believing and Knowing in the Fourth Gospel', *TS* 26 (1965), pp. 215-41.

represents the followers of Jesus who saw him physically, and having faith, were granted life. But, even more blessed are those who did not meet Jesus, but still have faith (that is, the Johannine Christians). Dodd summarizes: 'When Christ was on earth, to have faith was to "see His glory"... Now that He is no longer visible to the bodily eye, faith remains the capacity for seeing His glory.'[2]

Wilhelm Bousset further refined the connection between vision mysticism or, as he defines it, 'deification through the vision of God', and the Johannine usage of 'faith'.[3] He notes that the apostles and eye-witnesses of the life of Jesus experienced the *visio Dei* through Jesus, the 'image of God'.[4] He suggests that the Johannine community is also to experience this vision in the image of Jesus, particularly through worship, sermons, sacramental participation, and, above all, through faith.[5]

Dodd and Bousset certainly recognized the centrality of faith as vision in the Gospel of John. Unfortunately, neither fully developed their interpretations nor saw the connections between John's substitution of faith for vision and his polemic against proleptic visionary flights into heaven. Thus, in this chapter, I will reconstruct the tenets of what I call 'faith mysticism', the new theology or Synthetic End Point that the Johannine author presents in response to the mystical soteriology of the Thomasine Christians.

He does this by disarticulating himself from the Religio-historical and Traditio-religious Horizons. This disarticulation empties a space for his own creative theological thinking about faith and salvation, the development of his own Interpretative Trajectory. At the same time as he disarticulates from these horizons, however, he also articulates within their spheres. Thus he salvages the underpinnings of vision mysticism but transforms these tenets into something of value to him and his community: a salvific mystical experience centered on faith rather than ecstatic vision. As we will see, the Synthetic End Point or 'faith mysticism' is a form of mysticism that is developed by the Johannine author through his division of time into three eras: the pretemporal existence of Jesus when Jesus was with God, the historical presence of

2.   Dodd, *The Interpretation of the Fourth Gospel*, p. 186.
3.   W. Bousset, *Kyrios Christos* (trans. J.E. Steely; New York: Abingdon Press, 1970), pp. 221-32.
4.   Bousset, *Kyrios Christos*, p. 228.
5.   Bousset, *Kyrios Christos*, p. 230.

Jesus when people who saw Jesus were transformed, and the author's own time characterized by the historical absence of Jesus when transformation occured through faith in Jesus rather than vision.

1. *The Pretemporal Existence of Jesus*

The Prologue makes clear the pretemporal existence of Jesus as the Logos of God who was with God prior to creation and who aided in creation before his incarnation in human form. The most current interpretation of the Prologue by Jarl Fossum correctly challenges the widespread opinion since the works of J. Rendel Harris and Rudolph Bultmann that the Logos in the Prologue is best understood in terms of Sophianology.[6] Fossum contends that Sophia traditions cannot explain the incarnation of the Logos in one individual person,[7] nor the identification of the Logos with God who existed from the beginning. Rather, the Johannine author is utilizing Jewish traditions about the Angel of the Lord who is indistinguishable from the Tetragrammaton. The Name of God was understood in the traditions to be a hypostasis of God's eternal nature and thus equivalent to him. It helped with creating the world and was present in the Angel of the Lord who was known to descend to earth and take on a human form. Thus, according to John, Jesus is the final dwelling place of the Name of God.[8]

The association of this pretemporal existence of Jesus as the Name with the dynamics of vision is vividly expressed in the first few verses. It is stressed that not only was Jesus with God prior to his incarnation (Jn 1.1-18), but he also has seen God while he was with the Father in heaven (Jn 1.18). So John dictates in the introduction to his Gospel that 'no one has ever seen God (θεὸν οὐδεὶς ἑώρακεν πώποτε)'[9] except the

6.   J. Rendel Harris, 'The Origins of the Prologue to St. John's Gospel', *Expositor* 8.12 (1916), pp. 147-60, 161-70, 314-20, 388-400; R. Bultmann, 'Der religionsgeschichtliche Hintergrund des Prologs zum Johannes-Evangelium', in H. Schmidt (ed.), *Eucharisterion: Festschrift für Hermann Gunkel* (FRLANT, 37.2; Göttingen: Vandenhoeck & Ruprecht, 1923), pp. 3-26.

7.   There is no evidence for the incarnation of Sophia, only of her transmigration (Wis. 7.27).

8.   J. Fossum, 'In the Beginning was the Name: Onomanology as the Key to Johannine Christianity', in *idem*, *The Image of the Invisible God: Essays on the Influence of Jewish Mysticism on Early Christology* (NTOA, 30; Göttingen: Vandenhoeck & Ruprecht, 1995), pp. 109-33.

9.   P. Borgen, *Philo, John and Paul: New Perspectives on Judaism and Early*

Son who was in 'the bosom of the Father' (Jn 1.18). John continues to emphasize that no one has 'seen' God except Jesus: 'Not that anyone has seen the Father except him who is from God; he has seen the Father (οὐχ ὅτι τόν πατέρα ἑώρακέν τις εἰ μὴ ὁ ὢν παρὰ τοῦ θεοῦ, οὗτος ἑώρακεν τὸν πατέρα)' (Jn 6.46). In Jn 5.37, the Johannine author even has Jesus polemicize against the Jews: 'his [the Father's] form you have never seen (οὔτε εἶδος αὐτοῦ ἑωράκατε)'.

There is a striking passage that contains ideas similar to these. This passage is described in the first-century Jewish writing quoted by Origen, the *Prayer of Joseph*. According to this text, Jacob is also 'Israel', an angel of God. Jacob claims that God called him Israel which means 'a man seeing God (ἀνὴρ ὁρῶν θεόν)', because he was 'the firstborn of every living thing to whom God gives life (ἐγὼ πρωτόγονος παντὸς ζῴου ζωουμένου ὑπὸ θεοῦ)'. Israel then descended to earth and tabernacled among men and was called Jacob: εἶπεν ὅτι κατέβην ἐπὶ τὴν γῆν καὶ κατεσκήνωσα ἐν ἀνθρώποις, καὶ ὅτι ἐκλήθην ὀνόματι Ἰακώβ (Origen, *Comm. in Joh.* 2.188-90).[10]

Thus there existed a tradition contemporaneous with John that a special angel of God existed before the rest of creation. This angel was given a special name based on the fact that he had seen God during his cohabitation with God. Later this angel descended to earth in human form.

The Johannine author, therefore, seems to be articulating at the same time as he is disarticulating with this Religio-historical Horizon as he begins to build the figural action in his Gospel. He writes of a preexistent Logos figure who cohabited with God and was given the *sole* visionary experience of that God. This pretemporal visionary experi-

---

Christianity (BJS, 131; Atlanta: Scholars Press, 1987), pp. 177-78, suggests that this theme that 'no one has ever seen God' is an interpretation of the theophany at Sinai in Exod. 33.20 where Moses was not allowed to see the face of God because no one can see God and live; according to John, the only heavenly figure to be able to see God is the Son; this figure may be associated with the angel Israel, 'he who sees God', in Philo (*Conf. Ling.* 1.46; *Leg. All.* 1.43). It should be noted, however, that Moses does see God or God's Glory! Cf. the interpretation of Exod. 33.20 (in light of Num. 12.8) in *Lev. R.* 20.10; see also *Exod. R.* 23.15. Jn 5.37 apparently looks back to 5.24-25. Thus, Jesus is equivalent to the 'form' or Glory of God. On this, see J. Fossum, *The Name of God and the Angel of the Lord* (WUNT, 36; Tübingen: J.C.B. Mohr, 1985), p. 295 n. 112.

10. C. Blanc, *Origène: Commentaire sur Saint Jean*, I (SC, 120; Paris: Cerf, 1966), pp. 334-37.

ence has made this entity special. He not only is the only one who truly knows the Father because he is the only one who has seen the Father (Jn 1.18), but he also participates in and embodies the deity. The Logos is God (Jn 1.1). Moreover, once this Logos has descended from heaven (Jn 3.13, 31-32; 7.29; 8.23; cf. 17.5)[11] and tabernacled with humans, he, as Jesus, can claim that 'the Father and I are one' (Jn 10.30) and 'believe me that I am in the Father and the Father in me' (Jn 14.11). He has been given God's Name and thus is one with God (Jn 17.11).

2. The Historical Presence of Jesus

a. The Kābôd
The key to unlocking the mysterious Christology of John is understanding the author's application of *kābôd* traditions to the historical manifestation of Jesus. This idea is compatible with John Ashton's conclusions found in his article, 'Bridging Ambiguities'. In this article, he demonstrates that Jewish angelology goes a long way to explain the perplexing Christology in John.[12]

It is unfortunate that James Dunn did not make this connection in his otherwise informed article on Christology in the Fourth Gospel.[13] He correctly notes that the Christology of Jesus as the manifestation of God descended from heaven reflects Johannine hostility towards Christian interest in Jewish mystical ascent and vision. The Johannine author, declaring this as too dangerous and too speculative, offers the alternative of the incarnate Logos who brings through himself the vision of the Father.[14] The deficiency in Dunn's argument is his reliance on Wisdom traditions to explain the equation of the Logos with God.[15] Sophia

11. For discussions about this theme, see especially, W. Meeks, 'The Man From Heaven in Johannine Sectarianism', *JBL* 91 (1972), pp. 44-72; for background of this motif, see C. Talbert, 'The Myth of a Descending–Ascending Redeemer in Mediterranean Antiquity', *NTS* 22 (1976), pp. 418-39.

12. J. Ashton, 'Bridging Ambiguities', in *idem*, *Studying John: Approaches to the Fourth Gospel* (Oxford: Clarendon Press, 1994), pp. 71-89.

13. J. Dunn, 'Let John be John: A Gospel for Its Time', in P. Stuhlmacher (ed.), *Das Evangelium und die Evangelium: Vorträge vom Tübinger Symposium 1982* (WUNT, 28; Tübingen: J.C.B. Mohr, 1983), pp. 309-39.

14. Dunn, 'Let John be John', p. 334.

15. Dunn, 'Let John be John', p. 337; Cf. J. Dunn, *Christology in the Making: A New Testament Inquiry into the Origins of the Doctrine of the Incarnation* (Philadelphia: Westminster Press, 1980), pp. 168-76.

traditions cannot explain the identification of a pre-existent Logos with God, nor the incarnation of the Logos in one individual as we find in John.

Fossum's interpretation, unlike prior ones such as Dunn's which focused on Sophianology, aligns with the representation of Jesus throughout the Gospel as God's manifestation, his *kābôd* or Glory, a figure from Jewish tradition that often bears God's Name.[16] Frequently in the Gospel of John we hear of 'seeing' the δόξα or Glory of God in Jesus and his works and words.

The Johannine usage of δόξα is distinctive. The Glory of Jesus is visible in his person (Jn 1.14), his signs or wonders (Jn 2.11; 11.40; 17.4), and his crucifixion (Jn 12.23, 28; 13.32; 17.1, 5).[17] In 1.14, for instance, the claim is made: 'we have seen his Glory (τὴν δόξαν αὐτοῦ), the Glory (δόξα) as of the Only Begotten from the Father'. The background of this vision may be found in Moses' vision of the Glory in Exod. 33.18–34.8.[18] Clearly here we have the personalizing of this term by connecting it to the personal being, the Only Begotten who is the visible manifestation of God (Jn 1.18).[19] Additionally, John implies that Isaiah's vision of 'the Lord' in Isaiah 6 was actually a vision of Jesus as the Glory (Jn 12.41):[20]

> For this reason they could not believe, because, as Isaiah says elsewhere: 'He has blinded their eyes and deadened their hearts, so they can neither see with their eyes, nor understand with their hearts, nor turn, and I would heal them'. Isaiah said these things because he saw his [Jesus'] Glory and he spoke concerning him [Jesus] (Jn 12.39-41).

16. For discussions on *kābôd* traditions in John, see, Dodd, *The Interpretation of the Fourth Gospel*, pp. 206-208, 373-79; C. Rowland, 'John 1.51, Jewish Apocalyptic and Targumic Tradition', *NTS* 30 (1984), pp. 498-507 (505); most recently, C. Gieschen, *Angelomorphic Christology: Antecedents and Early Evidence* (AGJU, 42; Leiden: E.J. Brill, 1998), pp. 271-80.

17. G. Kittel, δόξα, *TDNT* II, pp. 242-45.

18. J. Fossum, 'Glory כבוד δόξα', in K. van der Toorn *et al.* (eds.), *Dictionary of Deities and Demons in the Bible* (Leiden: E.J. Brill, 1995), pp. 1486-98.

19. For a discussion of this idea, see Gieschen, *Angelomorphic Christology*, p. 273.

20. It is most likely that John is following the same exegetical tradition found in the Targum of Isaiah here which reads that Isaiah saw the 'יקרא' of the Lord' (6.1) or the 'יקר שכינת' of the King of the worlds' (6.5). On this, see Fossum, *The Name of the God*, p. 295 n. 112; and Fossum, 'Glory'.

The Gospel claims that God sent his son to earth out of his own love so that the world might be saved through encountering him (Jn 3.16-17). This theme is expanded upon in 17.20-26 where Jesus is identified with the Glory who has been sent to earth out of God's love. By seeing Jesus the Glory, the disciples will experience a mystic union with Jesus, and thus with the Father. Because Jesus is the *kābôd*, the personal manifestation of the Father, he is identified with the Father: 'even as you, Father, are in me, and I, in you' (Jn 17.21). This Glory or divine essence is transferred to the disciple: 'The Glory which you have given to me, I have given to them, that they may be one even as we are one, I in them and you in me, that they may become perfectly one' (Jn 17.22-23). Such a transformation is possible through the mechanism of the visionary experience. Thus Jesus prays for the disciple 'to see my Glory (ἵνα θεωρῶσιν τὴν δόξαν τὴν ἐμήν) which you [the Father] have given to me in your love for me before the foundation of the world' (Jn 17.24). In the capacity of God's *kābôd*, Jesus makes the Father known to the world and makes available the opportunity for union with him (Jn 17.25-26).

Wilhelm Bousset made reference to this concept in his well-known work, *Kyrios Christos*: 'This vision which deifies men occurs in the image of the Son of God who has appeared on earth';[21] thus, 'the apostles and eyewitnesses of the life of Jesus have experienced the vision of God in the image of God, and are now themselves flooded by the utter abundance of the powers of the upper world'.[22]

This notion is quite vividly displayed in narratological form in Jn 6.30-40 where Jesus is asked what sign he does so that 'we may see, and believe you'. The questioners expect him to feed them manna as Moses did their forefathers. Jesus then replies that he is the manna come down from heaven and which gives life. Thus Jesus himself is the sign they seek to see. This is summed up neatly in Jn 6.40 which reads: 'For this is the will of my Father that everyone who sees the Son (πᾶς ὁ θεωρῶν τὸν υἱὸν) and believes in him should have eternal life (ἔχῃ ζωὴν αἰώνιον).'

Consequently, Jesus himself is literally 'the way (ἡ ὁδὸς)' (Jn 14.6) because he embodies the journey to the Father and mediates the knowledge of God or the vision of God.[23] Rudolph Bultmann explains that

21. Bousset, *Kyrios Christos*, p. 227.
22. Bousset, *Kyrios Christos*, p. 228.
23. Cf. Dodd, *The Interpretation of the Fourth Gospel*, pp. 404-405.

Jesus as 'the way' is the *only* access to God 'not in the sense of a mystagogue, who brings doctrines and celebrations that are the means to the vision of God'. Rather, Jesus is 'the way' in such a manner that he is:

> at the same time the goal; for he is also ἡ ἀλήθεια καὶ ἡ ζωή: the ἀλήθεια as the *revealed* reality of God, and the ζωή as the *divine* reality which bestows life on the believer in that it bestows self-understanding in God.[24]

Thus there is no rebirth apart from the Son of Man (Jn 3.3-13) and no one can ascend to heaven and enter the Kingdom of God unless through the Son of Man (Jn 3.13).[25]

In the Johannine tradition, therefore, the deity has been manifested historically. Ascent to heaven and a vision of God are not necessary to be transformed and achieve life because the divinity has come to earth and has brought this mystic experience with him. So John emphasizes that the vision of Jesus on earth substitutes for the vision of the Father in heaven: 'He who has seen me has seen the Father (ὁ ἑωρακὼς ἐμὲ ἑώρακεν τὸν πατέρα)' (Jn 14.9). Moreover, knowing Jesus on earth is knowing the Father in heaven: 'If you had known me, you would have known my Father also (εἰ ἐγνώκατέ με, καὶ τὸν πατέρα μου γνώσεσθε); henceforth you know him and have seen him' (Jn 14.7). And those who see Jesus shall live (Jn 14.19). The revelation of the divinity, in the words of Christopher Rowland, is not to be found 'in the visions of the mystics' but only 'in the earthly life of Jesus Christ'.[26]

Consequently, Rowland draws the provocative conclusion that the incarnation of Jesus as the *kābôd* in John is an attempt to downplay any claims to revelation apart from Jesus.[27] Rowland even sees Jn 1.51 ('You will see heaven opened, and the angels of God ascending and descending upon the Son of Man') as a verse whose function is to testify to the fact that the vision does not provide an avenue for the mystic

---

24. R. Bultmann, *The Gospel of John: A Commentary* (trans. G.R. Beasley-Murray; eds. R.W.N. Hoare and J.K. Riches; Oxford: Basil Blackwell, 1971), pp. 605-606.

25. Refer to discussions in H. Odeberg, *The Fourth Gospel Interpreted in its Relationship to Contemporaneous Religious Currents in Palestine and the Hellenistic-Oriental World* (repr.; Amsterdam: B.R. Grüner, 1974 [1929]), pp. 95-97; Borgen, *Philo, John and Paul*, p. 115.

26. Rowland, 'John 1.51', p. 505.

27. Rowland, 'John 1.51', p. 505.

to gaze into heaven, but teaches him that even the angels who are already *in* heaven must come to earth to see the revelation of God which is located in the historical figure Jesus.[28]

One could say, therefore, that the goal, so cherished by the Thomasine Christians, of mystic flights into heaven in order to gaze upon the Glory of God, is challenged by the Johannine author who insists that such visions can only be achieved in the historical encounter with Jesus who was the *kābôd* on earth glorified completely at Golgotha (Jn 12.32).

b. *The Body of Jesus as the New Temple*
As we have seen in earlier chapters of this monograph, speculation about a new Temple in the absence of the Jerusalem Temple was quite prevalent in early Jewish mystical thought. This tradition had elevated the Temple to the supernal realm where the adept now journeyed to worship God and experience a spiritual transformation often effected by gaze. Such speculation certainly became part of early Christian texts, particularly Revelation and Hebrews. In these texts, the Temple is a celestial house of God where God is enthroned in the Holy of Holies. It is noteworthy that John of Patmos is able to journey into this Temple in Revelation and join in the heavenly worship (Rev. 4–5), while in Hebrews, the 'priesthood' of Christians are encouraged to 'draw near to the throne of grace' (Heb. 4.16), and to 'enter the sanctuary by the blood of Jesus, by the new and living way which he opened for us through the veil, that is, through his flesh' (Heb. 10.19), in order to 'offer to God acceptable worship, with reverence and awe; for our God is a consuming fire' (Heb. 12.28-29). In both these cases, the Temple is identified with the space of heaven and is a 'building' which believers enter.

As I conjectured in the last chapter, Logion 71 may be evidence that the Thomasine Christians felt that the destruction of the earthly Temple was a positive historical development. It is plausible that they held this belief because they too were advocates of a celestial Temple through which they ascended in order to come before God's throne, as Logion

---

28. Rowland, 'John 1.51', pp. 498-507, esp. 506. J. Fossum has provided recent interpretation of this passage in his article, 'The Son of Man's Alter Ego: John 1.51, Targumic Tradition and Jewish Mysticism', in *idem, The Image of the Invisible God: Essays on the Influence of Jewish Mysticism on Early Christology* (NTOA, 30; Göttingen: Vandenhoeck & Ruprecht, 1995), pp. 135-51.

15 suggests: 'When you see one who was not born of woman, prostrate yourselves on your faces and worship him. That one is your Father.'

Because of the importance of the celestial Temple in these traditions, it is not surprising that John responds to them by reworking the ideas into a new Synthetic End Point that supports his position that ascent and visionary experiences are not necessary for salvation. He shifts the emphasis from a celestial Temple to another 'earthly' Temple: he argues that Jesus' body is the new tabernacle of God's presence (1.14).

Raymond Brown was one of the first scholars to notice that σκηνοῦν in Old Testament passages was used to indicate the Tabernacle and Temple, the 'site of God's localized presence on earth'.[29] This theme is found in Exod. 25.8-9 where Israel is commanded to make a σκηνή or Tabernacle so that God could dwell among the Israelites. Later this word was used to indicate the presence of God in the Jerusalem Temple (Joel 3.17; Zech. 2.10; Ezek. 43.7). Brown concludes:

> When the Prologue proclaims that the Word made his dwelling among men, we are being told that the flesh of Jesus Christ is the new local-ization of God's presence on earth, and that Jesus is the replacement of the ancient Tabernacle. The Gospel will present Jesus as the replacement of the Temple (ii 19-22), which is a variation of the same theme.[30]

Jarl Fossum also has drawn attention to this theme in his article, 'In the Beginning was the Name'. He investigates the use of the verb σκηνόω and its nominal forms and concludes that Jn 1.14 implies that 'Jesus is the new sanctuary, the dwelling-place of the Name of God'.[31] He states that the idea that 'Jesus is the new sanctum' is clearly spelled out in Jn 2.19-21:

> Jesus answered them and said to them, 'Destroy this temple, and in three days I will raise it up'. Then the Jews said, 'In forty days and six years was this temple built, and you will raise it in three days?' But he spoke of the temple of his body.

Furthermore, in ch. 7, Jesus teaches at the Temple during the Feast of Tabernacles, a festival that included daily water libations poured out on the altar in front of the Temple. The water libations were connected to Old Testament prophecies that in the age to come, a fountain of sal-

---

29. R. Brown, *The Gospel According to John* (2 vols.; AB, 29; Garden City, NY: Doubleday, 1985), I, pp. 32-33.

30. R. Brown, *John*, p. 33.

31. Fossum, 'In the Beginning was the Name', pp. 121-25.

vation would spring forth from the Temple (Isa. 12.3; Ezek. 47.1-2; Joel 3.18; Zech. 14.8). Thus, when Jn 7.37-38 writes that Jesus cries, 'If anyone thirsts, let him come to me. And let him drink who has faith in me. As Scripture says: "Out of his body shall flow rivers of living waters"', he is identifying Jesus as the source of the living waters, the new Temple.[32]

One of Fossum's students, Mark Kinzer, has developed these ideas further in a paper that he presented at the 1998 Society of Biblical Literature Annual Convention.[33] He argues that the portrayal of Jesus as the Temple of God by John 'serves as the integrating center for his cultic Christology'.[34] In addition to examining Jn 1.14; 2.20 and 7.37-39, Kinzer remarks on the story of the Samaritan woman in ch. 4. She is given 'living water' or the spirit (cf. Jn 7.37-39), by Jesus (Jn 4.10, 14). Jesus then contrasts worship in this spirit with the worship that was going on at both the Jerusalem and Gerizim Temples: 'The hour is coming when neither on this mountain nor in Jerusalem will you worship the Father... The hour is coming, and now is, when the true worshipers will worship the Father in spirit and in truth...' (Jn 4.21, 23). Kinzer states that these verses imply that 'a new and different kind of Temple is being established'.[35]

Kinzer expands Jesus' connection with the Feast of Tabernacles by pointing out that chs. 7–8 tell about Jesus and his critics, during the Feast, disputing over the two key themes of the festival: water and light. John identifies Jesus with 'the light of the world' (Jn 8.12) and has Jesus give out 'living water' (Jn 7.37-39). According to Kinzer, these themes are continued in ch. 9 with the healing of the blind man. The healing takes place at the starting point for the procession of the water-drawing ceremony during the festival: the pool of Siloam. Through this healing, Jesus is portrayed as the light of the world (Jn 9.5).[36] Additionally, he examines ch. 10, a scene that occurs during the Feast of Dedication. This feast commemorates the rededication of the Temple after it had been desecrated by Antiochus. In the discourse, Jesus refers to himself as the one 'consecrated and sent into the world' (Jn 10.36).

---

32. Fossum, 'In the Beginning was the Name', pp. 130-31.

33. M. Kinzer, 'Temple Christology in the Gospel of John' (SBLSP; Atlanta: Scholars Press, 1998), pp. 447-64.

34. Kinzer, 'Temple Christology', p. 447.

35. Kinzer, 'Temple Christology', p. 449.

36. Kinzer, 'Temple Christology', p. 449.

Kinzer concludes, 'He is thus the new and true Temple, consecrated by God himself'.[37]

He feels that Jesus as the Temple is intimately linked in John with several other Johannine themes: (1) Jesus as Sophia, the divine presence in the Temple (cf. Ps. 132; Sir. 24.8-12); (2) Jesus as the bearer of God's Name, the cultic term for the divine presence in the Temple; (3) Jesus as the vision of God, who traditionally was 'seen' during worship at the Temple (cf. Ps. 27.4; 63.2; 84.7); (4) Jesus as the Temple that linked heaven and earth; and (5) Jesus the giver of the Spirit during baptism, the true purification that allows the believer to worship at the Temple.[38] At the finale of his study, Kinzer concludes that 'whereas John focuses on the person of Jesus as the new Temple, other related traditions are oriented to the heavenly Temple, the eschatological Temple, and/or a particular community as earthly Temple'.[39] This sets John in the center of the mystical Temple traditions.

Most recently, Jonathan Draper has turned to this theme in an article which he promises will soon become a monograph.[40] He begins with Jn 1.14, stating that 'Jesus' incarnation is actually his "tenting" among us so that the divine glory usually understood to be present in the temple building may instead be experience by those with eyes to see in him'. Draper understands this ideology to be a 're-interpretation of the symbol of the temple in terms of *merkābâ* mysticism'.[41] He then examines, on a surface level, several Johannine passages which he links to key Merkavah themes: 1.47-51; 2.12-22; 2.23–3.21; 4.1-42; 7.37-39; 10.3-5, 34-36; 12.28-30, 37-41; 14.1-6; and 15.1-10. Later in this chapter, I will examine some of the difficulties with his interpretation of these particular passages.

It seems that there is solid evidence that demonstrates that the Johannine author understood Jesus, during his lifetime, to be the true dwelling place of God's presence, the replacement for the corrupt Temple in Jerusalem which Jesus violently condemned (Jn 2.13-22). His physical body was the Temple of Yahweh from which poured the waters of life. Furthermore, Jesus' physical body was indwelled by Jesus' spiritual

37. Kinzer, 'Temple Christology', p. 450.
38. Kinzer, 'Temple Christology', pp. 451-58.
39. Kinzer, 'Temple Christology', p. 458.
40. J.A. Draper, 'Temple, Tabernacle, and Mystical Experience in John', *Neot* 32 (1997), pp. 263-88.
41. Draper, 'Temple, Tabernacle', p. 266.

body, the *kābôd* or manifestation of God. Therefore, the people around Jesus could encounter the true presence of God who had taken up residence in the new Temple, the body of Jesus. This new locale meant that by making a pilgrimage to Jesus, people during his lifetime were journeying to the real Temple and would 'see' God there.

3. *The Historical Absence of Jesus*

This theology was functional for those who actually saw the 'historical' Jesus while he walked on earth. But what about after his death? How does the person who did not live during Jesus' lifetime gain eternal life, especially when the Johannine author has closed the open heaven and has crucified the new Temple?

a. *The Paraclete*
In ch. 16 we hear echoes of this very concern. Jesus prophecies that shortly his followers will not be able to see him, but soon, they will be able to see him again: 'A little while, and you will see me no more; again, a little while, and you will see me (μικρὸν καὶ οὐκέτι θεωρεῖτέ με, καὶ πάλιν μικρὸν καὶ ὄψεσθέ με)' (Jn 16.16).

The farewell discourse in ch. 14 where the coming of the Paraclete is discussed, is the antecedent to this statement. Here Jesus explains that he will come to his followers in the form of the Paraclete: 'And I will ask the Father, and he will give you *another* Paraclete (ἄλλον παρά-κλητον) to be with you forever... I will not leave you orphaned; I am coming to you' (Jn 14.16, 18). Jesus reassures them that 'it is to your advantage that I go away, for if I do not go away, the Paraclete will not come to you; but if I go, I will send him to you' (Jn 16.7). He tells them repeatedly that he will not leave his followers desolate, that 'I will come to you' (Jn 14.18).

The Paraclete, along with being 'another' Jesus is also identified with the 'Spirit of Truth (τὸ πνεῦμα τῆς ἀληθείας)' or the 'Holy Spirit (τὸ πνεῦμα τὸ ἅγιον)' who is invisible to the world but who is known to his followers (Jn 14.25-26; 15.26):

> This is the Spirit of Truth, whom the world cannot receive, because it neither sees him, nor knows him. You know him, because he abides in you, and he will be in you (τὸ πνεῦμα τῆς ἀληθείας, ὃ ὁ κόσμος οὐ δύναται λαβεῖν, ὅτι οὐ θεωρεῖ αὐτὸ οὐδὲ γινώσκει. ὑμεῖς γινώσκετε αὐτό, ὅτι παρ᾽ ὑμῖν μένει καὶ ἐν ὑμῖν ἔσται) (Jn 14.17).

The world may not be able to see Jesus, but his followers will because he will make himself manifest to them as the Paraclete and in the form of divine love (Jn 14.22-23).

Although much scholarship has been generated in the attempt to establish the origins and meaning of the Johannine Paraclete,[42] particularly scrutinizing the Jewish traditions of intercessory angels,[43] the most recent work by Charles Gieschen points to the probability of an 'angelomorphic' Paraclete. He demonstrates that the phenomenon of two Johannine Paracletes, Jesus and the Spirit, is probably tied directly to Jewish and Christian traditions about a pair of God's principle angels.[44] He bases his work on the research of Gilles Quispel who previously proposed that a parallel to John's two Paracletes is found in the contemporaneous Jewish-Christian literature of Elchasai and the *Ascension of Isaiah*.[45]

Thus, it is likely that John's representation of the Paraclete as another Jesus has its foundation in such traditions. But the concern of the Johannine author surfaces in his insistence that the community, in Jesus' absence, will not be left alone without the opportunity of the mystical encounter with the divine. This need for the ideology of the Paraclete has been analyzed by Jonathan Draper from a sociological perspective. He has determined that the Paraclete is developed in John due to the community's concern over 'the departure of Jesus'.[46] The death of the 'charismatic founder' of the religious movement raises the questions of

42. For a history of research on this subject, refer to G. Burge, *The Anointed Community: The Holy Spirit in the Johannine Tradition* (Grand Rapids: Eerdmans, 1987); J. Ashton, 'Paraclete', *ABD*, V, pp. 152-54.

43. On this, see H. Windisch, *The Spirit-Paraclete in the Fourth Gospel* (trans. J. Cox; Philadelphia: Fortress Press, 1968). In addition, N. Johannson, *Parakletoi: Vorstellungen von Fürsprechern für die Menschen vor Gott in der alttestamentlichen Religion, im Spätjudentum, und Urchristentum* (Lund: C.W.K. Gleerup, 1940); J. Behm, 'παράκλητος', *TDNT*, V, pp. 800-14; and O. Betz, *Der Paraklet* (Leiden: E.J. Brill, 1963).

44. Gieschen, *Angelomorphic Christology*, pp. 286-93.

45. G. Quispel, 'John and Jewish Christianity', *Gnostic Studies* 2 (Nederlands Historisch-Archaeologisch Instituut te Istanbul, 34.2: Leiden: E.J. Brill, 1975), pp. 210-29 (220-24); Quispel is informed by the research of G. Kretschmar, *Studien zur frühchristlichen Trinitätstheologie* (BHT, 21; Tübingen: J.C.B. Mohr, 1956), pp. 62-93; see also, G. Stroumsa, 'Le couple de l'ange et de l'espirit: traditions juives et chrétiennes', *RB* 88 (1981), pp. 42-61.

46. J.A. Draper, 'The Sociological Function of the Spirit/Paraclete in the Farewell Discourses in the Fourth Gospel', *Neot* 26 (1992), pp. 13-27 (14).

the 'succession of charisma' in the community, produces an increase in cognitive dissonance among members, and leads to a possible dissolution of the community in face of external hostility.[47] The Paraclete functions as the 'boundary maintenance over against a hostile world'. The Paraclete passages are interwoven into the Farewell Discourses in order to differentiate the community that possesses the Paraclete in Jesus' absence from the world, and give the community strength to maintain themselves against the world. Additionally, the possession of the Paraclete as the Spirit of Truth means that the community members can lay exclusive claim to salvation. According to Draper, 'There is no salvation outside the sect'.[48]

Thus John fleshes out the Interpretative Trajectory with his idea of the Paraclete, the Holy Spirit, who replaces Jesus in his absence. Although a theophany of this being is not realistic because he does not have a visible form, the community will 'know' him nonetheless. He will be manifested as the divine love of Jesus for his followers, a love that is mutually shared between the members of John's community. According to the Johannine author, this display of love becomes the new Torah just as Jeremiah predicted: 'I will put my law within them, and I will write it upon their hearts' (Jn 13.33). Furthermore, the true disciples of Jesus are identified by this mutual love:

> A new commandment I give to you, that you love one another; even as I have loved you, that you also love another. By this all people will know that you are my disciples, if you have love for one another (Jn 13.34-35).

This means that Jesus' command to love one another is the evidence that Jesus as the Paraclete dwells within the Johannine community:

> He who has my commandments and keeps them, he it is who loves me; and he who loves me will be loved by my Father and I will love him and manifest myself to him... If a person loves me, he will keep my word, and my Father will love him, and we will come to him and make our home with him (Jn 14.21-24).

So, even though the followers will no longer be able to 'see' Jesus, they will be able to 'know' the Paraclete. And the Paraclete, through this encounter with the believers, will mediate God. Proleptic visionary ascents are not necessary because the Paraclete has come down to earth in Jesus' absence.

---

47. Draper, 'Sociological Function of the Spirit', p. 14.
48. Draper, 'Sociological Function of the Spirit', pp. 22-23.

b. *The Eschatological Temple*
Since the Temple has been identified with Jesus' body, the Johannine
author recognizes that the Temple must be reconstituted after Jesus'
crucifixion. Instead of creating an ideology that the community of
believers was the newest Temple as other Christians argued (cf. 1 Cor.;
2 Cor.; Eph.; 1 Pet.), John interprets Jesus' resurrection as the
recreation of the Temple in the heavenly realm. Therefore, Jesus claims
in John to be able to raise up the destroyed Temple in 'three days' (Jn
2.19-21). Moreover, he tells his disciples in ch. 14 that in his Father's
'house (οἰκία)' there are many rooms (14.2). He is going there 'to
prepare a place' for his followers. In the future, he will come to earth
again, to collect his own and take them to himself (14.3). It seems that
the Johannine author understands Jesus' resurrected body to be the new
heavenly Temple which believers will be able to enter at the end of
time.

Jonathan Draper has made similar observations in his article. He
states, 'In John's Gospel, the concept of Jesus as the tented wilderness
presence of God with his people on earth, is supplemented it seems
with the idea of Jesus constituting or building the heavenly temple on
his return to the Father'.[49] Although I think that this is a very solid
conclusion, Draper goes on to state that 'in so doing, he opens the way
for his disciples to gain mystic experience of the heavenly throne room
by means of ascent and descent obtained through the worship of the
community'.[50] This latter statement is problematic in that it does not
recognize the eschatological nature of Jn 14.2-3. The Johannine author
is *not* stating that ascent and visionary experience in God's new Temple
is available to the believers *now*—but that this will be a future event
which the community members can only long and hope for now. Thus,
as we have seen, throughout the Gospel there are claims that no one can
see God except Jesus, or ascend into heaven, or follow Jesus there until
the prepared time. It should also be remembered that this is the
direction of the Johannine trajectory in 1 Jn 3.2: 'Beloved, we are
God's children now; it does not yet appear what we shall be, but we
know that when he appears we shall be like him, for we shall see him as
he is.'

Thus, Draper's interpretation of Jn 3.13 has difficulties: 'Jesus comes
from above to enable those below to ascend and experience the worship

49. Draper, 'Temple, Tabernacle', p. 278.
50. Draper, 'Temple, Tabernacle', pp. 278-79.

of the heavenly temple.'[51] He recognizes that previous scholars are correct to note here 'a polemic against the claims of mystics to ascend into heaven by their own work' but feels that we also have in 3.13 a passage which points out that 'access to the Father is open through Jesus, who takes his disciples to himself and provides birth "from above"' (Jn 14.3-6). He continues that 'it is no accident that the gospel so often uses the concept of seeing and believing (e.g. 1.39, 46; 9.1-41; though note 20.29). The vision of God is the goal of worship in the new Temple'.[52] Kinzer also seems to be reading the Gospel in this direction when he states:

> Like other Temple traditions of the time, John's Gospel promotes a visionary and mystical brand of Judaism, and roots the visionary and mystical knowledge it promotes in a type of Temple worship which is only indirectly tied to the Temple in Jerusalem.[53]

Unfortunately, neither scholar has made the distinction, which I contend is vital, between John's understanding of how Jesus functioned during his lifetime (as the new earthly Temple indwelled by the *kābôd*, to which people could journey in order to 'see' God), and how Jesus functioned after his death (as the heavenly Temple which the believers can only ascend to and enter when Jesus comes to take them there at the eschaton). This takes me to one final note: neither Draper nor Kinzer has tried to explain how Jn 20.29 fits into John's ideology. So it is to that task that I now turn.

c. *Faith*

The Johannine author also responds to the concern of Jesus' historical absence by repetitively linking the concept of *faith in Jesus* to the visionary experience. In this way he articulates with the Religio-historical Horizon by preserving the trappings of vision mysticism while simultaneously he disarticulates with this horizon by transforming the visionary experience into a faith experience. Thus, faith and vision are made to be correlative concepts.[54]

This theme surfaces in 6.36 when John suggests that vision alone will accomplish nothing unless it is accompanied by belief. So these words

---

51. Draper, 'Temple, Tabernacle', p. 281.
52. Draper, 'Temple, Tabernacle', pp. 281-82.
53. Kinzer, 'Temple Christology', p. 458.
54. Bousset, *Kyrios Christos*, pp. 230-32.

are attributed to Jesus: 'But I said to you that you have seen me and yet
do not believe (ἑωράκατέ [με] καὶ οὐ πιστεύετε).' Closely following
in v. 40, Jesus claims that the will of God is that 'everyone who sees the
Son and believes in him should have eternal life (πᾶς ὁ θεωρῶν τὸν
υἱὸν καὶ πιστεύων εἰς αὐτὸν ἔχῃ ζωὴν αἰώνιον).' John combines
vision and faith in 12.44-45 where belief in Jesus and a vision of Jesus
are equivalent to belief in God and a vision in God: 'He who believes in
me, believes not in me but in him who sent me. And he who sees me
sees him who sent me (ὁ πιστεύων εἰς ἐμὲ οὐ πιστεύει εἰς ἐμὲ ἀλλὰ
εἰς τὸν πέμψαντά με, καὶ ὁ θεωρῶν ἐμὲ θεωρεῖ τὸν πέμψαντά με).'
Faith, in the Gospel of John, according to Bousset, 'is nothing other
than this looking upon the likeness of Jesus in his divine Doxa'.[55]

Noteworthy as well is the story of the serpent in the wilderness in
Jn 3.14-15. According to Num. 21.8, those who *look* at the serpent will
live. So Moses is instructed by God to 'make a fiery serpent, and set it
on a pole; and everyone who is bitten, when he *sees* it, shall live (והיה
כל־הנשוך וראה אתו וחי); πᾶς ὁ δεδηγμένος ἰδὼν αὐτὸν ζήσεται
[LXX])'. In John's reference to this story, we find that he has intentionally altered the image: 'And as Moses lifted up the serpent in the wilderness, so must the Son of Man be lifted up, that whoever *believes in*
him (ὁ πιστεύων ἐν αὐτῷ) may have eternal life.' By making such an
alteration, John is making the statement that faith has replaced vision.

Additionally, whenever the vision of Jesus is mentioned, the Johannine author insists that this vision unaccompanied by faith in Jesus as
the manifestation of God is of no avail. Thus John the Baptist 'sees' at
the same time as he acknowledges that Jesus is the Son of God
(Jn 1.34). Sight accompanied by belief is the foundation of Nathanael's
call (Jn 1.45-51): he saw and believed that Jesus is the Son of God
(Jn 1.49). Martha is told in 11.40 that if she will believe, she will see
God's Glory: ἐὰν πιστεύσῃς ὄψῃ τὴν δόξαν τοῦ θεοῦ. Even the
Beloved Disciple in 19.35 claims that he bears witness because he saw
and he shares this discovery so that others may believe too: 'He who
saw it has borne witness. His testimony is true, and he knows that he
tells the truth that you also may believe (ὁ ἑωρακὼς μεμαρτύρηκεν,
καὶ ἀληθινὴ αὐτοῦ ἐστιν ἡ μαρτυρία, καὶ ἐκεῖνος οἶδεν ὅτι ἀληθῆ
λέγει, ἵνα καὶ ὑμεῖς πιστεύ[σ]ητε).'

The story of the blind man summarizes John's point well. The blind
man in ch. 9 is asked by Jesus, 'Do you believe in the Son of Man?'

55. Bousset, *Kyrios Christos*, p. 230.

(Jn 9.35). The blind man wants to know who the Son of Man is so that he can believe (Jn 9.36). Jesus responds: 'You have seen him (ἐώρακας αὐτὸν), and it is he who speaks to you' (Jn 9.37). Then the blind man confesses, 'Lord, I believe' (Jn 9.38). Jesus says that one of his purposes for coming into the world is so that 'those who do not see may see, and that those who see may become blind (οἱ μὴ βλέποντες βλέπωσιν καὶ οἱ βλέποντες τυφλοὶ γένωνται)' (Jn 9.39). Thus John reinforces the idea that sight without belief is blindness and will not bring salvation. But sight accompanied by faith will ensure redemption.

When it comes down to it, however, the vision itself is not the necessary ingredient for eternal life, according to the Johannine author. This is the effect of the climactic story about Thomas in ch. 20 when Jesus blesses those who believe without having seen Jesus (Jn 20.29): 'Blessed are those who have not seen and yet believe.' C.K. Barrett concludes that this is so that the successors of the eyewitnesses 'equally may believe, and that their faith places them on the same level of blessedness with the eyewitnesses, or even above it'.[56] Thus the original Gospel ended: 'and that believing you may have life in his name' (Jn 20.31).

It is arguable that the Johannine author creates the Synthetic End Point, faith mysticism, in response to vision mysticism promoted by the Thomasine Christians. He brilliantly utilizes the mechanism of visionary transformation but replaces the visionary experience with one of faith. In this way, his audience is secure in his articulation with the Religio-historical and Traditio-religious Horizons, but can accept his disarticulation and endeavor to offer a creative solution or End Point to this discourse.

According to John, therefore, one need not worry about visions now that Jesus has ascended to the Father and the eyewitnesses have died, because it is one's faith in Jesus that truly brings life. In a sense the deifying function of a vision of Jesus as God's manifestation has been replaced by faith in Jesus as God's historical manifestation: vision mysticism has become 'faith mysticism'. Or as C.H. Dodd so aptly said: 'Faith, then, is a form of vision.'[57]

56. C.K. Barrett, *The Gospel According to St John* (London: SPCK, 1956), p. 478.

57. Dodd, *The Interpretation of the Fourth Gospel*, p. 186.

d. *Sacramental Experience*

In John, however, faith is more than cognitive belief. It is encounter with God's presence. As we have discovered, for those who saw Jesus during his career, it was encounter with the *kābôd*, Jesus manifesting God on earth and embodying the new Temple. After the death and ascent of Jesus, it was encounter with the Spirit. For the believers, the historical distance between Jesus of Nazareth and the experience of the Johannine community was bridged by the Paraclete who gave them direct and immediate contact with Jesus. Such an understanding is reflected in the remarks of the author of 1 Jn 4.13: 'by this we know that we abide in him and he in us, because he has given us of his own Spirit (Ἐν τούτῳ γινώσκομεν ὅτι ἐν αὐτῷ μένομεν καὶ αὐτὸς ἐν ἡμῖν, ὅτι ἐκ τοῦ πνεύματος αὐτοῦ δέδωκεν ἡμῖν)'.

But how did the believers enter into this contact? I support the position that the encounter with the Spirit, according to the Gospel of John, is available through the sacramental experience: initially through baptism and continually through the Lord's Supper.[58] Even though several scholars have criticized Oscar Cullmann's celebrated piece, *Early Christian Worship*, in which he makes a case for the sacramental background of John, his thesis that 'the Gospel of John regards as one of its chief concerns to set forth the connexion between contemporary Christian worship and the historical life of Jesus' remains steadfast.[59] He concludes that the Gospel of John treats the sacraments of Baptism and the Lord's Supper as 'expressions of the whole worship life of the early community' and correspondingly John presents the relation between the

58. Scholars argue both sides of this issue. For a full bibliography, refer to H. Klos, *Die Sakramente im Johannesevangelium* (Stuttgart: Katholisches Bibel-werk, 1970); R. Kysar, *The Fourth Evangelist and His Gospel: An Examination of Contemporary Scholarship* (Minneapolis: Augsburg, 1975), pp. 249-59; E. Malatesta, *St. John's Gospel 1920–1965* (Rome: Biblical Institute Press, 1967); H. Thyen, 'Aus der Literatur zum Johannesevangelium', *TRu* 44 (1979), pp. 97-134; cf. W. Michaelis, *Die Sakramente im Johannesevangelium* (Bern: BEG-Verlag, 1946); W. Howard, *The Fourth Gospel in Recent Criticism and Interpretation* (London: Epworth Press, 1955), pp. 195-212; R. Bultmann, *The Theology of the New Testament* (trans. K. Grobel; 2 vols.; London: SCM Press, 1955), II, pp. 3-14; R. Brown, 'The Johannine Sacramentary Reconsidered', in *New Testament Essays* (Milwaukee: Bruce, 1965), pp. 51-76.

59. O. Cullmann, *Early Christian Worship* (SBT, 10; Chicago: Henry Regnery, 1953), p. 37.

Lord and the community 'present especially in these two sacraments'.[60]

There are opponents to the argument that, in the Gospel of John, we discover expressions of sacramental imagery.[61] These scholars point to the absence of the baptismal commission of Matthew 28 and the lack of the words of institution. The obvious problem with this non-sacramental stance is that it is hard to imagine any early Christian community not being aware of baptism and the Eucharist. The Gospel of John clearly knows of baptism, even Jesus' own (1.29-34). In Jn 3.26 and 4.1, we are told that baptism was part of Jesus' ministry as well! The argument that John does not contain a reference to the baptismal commission is an argument from silence and must take into account that, in addition, neither Mark nor Luke mentions the commission. Also, I would contest that John did know about a tradition concerning words of institution, and that this tradition is reflected in ch. 6.

Certainly this is not the place to repeat the detailed arguments of past scholars on the subject of sacramentalism in the Gospel of John. But I do want to briefly point out some of the cultic nuances in chs. 3, 4, and 6 and how the ideology of faith mysticism has been interwoven with them.

In Jn 3.5, Jesus speaks of being reborn 'of water and spirit (ἐξ ὕδατος καὶ πνεύματος)' in order to enter the Kingdom of God.[62] There must be a baptismal reference behind this statement, especially since the story framing this dialogue regards the baptismal activities of Jesus and John the Baptist (Jn 3.22-36). It is plausible that 3.5 reflects the idea that the baptismal experience brings the initiate into the presence of the Spirit. This experience is one of birth into the sacred: 'that which is born of the Spirit is spirit (τὸ γεγεννημένον ἐκ τοῦ πνεύματος πνεῦμά ἐστιν)

60. Cullmann, *Early Christian Worship*, p. 58.

61. For instance, see E. Schweizer, 'Das Johanneische Zeugnis vom Herren-mahl', *EvT* 12 (1953), pp. 341-63; Bultmann, *Gospel of John*, p. 471; Bultmann, *The Theology of the New Testament*, II, pp. 58-59; G. Bornkamm, 'Die eucharist-ische Rede im Johannesevangelium', *ZNW* 47 (1956), pp. 161-69; H. Koester, 'Geschichte und Kultus im Johannesevangelium und bei Ignatius von Antiochien', *ZTK* 54 (1957), pp. 56-59. E. Lohse, 'Wort und Sakrament im Johannes-evangelium', *NTS* 7 (1960–61), pp. 110-25; Klos, *Die Sacramente*, pp. 11-21; Kysar, *The Fourth Evangelist*, p. 259.

62. Some have argued that ὕδατος καί was penned by a later ecclesiastical redactor: Bultmann, *Gospel of John*, p. 138 n. 3; Lohse, 'Wort und Sakrament', pp. 110-25; F.-M. Braun, 'Le don de Dieu et l'initiation Chrétienne', *NRT* 86 (1964), pp. 1025-48.

(cf. Jn 3.5-8). The heavenly mystical encounter has been brought to earth first through Jesus' descent and historical presence, and then after his ascent through the sacramental encounter with the Spirit. Thus Jesus stresses to Nicodemus that only the Son of Man has descended from and ascended into heaven (Jn 3.13) so that eternal life can be given to the believer (Jn 3.15). Through baptism, Jesus as Spirit becomes present to the faithful.

This is supported by the story of the Samaritan woman at the well in the following chapter. Jesus speaks of giving to the faithful, 'the living water (ὕδωρ ζῶν)' which will well up to eternal life (Jn 4.10-14). Further, we find embedded in the story a metaphor for divine trans-formation when Jesus states that the believer will never thirst again: οὐ μὴ διψήσει εἰς τὸν αἰῶνα (Jn 4.14). It is plausible that these words allude to baptism, reminding the reader that this sacrament effects the initial encounter with the divine presence and the consequent trans-formation.

This initial encounter with the divine presence is perpetuated by par-ticipating in the Eucharist meal. In ch. 6, eucharistic references are behind Jesus' claim to be the 'bread of life (ὁ ἄρτος τῆς ζωῆς)' who has 'come down from heaven (ὁ καταβὰς ἐκ τοῦ οὐρανοῦ)' (Jn 6.35, 41, 51). This bread is his 'flesh (ἡ σάρξ μου)' and, if the faithful consume it, they will live forever (Jn 6.51). This reference is expanded to include Jesus' blood (αὐτοῦ τὸ αἷμα) which must be drunk by the faithful in order to have life everlasting (Jn 6.53-55). Participating in this ritual brings about mystical encounter and identification with Jesus as well as eternal life seemingly because the incorporation of the sacred food serves to immortalize the person—the person literally has incorporated Jesus:[63] 'He who eats my flesh and drinks my blood abides in me, and I in him (ὁ τρώγων μου τὴν σάρκα καὶ πίνων μου τὸ αἷμα ἐν ἐμοὶ μένει κἀγὼ ἐν αὐτῷ)' (Jn 6.56).

How has this been effected? Through the ascent of Jesus to heaven (Jn 6.62) and the release and descent of the Spirit (Jn 6.63). The text makes clear that it is not speaking of eating the flesh and drinking the blood of the body of the 'historical' Jesus, but of an action made effective through the presence of Jesus' Spirit in the elements (Jn 6.63).

63. On this idea, refer to A. Lieber, *God Incorporated: Feasting on the Divine Presence in Ancient Judaism* (PhD dissertation, Columbia University Press, 1998), pp. 204-212.

Thus the faithful can encounter Jesus through their participation in the Eucharist even though Jesus is no longer physically alive.

4. *Conclusion*

In conclusion, it is historically plausible that the Johannine author created a 'faith mysticism' as a polemical response to the mystical ascent soteriology such as that found in the *Gospel of Thomas*. According to the Johannine polemic, salvation could not be wrought by personally ascending into heaven in order to see the deity and thus become deified. Rather Jesus was the Temple and the historical embodiment of God on earth. Yet even so, a historical vision of Jesus alone was not enough to effect salvation; it had to be accompanied by faith in Jesus as God's manifestation. Faith, however, was the vital ingredient and, in Jesus' historical absence, functioned as if it were a vision, bringing the believer eternal life. This was effected for the Johannine Christians largely through the sacramental experiences, particularly Baptism and the Eucharist.

Moreover, Jesus' new manifestation, although invisible to the worldly eye, will now be in the experience of the Paraclete and the sharing in divine love. It seems that it is only at the end of the world that the believer will be able actually to see Jesus himself when Jesus returns in order to guide his followers to the heavenly Temple that he has prepared for them. This is aptly stated in 1 Jn 3.2: 'it does not yet appear what we shall be, but we know that when he appears we shall be like him, for we shall see him (ὀψόμεθα αὐτὸν)'. As Wilhelm Bousset noted: 'Deification through vision of God is postponed to the blessed future.'[64] But, in the Gospel of John, the vision and ascent to heaven at the eschaton clearly is overshadowed by the movement of the divinity down from heaven in the form of the Paraclete who will take up its home in the meantime with the faithful.[65]

It is noteworthy that the eschatological interpretation of the vision of God is developed in the later Johannine writing, 1 John. The community at this point in its history, believes that the eschaton is imminent: 'Children, it is the last hour' (1 Jn 2.18). So it is very important for Christians in the community who hope to have an eschatological vision of Jesus and experience divine transformation to 'purify'

64. Bousset, *Kyrios Christos*, p. 222.
65. Ashton, *Understanding the Fourth Gospel*, p. 465.

themselves even as Jesus is pure (1 Jn 3.3). This common mystical theme, however, is not understood in terms of ascetic or encratitic behavior as we saw in the *Gospel of Thomas*. Rather, purification is effected through the indwelling of the Spirit which enables believers to follow Jesus' commandment to love one another (1 Jn 4.13, 19-21).

Since believers cannot see God now, in order to be perfected, purification must be achieved through the Spirit that 'abides' in them:

> No one has ever seen God; if we love one another, God abides in us and his love is perfected in us. By this we know that we abide in him and he in us, because he has given us of his own Spirit (1 Jn 4.12-13).

Thus the Spirit aids the believer in keeping Jesus' commandment to love. In this way, the loving action of the believer toward his or her neighbor mirrors the loving action of the believer toward the unseen God:

> If anyone says, 'I love God', and hates his brother, he is a liar; for he who does not love his brother whom he has seen, cannot love God whom he has not seen. And this commandment we have from him, that he who loves God should love his brother also (1 Jn 4.20-21).

Through the believer's actions of love, God is revealed to others, and the believer is purified.

In addition, though, this text makes it clear that faith in the testimony of the community about Jesus' historical presence as God-Manifest is essential (1 Jn 1.1-3). Believers must have faith in the witness of those who saw Jesus during his lifetime (1 Jn 4.14). Now that Jesus is absent, it is only necessary to 'confess' Jesus as 'Son of God', the one who originally manifested God's love to humans (1 Jn 4.15-16). Moreover, like the *Gospel of John*, the victory over this world is faith expressed in terms of the sacraments, baptism and the Eucharist, which insure the indwelling of the Spirit (1 Jn 5.6-8). All in all, 1 John preserves evidence that tenets of Johannine faith mysticism continued to be taught and developed in the early second century.

Chapter 6

VISION MYSTICISM IN EARLY SYRIAN CHRISTIAN TEXTS:
THE DISCOURSE CONTINUES

> John, do not be faithless,
> but believing…
> (*Acts of John* 90).

This monograph has been an attempt to apply a new methodology to two contemporaneous Christian texts: the Gospels of John and *Thomas*. This application has been successful in identifying a link between the two communities responsible for these documents. This link is a discourse over the 'correct' soteriological system.

The Johannine author has textualized this discourse in his Gospel by articulating the Point of Discourse on a symbolic level, presenting the actor Thomas as the representative of the Thomasine community. Jesus' responses to Thomas express the Johannine community's views. Thus the actual historical discourse has become a theoretical construct in the Johannine narrative. As such, it only partially mirrors the reality of the discourse and intentionally presents Thomas in a negative manner.

Because of this, it is necessary to turn to the *Gospel of Thomas* in order to balance the historical scales and fill the empty space of the opponent's Traditio-religious Horizon. This document verifies the earlier conclusion that John had identified Thomas with a mystical form of Christianity concerned with ascent and visions. Indeed, according to *Thomas* itself, salvation hinges on one's faithfulness to the encratite lifestyle which provided the necessary state of purity before ascent into the dangerous zone of the sacred. The goal of the flight into heaven was a vision of the divine, either of one's heavenly double or God. This experience was mystically transforming. It translated the person from the realm of mortality and death to that of immortality and life. One entered God's Kingdom and united with the divine.

The Johannine author responds negatively to the soteriological system of the Thomasine Christians. He insists that no one has ever

ascended into heaven except Jesus and no one has ever seen God except
the Son. He repeats the theme constantly that his followers will not be
able to follow him into heaven until the eschaton itself. He villianizes
Thomas as the false hero who misunderstands the 'way' to God to be
that of ascent and who needs visions of Jesus to believe.

In this articulation, John offers an alternative albeit 'correct' system
of salvation by preserving the transformative mechanism of visionary
mysticism but substituting the faith experience for the visionary one.
He forwards this Interpretative Trajectory by ingeniously using his
adversary Thomas as the figural character, the character whose words
and actions serve to illicit the Johannine truth. This is particularly the
case in Jn 20.24-29 where Thomas's need for the vision is harshly
rebuked by Jesus and the blessedness of faith is lauded.

Moreover, according to John, ascent into heaven is not necessary
because the mystical encounter with the divine can occur now on earth.
The reason for this, in John's system, is that the divine has descended,
first (during Jesus' lifetime) in the form of Jesus as God's *kābôd*, and
consequently (after Jesus' death) in the form of the Paraclete, God's
Spirit. For John, salvation hinges on faith in the historical manifestation
of God on earth and the mystical encounter with him now as the Paraclete who resides among the believers in Jesus' absence and is continually met in the sacramental elements. Only when Jesus comes again at
the eschaton, will the faithful achieve the long-awaited vision of Jesus,
when they enter the celestial Temple (Jn 14.2-4) and fully become 'like
him' (1 Jn 3.2).

Thus a negative image of Thomas is preserved for us in the Gospel of
John due to the textualization of the discourse between the respective
communities over the issue of soteriology. The result is an image of
Thomas as the 'Doubter', an image that must have shocked and disturbed the early Thomasine community who clearly remembered
Thomas differently. Their records show us a Thomas who was the cham-
pion of soteriology, the mystic who learned the secrets of immortality
from the great mystic himself, Jesus. By the time the *Acts of Thomas*
was written, Thomas was known as the hero who achieved deification
during his lifetime. He had experienced a mystical metamorphosis into
Jesus himself—he had become his twin—and thus had fulfilled the
promise of transformation into Jesus as purported in Logion 108.

It is most interesting that even when the Gospel of John became a
revered scriptural text in Syria, many of the Syrian Christians inter-

preted the 'Doubting Thomas' pericope in a positive manner. This is most evident in the creation of the Doubting Thomas ampullae which were popular objects of early Byzantine pilgrimage and which were believed to have contained sanctified oil from the Golgotha Cross. According to Gary Vikan, the portrayal of this scene on these objects was intended to remind the pilgrim that Thomas was rebuked by Jesus because of his lapse of faith, a faith that was restored *only after* Thomas had *seen* and *touched* Jesus. Thomas was the model for the early pilgrims whose experiences of seeing and touching were basic to their faith. He was the biblical parallel for the pilgrim and his own experience. It is quite significant that the words on the object, 'My Lord and my God', are voiced by Thomas at the moment when he, like the pilgrim, sees, touches, and believes.[1]

Thus, I would propose that the discourse between the Johannine and Thomasine communities continued even after the composition of the Gospel of John. These two traditions continued to compete for the 'orthodox' position on mystical experience. On the one hand, there were Christians in the east who revered the Gospel of John and argued that mystical encounter with God occured through the faith and sacramental experience; visions of God were not one's goal. On the other hand, there were Christians in Syria who contended the opposite: Jesus came as a mystagogue opening the way into heaven so that the believer could follow him into the celestial Temple and receive visions of God. These visions were understood to be the basis for belief and the authority behind their traditions. These Christians, I would contend, continued to produce religious literature in the early second century which supported this position or modified it slightly. What is this literature and how does it develop this Christian discourse?

1. *Preachings of John*

A passage from the *Preachings of John* preserved in the *Acts of John* 90,[2] written in Syria shortly after the Gospel of John and contempor-

---

1.   G. Vikan, *Byzantine Pilgrimage Art* (Washington, DC: Dumbarton Oaks Center for Byzantine Studies, 1982), pp. 24-25.

2.   M. Bonnet, 'Acta Ioannis', in R.A. Lipsius and M. Bonnet (eds.), *Acta apostolorum apocrypha*, II/1 (repr. Hildesheim: Georg Olms, 1959 [1898]), pp. 193-203; K. Schäferdiek, 'Johannesakten', in W. Schneemelcher (ed.), *Neutestamentliche Apokryphen*, II (Tübingen: J.C.B. Mohr, 1989), pp. 138-55.

aneous with the competitive circulation of 1 John,[3] records a story in which John, *not* Thomas, is rebuked by Jesus: 'John, do not be faithless, but believing, and not inquisitive.' And what provoked this rebuke? That John went up a mountain (a metaphor for ascent in mystical traditions!), and was afraid of the vision he had of Jesus as the gigantic *kābôd*![4] The text reads in full:

> He took us three [John, James and Peter] likewise up the mountain, saying 'Come with me'. And again we went; and we saw him at a distance praying. Then I, since he loved me, went quietly up to him, as if he could not see me, and stood looking at his hinder parts; and I saw him not dressed in clothes at all but stripped of those we (usually) saw (upon him), and not like a man at all. (And I saw that) his feet were whiter than snow, so that the ground there was lit up by his feet; and that his head stretched up to heaven, so that I was afraid and cried out; and he, turning about, appeared as a small man and caught hold of my beard and pulled it and said to me, 'John, do not be faithless, but believing, and not inquisitive'.

So here, I believe, we have a rebuttal from the early Syrian Christians against the Johannine position. We have their counterattack textualized as a narrative about John's cowardice in face of ascension and the visionary experience. It is certainly plausible that this represents the theoretical construction of continued discourse between the mystic Christians of Syria who applauded Thomas and those who continued to revere John's position. It symbolized the perpetual esteem that the Syrian Christians held for Thomas and their own creative articulation of their side of the discourse.

2. *Gospel of the Savior*

Fragments from a previously unknown Coptic 'gospel', Papyrus Berolinensis 22220, were recovered from the archives of the Berlin Museum in the early 1990s. Recently, they have been restored, edited and published by Charles Hedrick and Paul Mirecki under the title, *The Gospel of the Savior: A New Ancient Gospel*.[5] When Paul Mirecki asked to

3. R. Cameron, *The Other Gospels* (Philadelphia: Westminster Press, 1982), pp. 88-89; cf. H. Koester, *Introduction to the New Testament. II. History and Literature of Early Christianity* (Philadephia: Fortress Press, 1982), pp. 196-98.
4. Refer to Fossum, '*Partes posteriores dei*: The "Transfiguration" of Jesus in the Acts of John', in *The Image of the Invisible God*, pp. 95-108.
5. Sonoma, CA: Polebridge Press, 1999.

consult with me on this find in the spring of 1998, I was both delighted and shocked with the manuscript. Here we have a splendid example of an early Christian text exhibiting features associated with Jewish mystical ascent traditions.[6]

What does a preliminary reading of this text tell us and how might it help us reconstruct the continued dialogue between the Syrian vision mystics and the Johannine faith mystics? In particular, these fragments provide an exegesis of some early version of Mt. 26.26-46 via Jewish mystical traditions (*Gos. Sav.* 97.1-30; 97.57–99:3; 99.33–100.51; 107.2-4; 113.1–115.32; 14FH). Furthermore, the author seems to be familiar with the Johannine tradition which he creatively rewrites, correcting elements with which he disagrees (*Gos. Sav.* 98.60-62; 99.3-20; 107.5-64; 108.45-46, 59-64). Also the author seems to be familiar with a Syrian sayings tradition such as we find in the *Gospel of Thomas*. Among the sayings found in these new fragments is a version of a saying of Jesus also preserved in the *Gospel of Thomas*:

> *Gos. Thom.* 82: The one who is near me is near the fire and the one who is far from me is far from the Kingdom (пєт2нн єроєі єц2нн єтсатє аүω пєтоүнү ммоєі цоүнү нтмнтєро).

> *Gos. Sav.* 107.43-48: The one who is near me is near the fire. The one who is far from me is far from life (п[єт2нн] є2оүн єро[ї єц]2нн є2оүн є[пк]ψ2т пєтоүнү євоλ ммоï єцоүнү євоλ мпωн2).

Because the versions of this particular saying were also known to Origen (*Hom. in Jer.* 20.3), Didymus the Blind (*PG*, 39 1488D), and are found in an Armenian text,[7] it is probable that the use of the saying in P22220 is due to oral tradition rather than direct literary dependence on the *Gospel of Thomas*.

The genre of the *Gospel of the Savior* is remarkably similar to the *Dialogue of the Savior* and the *Apocryphon of James*: dialogues between the 'Savior' and his disciples constructed out of variations of Jesus-sayings during which the disciples participate in an ascension into

6.   Thus it is probably better understood as an early Christian apocalypse than a gospel.

7.   Joseph Schäfers, *Eine altsyrische antimarkionitische Erlärung von Parabeln des Herrn und Zwei andere altsyrische Abhandlungen zu Texten des Evangeliums mit Beiträgen zu Tatians Diatessaron und Markions Neuem Testament* (NTAbh, 6.1-2; Münster: Aschendorff, 1917), p. 79. Also see the translation by G. Eagen, *Saint Ephrem: An Exposition of the Gospel* (CSCO, 5 and 6; Louvain: Secrétarit CSCO, 1968), 6.62.

heaven with Jesus. For instance, in the *Dialogue of the Savior*, after several pages of dialogue, Jesus takes Judas, Matthew, and Mary to 'the edge of heaven and earth' (*Dial. Sav.* 36). They receive two visions, one of the fiery abyss and one of the Son of Man bestowing a 'garment' or spiritual body on someone entering heaven. This leads into more dialogue in which Jesus explains the nature of their visions (*Dial. Sav.* 42-44). In the *Apocryphon of James*, James and Peter dialogue with Jesus. At the end of the dialogue, Peter and James ascend into heaven and receive a vision of angels hymning before the 'Majesty' (*Ap. Jas.* 15.5-30).

Similarly, the *Gospel of the Savior* is a dialogue between the Savior and his disciples (Andrew, John, and Judas are named in the fragments). Inserted within the dialogue are three visionary experiences: an ascent into heaven while on the Mount Olives in order to witness Jesus sing a hymn to the Cross (*Gos. Sav.* 99.33–100.51); an ascent into heaven while in the Garden of Gethsemane in order to observe Jesus ask the Father to 'let this cup pass by me' (*Gos. Sav.* 113.1–115.32); and an ascent into heaven to view the heavenly Jerusalem (*Gos. Sav.* 14FH). Thus, the *Gospel of the Savior* can be broken into the following seven sections.

a. *Dialogue* (*Gospel of the Savior* 97.1–99.20)

This section represents a Christian midrash of an early form of Mt. 26.26-35. The first passage to be examined in the midrash is Mt. 26.26-29:

> Now as they were eating, Jesus took bread, and blessed, and broke it, and gave it to the disciples and said, 'Take, eat; this is my body'. And he took a cup, and when he had given thanks he gave it to them saying, 'Drink of it, all of you; for this is my blood of the covenant, which is poured out for many for the forgiveness of sins. I tell you I shall not drink again of this fruit of the vine until that day when I drink it new with you in my Father's Kingdom' (Mt. 26.26-29).

> ...the kingdom of [the] heavens at your right hand. Blessed is [the one] who will eat with me in the [kingdom] of the heavens (ⲛⲁⲓ̈ⲁⲧϥ ⲙ̄ⲡⲉⲧⲛⲁⲟⲩⲱⲙ ⲛⲙ̄ⲙⲁⲓ̈ ϩⲛ̄ ⲧⲙⲛ̄ⲧⲉⲣⲟ ⲛ̄ⲙ̄ⲡⲏⲩⲉ). You are the salt of the earth, and you are the lamp that illuminates the world (ⲛ̄ⲧⲱⲧⲛ̄ ⲡⲉ ⲡⲉϩⲙⲟⲩ ⲙ̄ⲡⲕⲁϩ ⲁⲩⲱ ⲛ̄ⲧⲱⲧⲛ̄ ⲡⲉ ⲧⲗⲁⲙⲡⲁⲥ ⲉⲧⲣ̄ⲟⲩⲟⲉⲓⲛ ⲉⲡⲕⲟⲥⲙⲟⲥ). Do not sleep nor [slumber]...in the garment of the kingdom, which I bought with the blood of the grape (ⲙ̄ⲡⲉⲛⲇⲩⲙⲁ ⲛ̄ⲧⲙⲛ̄ⲧⲉⲣⲟ ⲡⲁⲓ̈ ⲉⲛⲧⲁⲓ̈ϣⲟⲡϥ ϩⲛ̄ ⲡⲉⲥⲛⲟϥ ⲙ̄ⲡⲉⲗⲟⲟⲗⲉ) (*Gos. Sav.* 97.13-30).

In this section of the *Gospel of the Savior*, the author develops the apocalyptic and eucharistic themes of Matthew by collecting Jesus sayings with similar themes and editing them into a dialogue. This was apparently meant to provide the reader with a deeper understanding of the Matthean passage.

So we find a saying in which Jesus blesses the person who will 'eat (oγωм) with me in the [kingdom] of the heavens' (*Gos. Sav.* 97.15-18; variant in Lk. 14.15) used to develop the notion that the believers will dine with Jesus in a heavenly banquet. The previous saying seems to indicate that the disciples are also present, enthroned in heaven with something or someone on their right hand (*Gos. Sav.* 97.13-15). The believers are described as 'the salt of the earth (ѝтωтѝ пе пе2моγ ѝпка2)' (cf. Mt. 5.13) and 'the lamp that illuminates the world (ѝтωтѝ пе тлампас етроγоеін епкосмос)' (cf. *Gos. Thom.* 24; Mt. 5.14-15).

Apparently, the Eucharist is understood by the author to represent this heavenly banquet either as an anticipation of an apocalyptic event or as the periodic ascension into heaven in order to partake of the feast mystically. The Eucharist is described as a 'garment (енлγма)' which the believer seemingly puts on. The 'garment' symbolizes a new spiritual body which the believer is given.[8] This garment was purchased by Jesus with his blood which is the eucharistic wine or 'the blood of the grape (песноq ѝпелооле)'.[9]

It is noteworthy that the *Gospel of Philip* witnesses to a similar understanding of the Eucharist. The Eucharist is described as 'Jesus' (63.21-25) and the 'Perfect Man' (55.11-14; 70.5-10; 75.15-25; 76.23-30) which the believer 'puts on' (75.15-25) like a piece of clothing (56.33–57.9). The eucharistic cup 'is a body' which the believers don after their baptism during which they had removed their old clothing (75.15-25). This new garment is a spiritual body that will make it possible for the believer to ascend into heaven without being detained by the Powers (70.5-10; 76.23-30; 86.6-11).

Such similarities suggest to me that the early Christians were developing esoteric meanings to explain the Eucharist ceremonies. Because the ceremony involved imbibing Jesus' perfect body, they conjectured

---

8. On this theme, refer to J. Fossum, 'Ascensio, Metamorphosis: The "Transfiguration" of Jesus in the Synoptic Gospels', in *The Image of the Invisible God*, pp. 82-86.

9. A Jewish euphemism for 'wine'; cf. Deut. 32.14; Sir. 39.26; 50.15.

that they were receiving their spiritual bodies which would enable them to ascend into heaven like Jesus. This type of theology was certainly influenced by exegesis of 1 Corinthians 15 where Paul discusses the transformation of our mortal bodies into spiritual bodies, 'for the perishable nature must put on the imperishable, and this mortal nature must put on immortality' (15.53). As a spiritual body, death is 'swallowed' up, and the believers are resurrected (15.54).

Not suprisingly, the next part of the dialogue in the *Gospel of the Savior* turns to the discussion of the fleshly body in contrast to the spiritual. The 'man who is [his] own authority (ⲡⲣⲱⲙⲉ ⲟⲩⲁⲩⲧⲟⲍⲟⲩⲥⲓⲟⲥ)' appears to be the one who while 'in the body', does not let matter be the master controlling him ([ⲉⲛⲍⲟ]ϭⲟⲛ ⲧⲉⲧⲛ̄[ϣⲟⲟ]ⲡ ⲍ̄ⲙ ⲡⲥⲱⲙ[ⲁ] ⲙ̄ⲡⲣ̄ⲧⲣⲉⲑⲩⲗⲏ ⲣ̄ ⲭⲟⲉⲓⲥ ⲉⲣⲱⲧⲛ̄) (98.31-46). This passage serves to expound on the meaning of Mt. 26.41: 'Watch and pray that you may not enter into temptation; the spirit indeed is willing, but the flesh is weak.' The author of the *Gospel of the Savior* seems to be leaning towards an ascetic interpretation of Matthew, emphasizing that the believer must control the bodily passions in order to become spiritual person, a position that was common in early Christianity, especially in mystical forms such as those represented by the *Gospel of Thomas*.

The *Gospel of the Savior* then interjects a reference to Mt. 26.46: 'Rise, let us be going; see, my betrayer is at hand.' In the *Savior*, it reads: 'Arise, let us go away from this place. For the one who will hand me over is near' (*Gos. Sav.* 98.47-51). The author seems to be familiar with Jn 14.31, 'Let us go away from this place', which he affixes to his version of Matthew's verse. In the canonical Gospel stories, this statement is made in the Garden of Gethsemane, but in the *Gospel of the Savior*, the author seems to understand it as referring to the house in which the disciples just finished the Passover meal. Perhaps he made this adjustment for editorial reasons in order to provide a way for Judas to become separated from the rest of the disciples who, very soon, will experience a heavenly journey. Since Matthew's Gospel does not have Judas exit the meal, it seems that he is in the company of the rest of the disciples on the Mount of Olives and then in Gethsemane. The author of the *Savior* wants to make clear that Judas did not take part in these experiences, since he understands these experiences to be spiritually transformative journeys with Jesus.

The author returns to the storyline in Matthew, exegeting verse 26.31: 'Then Jesus said to them, "You will all fall away because of me this night; for it is written, I will strike the shepherd, and the sheep of the flock will be scattered".' According to the *Gospel of the Savior*, even though all of the disciples will 'flee' from Jesus because they will be 'scandalized' by him, Jesus will not be left alone. Drawing off the Johannine tradition, the reader is told that Jesus will not remain alone 'for my Father is with me. I and my Father, we are a single one (ⲁⲛⲟⲕ ⲙⲛ̄ ⲡⲁⲓ̈ⲱⲧ ⲁⲛⲟⲛ ⲟⲩⲁ ⲛ̄ⲟⲩⲱⲧ)' (98.51-62; cf. Jn 10.30 and 17.21). This divine-centered Christology is supported by another passage in the *Savior* in which Jesus states that he was a god who 'became a man (ⲁⲛ[ⲅ̄ ⲟⲩ]ⲛⲟⲩⲧⲉ ⲁ̈ⲓⲣ̄ⲣⲱ[ⲙⲉ])' (99.18-19). It is plausible that this too echoes the Johannnine tradition (cf. Phil. 2.6-11), 'the Logos became flesh' (Jn 1.14), especially since the Logos is identified as 'god' in this tradition (Jn 1.1).

As in Matthew, the abandonment of Jesus by his disciples is compared to the scattering of sheep in the *Gospel of the Savior* (98.63–99.3). Then the author turns to the Johannine tradition again to provide further exegesis of this theme. He identifies Jesus as 'the good shepherd (ⲁⲛⲟⲕ ⳓⲉ ⲡⲉ ⲡϣⲱⲥ ⲉⲧⲛⲁⲛⲟⲩϥ)' who will lay down his life for his believers (99.3-6; cf. Jn 10.11). In order to be as pleasing to the Father as Jesus is, the believers also must lay down their lives (99.6-10; cf. 15.13). The greatest commandment is said to be that Jesus should lay down his life for the people. Because of this, the Father loves Jesus (99.11-18). This is probably a creative midrash of Jn 15.12-13 in light of 10.15, 17: 'This is my commandment, that you love one another as I have loved you. Greater love has no man than this, that a man lay down his life for his friends' and 'I lay down my life for the sheep... For this reason, the Father loves me, because I lay down my life, that I may take it again'. Thus this dialogue section concludes that Jesus completed God's will (*Gos. Sav.* 99.17-18).

b. *Ascent Narrative (Gospel of the Savior 99.33–100.51)*
The ascent narrative beginning in 99.33 represents the author's midrash of Mt. 26.30: 'And when they had sung a hymn, they went out to the Mount of Olives.' The author interprets their journey up the Mount of Olives to be an ascension into heaven where they will witness Jesus singing a hymn to the Cross. Thus, they ask Jesus to 'take us out of the world [that] we may come to you (ⲛ̄ⲅⲛ̄ⲧⲛ̄ ⲉⲃⲟⲗ ϩⲛ̄ ⲡⲕⲟⲥⲙⲟ[ⲥ ⲛ̄]ⲧⲛ̄ⲉⲓ ϣⲁⲣⲟⲕ)' (99.36-39). That the author should understand the climbing of a mountain to be a metaphor for ascension into heaven should not be

surprising since this was a stock image in ancient Judaism and early Christianity (cf. Mk 9.2-8 and parallels; *Asc. Isa.* 2.8; *T. Levi* 2.5-7). This idea probably originated in the exegetical tradition about Moses' Sinai experience (cf. *Targ. Ps.-J.* 69.19; *Sifre Deut.* 357; *b. Soṭ.* 13b; *Yal Shim'oni* on Deut. 962, 965; *Ps.-Philo* 12.1; *Ezek. Trag.* 68–81, quoted by Eusebius, *Praep. Ev.* 9.28.2). For instance, Philo of Alexandria interprets Exod. 24.12, 'The Lord said to Moses: "Come up to me on the mountain"', in this manner:

> This signifies that a holy soul is divinized by ascending not to the air or to the ether or to heaven [which is] higher than all, but to [a region] above the heavens. And beyond the world there is no place but God (*Quaest. in Exod.* 2.40).

Due to the fragmentary nature of this leaf and the next, we cannot reconstruct what happened during the ascent until *Gos. Sav.* 100.33 when the disciples state that while they were 'upon the mountain, we too became like spiritual bodies (ⲉⲝⲚ ⲠⲦⲞⲞⲨ ⲀⲚ[ⲞⲚ] ϨⲰⲰⲚ ⲀⲚⲢ̄ⲞⲈ Ⲛ̄ ⲚⲒⲤⲰⲘⲀ Ⲛ̄ⲠⲚ̄Ⲓ̄Ⲁ̄)'. This comment suggests that they had just witnessed Jesus' body being transformed likewise.

Hedrick and Mirecki understand this to be a misplaced transfiguration or post-resurrection story.[10] But there are problems with this interpretation. For instance, Moses and Elijah never appear, the voice of God is not mentioned, and the construction of the tabernacles is not found. In addition to Jesus, the disciples themselves are transformed. So what we probably have is a completely different story interpreting Mt. 26.30 as an ascension of Jesus with his disciples into heaven to worship in song before God's throne.

So why is transformation language present? Because this is stock language used by the ancient Jews and Christians to describe what happens to the body when a person enters heaven. Generally, the body is said to become 'glorified', 'angelic', 'white', 'spiritual', or dressed in a new 'garment'. This type of language of transformation probably originated in the pattern of installation of a king or priest in Israel's cult. During the Second Temple period, this imagery was connected with heavenly installations in the celestial Temple of righteous men like Enoch (*2 En.* 22.8-10; *3 En.* 10.1, 12.1-2), Levi (*T. Levi* 8.5), Isaiah (*Asc. Isa.* 7.25, 9.2), and Zephaniah (*Apoc. Zeph.* 8.2-3).

---

10. Hedrick and Mirecki, *Gospel of the Savior*, p. 96.

This notion became democratized to all righteous people who were promised a similar fate following death (Dan. 12.3; *1 En.* 108.11-15; *Asc. Isa.* 62.15-16; *Apoc. Abr.* 15.4–16.4). For example, in an early Christian text contemporary with the *Gospel of the Savior*, when Matthew tells Jesus that he wants to have a vision of the 'Place of Life (ⲡⲙⲁ ⲛ̄ⲡⲱⲛϩ)', Jesus replies that this is impossible as long as he 'carries the flesh (ⲉⲕϥⲟⲣⲓ ⲛ̄ⲧⲥⲁⲣⲝ)' (132.10-11). Later on in this text, the disciples witness a dead soul arriving in heaven. The soul is given a 'garment (ϩⲃ̄ⲥⲱ)' and is transformed (136.16-22; 138.20–139.8). In mystical circles, some thought that they could achieve this condition prior to their actual death by invading heaven. As we have seen in our discussion of the *Gospel of Thomas*, such a journey was believed to be transforming for the practioner. Even Paul claims to have participated in such a pre-mortem mystical event (2 Cor. 12.2-4). Paul uses the concept of spiritual transformation not only when describing the resurrected or 'spiritual body' (1 Cor. 15.35-55; cf. Rom. 6.5; 8.29; 12.2; Phil. 3.10-21) but also when discussing the spiritual transformation that believers could expect to experience during their lifetimes (Gal. 4.19; 2 Cor. 3.7-18; cf. Col. 3.9).

Connections with imagery found in mystical literature can also be seen in the expression made by the disciples: 'Our eyes opened up to every side (ⲁⲛⲉⲛⲃⲁⲗ ⲟⲩⲱⲛ ⲛ̄ ⲥⲁⲥⲁ ⲛⲓⲙ)' (*Gos. Sav.* 100.36-39). Certainly it is common to find in ascent literature the motif of 'opening eyes' such as in the *Ascension of Isaiah*: 'And I saw the great Glory while the eyes of my spirit were open' (*Asc. Isa.* 9.37). But in the *Gospel of the Savior*, we find an additional motif: The notion that the disciples were transformed into 'spiritual bodies' with eyes *on every side*. This phrase must be a reference to their new angelic status since it is not uncommon in mystical literature to find references to angels whose bodies are 'full of eyes' (cf. *3 En.* 9.4-5; 22.9; 25.2-6; 26.6). The angels are even known as God's 'many-eyed ones' (*2 En.* 22.2). The idea that the angels have eyes on every side of their bodies probably derives from exegesis of Ezek. 1.5-10 where the angels are said to have four sides (right, left, front, and back) with four faces (lion, ox, man, and eagle). Certainly this is the case in Rev. 4.6-8 where these four living creatures surround the celestial throne, being 'full of eyes all round and within' and 'full of eyes in front and behind'.

The next passage in the *Gospel of the Savior* reflects vision mystical traditions as well: 'We [approached] the heavens, and they [rose up] against each other (ⲁⲩⲧ[ⲱ]ⲱⲛ ⲉ[ⲟ]ⲣⲁ̈ ⲛⲥⲁ ⲛⲉⲩⲉⲣ[ⲏ]ⲩ). Those who watch the gates were disturbed (ⲛⲉⲧⲣⲟⲉⲓⲥ ⲉⲙⲡⲩⲗⲏ ⲁⲩϣⲧⲟⲣⲧⲣ̅). The angels were afraid (ⲣ̅ ⲟ̅ⲟⲧⲉ), and they fled to the... [They] thought [that] they were all about to be destroyed' (*Dial. Sav.* 100.40-48). Clearly the disciples are describing their initial entry into heaven, a place where the lowest of the angels were believed to dwell. These heavens were often described as a place of chaos and fighting. For example, in the *Ascension of Isaiah*, we find that the 'angels of the firmament' were 'fighting one another in envy' (*Asc. Isa.* 10.29) while the 'angels of the air' were 'plundering and doing violence to one another' (*Asc. Isa.* 10.31).

This tradition seems to be the opposite of the famous theme of angelic hostility to humans invading heaven.[11] Here we have a situation where the metamorphosized Jesus and his disciples enter heaven and provoke disturbance and fear among the angels residing there. Certainly what we are encountering in this text is the belief that Jesus' entry into heaven marks the beginning of the End. Jesus is recognized by the angelic populations as a warrior Messiah who is in the process of conquering the powers that rule the world: Satan and his angels. Thus they are afraid and try to flee their inevitable destruction.

The basis for these eschatological ideas derives from the familiar myth of the fallen angels and the cosmic drama of their battle for power. One version of this myth is found in *1 Enoch* where the Watchers or fallen angels descend to earth, mate with human women, bear giants and their demonic offspring, and corrupt the human race with their teachings (*1 En.* 6–36). A second version of the myth tells of a rebellion in heaven before the fall of the angels in which Satan or Lucifer believed that he should set up his throne higher than the clouds in order to be equal in rank with God (*2 En.* 29.4). God casts him down together with his angels and he is left 'flying in the air continually above the abyss' (*2 En.* 29.5). Satan and his host are thrown down to earth where they plot against Adam and Eve (*2 En.* 31.3-6; *LAE* 12–17; *Apoc. Mos.* 15–17) and bring humans under their rule. Some of the Watchers who rebelled with him were imprisoned in the second heaven (*2 En.* 7.3; 18.4), while others fell to earth, seduced the women (*2 En.* 18.4), and were imprisoned beneath the earth afterwards (*2 En.* 18.6-7). It is the apocalyptic expectation that God eventually will conquer Satan

11. On this topic, refer to A. DeConick, *Seek to See Him: Ascent and Vision Mysticism in the Gospel of Thomas* (VCSup, 33; Leiden: E.J. Brill, 1996), pp. 56-57.

and his host in the final eschatological battle, mete judgment on the fallen angels, and cast them into the fiery abyss (cf. *T. Jud.* 25.3; *T. Zeb.* 9.8; *T. Levi* 18.12; Rev. 20.10).

The angels' fear in the *Gospel of the Savior*, however, seems to be premature: this particular ascent of Jesus was *not* the beginning of the eschatological judgment. The purpose of Jesus' ascent with his disciples is to pierce through 'all the heavens (ⲛ̄ⲡⲏⲩⲉ̄ ⲧⲏⲣⲟⲩ)' (*Gos. Sav.* 100.49-51) and come directly before the throne of God in order to sing a hymn to the Cross.

c. *Hymn to the Cross (Gospel of the Savior 105.4–106.47; 122; 5FH; 7FH; 11FH)*

The author of the *Gospel of the Savior* seems to understand that as Jesus and the disciples venture up the Mount of Olives, Jesus sings the hymn referred to in Mt. 26.30. On an esoteric level, however, a heavenly journey was taking place. According to the author, Jesus and his disciples were ascending into heaven so that Jesus could join the angelic song before God's throne. Yet, he was to be distinguished from the rest of the angelic host because he prayed a special song: the hymn to the Cross. This hymn, although fragmentary, can be found on pages 105-106 of the *Gospel of the Savior*. Pages 101-104 are 'missing' according to Hedrick and Mirecki,[12] but I believe that the fragments they identify as 122, 5FH, 7FH, and 11FH are these missing four pages, belonging to the Cross hymn that Jesus offers to God while in heaven. Each of these fragments mentions the Cross and seems to be written in the same concise verse.

Creating stories which speculated about the nature of the hymn sung in Mt. 26.30 is not without precedent in other early Christian literature. For instance, in the *Preachings of John* 94.1–96.51, we find an interpretation of Mt. 26.30 in which Jesus has the disciples form a circle around him. He stands in the middle and sings a lengthy hymn to God and asks the disciples to sing after each verse the traditional choral response, 'Amen'. Each verse is short and simple, lauding the nature of Jesus. For instance, after Jesus sings, 'I am the lamp to you who see me', the disciples reply, 'Amen' (95.24). This is followed by the verse, 'I am a mirror to you who know me'. The disciples sing, 'Amen' (95.25). And so on.

---

12. Hedrick and Mirecki, *Gospel of the Savior*, p. 97. However, see p. 6.

In the *Gospel of the Savior*, Jesus sings about the Cross using an identical genre. Although the text is full of lacunae, each verse of the hymn seems to have been followed by the phrase, 'Amen' (cf. *Gos. Sav.* 105.7, 10, 15; 106.15). It is unclear who is singing the 'Amen' phrase due to the broken nature of the manuscript, but I would not doubt that, just as in the *Preachings of John*, the disciples are the chorus. In the fragments of the Cross hymn, Jesus sings about his readiness for the Cross ('You were ready for me, O Cross; I also will be ready for you' [*Gos. Sav.* 106.44-47]); his desire to fill the Cross with his wealth (O Cross, do not be afraid; I am rich. I will fill you with my wealth. I will mount you, O Cross' [5H: 58-63]); his plan to perfect the Cross (['A little longer], O Cross, and that which is lacking is perfected, and that which is diminished is full' [5F: 23-26]); and to raise it ('A little longer, O Cross, and that which [fell] arises' [5F: 27-29]). He sings about his resurrection after three days when he will take his disciples to heaven in order to teach them: '...[in] three days, [and I will] take you to [heaven] with me, and teach you' (122.60-63).

It is not surprising that the author interprets the hymning in Mt. 26.30 in this manner since, in mystical literature, the angelic host is known to sing before God's throne (cf. *1 En.* 61.9-11; *2 En.* 19.6; Rev. 4.8; *Asc. Isa.* 10.1-3; *Apoc. Abr.* 18.3; *Hekh. Rab.* 185, 187; *Sefer Hekh.* 57-58, 67; *M. Merk.* 553). In fact, one of the reasons to participate in a heavenly journey was to join the angelic beings and worship God in song (cf. *Asc. Isa.* 9.33; *Apoc. Abr.* 17.5-21; 18.1-3).

d. *Dialogue (Gospel of the Savior 107.1–108.64)*

The dialogue that ensues is the author's attempt to provide an interpretation of Mt. 26.32: 'But after I am raised up, I will go before you to Galilee.' In the process of his interpretation, the author seems to be responding to Jn 20.11-29 by critiquing the Johannine statement: 'Blessed are those who have not seen and yet believe.' This critique places the *Gospel of the Savior* squarely in the middle of the ongoing vision–faith debate, providing another example of the Syrian Christian response to Jn 20.29. The author of the *Savior* reassures the reader that, after death, Jesus appeared visually as a resurrected being with a body. Jesus' disciples are told that they should not be disturbed when they see him raised. The disciples then ask Jesus, 'O Lord, in what form will you reveal yourself to us (ⲡⲭ[ⲟ]ⲉⲓⲥ ⲉⲕⲛⲁⲟⲩⲟⲛ[2]ⲕ ⲉⲣⲟⲛ ⲛ̄ [ⲁ]ⲱ ⲛ̄ϭⲙⲟⲧ), or in what kind of body will you come (ⲏ ⲉⲕⲛ̄]ⲁⲉⲓ 2ⲛ̄ ⲁⲱ ⲛ̄ⲥⲱ[ⲙ]ⲁ ⲙⲁⲧⲁⲙⲟⲛ)? Tell us' (107.5-9). Then John, replies:

Oh Lord, when you come to reveal yourself to us, do not reveal yourself to us in all your glory, but change your glory into [another] glory in order that [we] may be able to bear it, [lest] we see [you and despair] from fear… (ⲡⲭⲟⲉⲓⲥ ⲉⲕϣⲁ[ⲛ]ⲉⲓ ⲉⲕⲛⲁⲟⲩⲟⲛⲅ̅ ⲉⲣⲟⲛ ⲙ̅ⲡⲣⲟⲩⲟⲛⲅ̅ ⲉⲣⲟⲛ ⲅ̅ⲙ ⲡⲉⲕⲉⲟⲟⲩ ⲧⲏⲣϥ. ⲁⲗⲗⲁ ⲡⲱⲱⲛⲉ ⲉⲕ[ⲉ]ⲟⲟⲩ, ⲭⲉⲕⲁⲥ ⲉⲛⲉϣϭⲓ ⲅⲁⲣⲟϥ. ⲙⲏ[ⲡⲟ]ⲧⲉ ⲛ̅ⲧⲛ̅ⲛⲁⲩ ⲉ[ⲣⲟⲕ ⲛ̅] ⲧⲛ̅ⲕⲁ ⲧⲟ[ⲟⲧⲛ̅ ⲉⲃⲟⲗ] ⲅⲁ ⲑⲟⲧ[ⲉ] ⲁϥⲟⲩ[ⲱⲱⲃ ⲛ̅ϭⲓ ⲡⲥⲱⲧⲏⲣ]) (107.12-23).

It is not surprising that John is concerned about his reaction to the glorified Jesus since visions of the Glory or *kābôd* can be terrifying and even deadly. So proper visionary etiquette required the practioner to approach the *kābôd* with fear and trembling, to fall prostrate before the awesome deity. Usually the practioner has to be commanded by God, 'Don't be afraid!' (cf. *1 En.* 14.14, 24-25; *2 En.* 20.1-2; 21.2-3; 22.4-5).[13] So, in the *Gospel of the Savior*, Jesus rebukes John and the rest of the disciples for being 'afraid' and says that he must appear transformed before them 'in order that you might see and believe (ⲭⲉⲕⲁⲥ ⲛ̅ⲧⲉⲧⲛ̅ⲛⲁⲩ ⲛ̅ⲧⲉ ⲧⲛ̅ⲡⲓⲥⲧⲉⲩⲉ)' (*Gos. Sav.* 107.27-30).

So here we find a visionary mystical tradition that seems to be responding to the Johannine story that rebuked the disciple Thomas because he had to see the risen Jesus in order to believe. The author of the *Gospel of the Savior* 'remembers' a different story. He insists that the problem is with the disciple John who was afraid of having visions of Jesus in his glorious divine body. For this reason, the Savior has to remind John that it is necessary for him to participate in the vision of Jesus as a fully divine being because such a vision is the basis for faith and, ultimately, salvation.

The themes of Jn 20.19-29 are furthered in the next verse where the author focuses on *not* 'touching' the glorified Jesus. Instead of telling Thomas, 'Put your finger here, and see my hands; and put out your hand, and place it in my side; do not be faithless but believing', as we find in Jn 10.27, Jesus commands John in the *Gospel of the Savior*, 'Do not touch me, until I go up to [my Father] (ⲙ̅ⲡⲣ̅ⲭⲱⲅ ⲛ̅ⲧⲟϥ ⲉⲣⲟⲓ ϣⲁⲛ†ⲃⲱⲕ' ⲉⲅⲣⲁⲓ ϣⲁ [ⲡ]ⲁⲓϣ[ⲧ]) who [is] your [Father], and [my God, who] is my Lord, who is your Lord' (107.31-38)! By echoing an earlier Johannine passage in which Jesus speaks similar words to Mary

---

13. I. Chernus, 'Visions of God in Merkabah Mysticism', *JSJ* 13 (1983), pp. 123-46 (128-30); C. Morray-Jones, 'Transformational Mysticism in the Apocalyptic-Merkabah Tradition', *JJS* 48 (1992), p. 25.

Magdalene (Jn 20.17: 'Do not touch me, for I have not yet ascended to the Father; but go to my brethren and say to them, I am ascending to my Father and your Father, to my God and your God'), the author of the *Savior* creates an interesting interpretation of Jn 20.19-29.

Why does the author feel that Jesus' glorified body should not be touched while it is in this earthly sphere? The answer is made obvious by the subsequent verse:

> If one is [near] to me, he will [burn]. I am the [fire that] blazes; the one who [is near to me, is] near to [the fire]; the one who is far from me, is far from life (ⲉϣⲱⲡⲉ ⲇⲉ ⲉⲣϣⲁ[ⲛ]ⲟⲩⲁ̀ ϩⲱ[ⲛ] ⲉϩⲟ[ⲩⲛ] ⲉⲣⲟⲓ̈ ϥⲛⲁ[ⲣ]ⲱ[ⲕ]ϩ̅ [ⲁ]ⲛⲟⲕ ⲡⲉ ⲡⲕ[ⲱϩ]ⲧ̅ [ⲉ]ⲧϫⲉⲣⲟ ⲡ[ⲉⲧϩⲏⲛ] ⲉϩⲟⲩⲛ ⲉⲣⲟ[ⲓ̈ ⲉϥ]ϩⲏⲛ ⲉϩⲟⲩⲛ ⲉ[ⲡⲕ]ⲱϩ̅ⲧ̅ ⲡⲉⲧⲟⲩⲏⲩ ⲉⲃⲟⲗ ⲙ̅ⲙⲟⲓ̈ ⲉϥⲟⲩⲏⲩ ⲉⲃⲟⲗ ⲙ̅ⲡⲱⲛ̅ϩ̅) (107.39-48).

Jesus has identified his glorified body with fire, an image commonly connected to the *kābôd*, the manifestation of God (cf. Exod. 16.10; 24.16-17, 43-44; 40.34-35, 38; Num. 17.7; 1 Kgs 8.10-11; Lev. 9.23-24; 1 Sam. 3.3; 4.21). Because his transformed body is a body of fire, any human who touches him will be burned and destroyed. However, now that he resides in heaven, his followers are supposed to ascend there in order to be near him and have access to 'life'. When they reach heaven, they too will have spiritual bodies of like substance and will be able to touch him without harm. For now, though, he tells the disciples that he is with them on earth 'a little longer' (ⲕⲉⲕⲟⲩⲓ̈ ⲡⲉ ⲉⲓ̈ϩⲛ ⲧⲉⲧⲛ̅ⲙⲏⲧⲉ, *Gos. Sav.* 107.62-63)—another possible reference to the Johannine text (Jn 7.33; 13.33; 14.19)—and should not be touched because they might be harmed by his body's fiery substance.

While in heaven, Jesus continues to teach the disciples about himself and his destiny. He identifies himself as a 'child (ϣⲏⲣⲉ ϣ[ⲏⲙ])' (*Gos. Sav.* 107.58-60) and a 'king (ⲣⲣⲟ)' (108.17) who will 'suffer because of the [sins] of the world (ϯ[ⲗ]ⲩⲡⲏ ⲉⲧⲃⲉ ⲛ̅ⲛⲟ[ⲃⲉ] ⲙ̅ⲡⲕⲟⲥⲙⲟⲥ)' (108.5-8). He admonishes his disciples not to weep, but to rejoice, because he has overcome the world (108.42-49): [ⲙ̅]ⲡ̅ⲣⲣⲓⲙⲉ ϫⲓⲛ ⲧⲉⲛⲟⲩ ⲁⲗⲗⲁ ⲣⲁϣⲉ ⲛ̅ⲧⲟϥ ϩⲁⲙⲏⲛ ⲁⲓ̈ϫⲣⲟ ⲉⲡⲕⲟⲥⲙⲟⲥ ⲛ̅ⲧⲱⲧⲛ̅ ⲇⲉ ⲙ̅ⲡ̅ⲣⲧⲡⲉ ⲡⲕⲟⲥⲙⲟⲥ ϫⲣⲟ ⲉⲣⲱⲧⲛ̅ ϩⲁⲙⲏⲛ. Like Jesus, who says he has become free from the world, the disciples will become free from it too (108.49-53): ⲁⲓ̈ⲣ̅ⲣⲙ̅ϩⲉ ϩⲙ̅ ⲡⲕⲟⲥⲙⲟⲥ ⲛ̅ⲧ[ⲱⲧ]ⲛ̅ ϩⲱⲧⲧⲏⲩⲧⲛ̅ [ⲉⲣⲣ]ⲙ̅ϩⲉ ⲉⲃⲟⲗ ⲙ̅[ⲙⲟϥ ϩ]ⲁⲙⲏⲛ. He prophesies that he 'will be pierced with a lance [in my] side (ⲥⲉⲛⲁⲕ[ⲟⲛ]ⲥ̅ⲧ̅ ⲛ̅ⲟⲩⲗⲟⲅⲭⲏ [ⲙ̅ⲡ]ⲁⲥⲡⲓⲣ)' (108.59-60). It is plausible that this is a reference to Jn 19.34, especially when the subsequent verse is taken into consideration: 'He who saw, let him bear witness. And his witness is true (ⲡⲉⲛⲧⲁϥⲛⲁⲩ ⲙⲁⲣⲉϥⲣ̄ⲙ̄ⲛ̄ⲧⲣⲉ ⲁⲩⲱ ⲟⲩⲙⲉ̓ ⲧⲉ ⲧⲉϥⲙ̄ⲛ̄ⲧⲙ̄ⲛ̄ⲧⲣⲉ)' (108.61-64; cf. Jn 19.35).

e. *Missing Pages (Gospel of the Savior 109.1–112.64)*
Although there is not much one can say about the content of missing pages, I think that it is a logical conclusion that these leaves probably continued exegeting Mt. 26.33-35: Peter's denial.

f. *Ascent Narrative (Gospel of the Savior 113.1–115.32)*
This section describes a second ascent of the disciples with the Savior into heaven in order to observe Jesus ask the Father to take away the cup. Thus, this section is a midrash of Mt. 26.36-46:

> Then Jesus went with them to a place called Gethsemane, and he said to his disciples, 'Sit here, while I go yonder and pray'. And taking with him Peter and the two sons of Zebedee, he began to be sorrowful and troubled. Then he said to them, 'My soul is very sorrowful, even to death; remain here, and watch with me'. And going a little farther he fell on his face and prayed, 'My Father, if it be possible, let this cup pass from me; nevertheless, not as I will, but as you will'. And he came to the disciples and found them sleeping...' Again, for the second time, he went away and prayed, 'My Father, if this cannot pass unless I drink it, your will be done'. And again he came and found them sleeping, for their eyes were heavy. So, leaving them again, he went away and prayed for the third time, saying the same words...'

We are told that the 'world became as the darkness (ⲁⲡⲉïⲕⲟⲥⲙⲟⲥ ϣⲱⲡⲉ ⲛ̄ⲑⲉ ⲛ̄ⲛⲓⲕⲁⲕⲉ)' to the disciples (*Gos. Sav.* 113.2-6). This phrase seems to be providing an explanation for the disciples' sleeping behavior: their sleeping was not ordinary. Rather it was the occasion of their second ascent into the heavens with Jesus. It is a common motif for visionaries to receive revelations while they are asleep, revelations which are then interpreted in texts as heavenly journeys (cf. Dan. 7.1-15; *1 En.* 13.7–36.4; *T. Levi* 2.5–5.7). So it is not surprising that the author of the *Gospel of the Savior* would understand the sleeping disciples as recipients of revelation and participants in a heavenly journey.

Next, the disciples state that they were transformed into heavenly beings: 'We became as [those] among the aeons [of Glory] (ⲁⲛⲣ̄ⲑⲉ [ⲛ̄ⲛ]ⲉⲧ2ⲛ̄ ⲛⲁⲓⲱⲛ [ⲙ̄ⲡⲉ]ⲟⲟⲩ)' (*Gos. Sav.* 113.6-8). Moreover, the ascent was the occasion for their investment with their 'apostleship (ⲙ̄ⲛ̄ⲧⲁ[ⲡ]-ⲟⲥⲧⲟⲗⲟⲥ)' (*Gos. Sav.* 113.11-12). Certainly we see here the understanding of the ascent of the disciples as heavenly priests. Like Levi and Enoch who were transformed and invested as priests in God's heavenly temple (*T. Levi* 8.1-10; *1 En.* 22; *3 En.* 12.1-5), the disciples are transformed and invested as apostles in heaven, seemingly to replace the priesthood of old.

Then the disciples watch as the Savior 'attained to the [fourth] heaven (ⲡⲱϩ ⲉⲧⲙⲉϩϥⲧⲟⲉ ⲙ̄ⲡⲉ)' (*Gos. Sav.* 113.13-16). As in their previous vision, Jesus' eruption into the heavenly sphere causes a great 'disturbance (ϣⲧ[ⲣ]ⲧⲣ̄)' (113.23). The angelic host is 'disturbed' because Jesus enters heaven, normally a place of worship and rejoicing, 'weeping and distressed' (113.53-57): ⲉⲧⲃ[ⲉ ⲟⲩ] ⲕⲣⲓⲙⲉ. ⲁⲩ[ⲱ ⲉⲕⲙⲟ]ⲕ̄ϩ ⲛ̄ϩⲏⲧ ⲛ̄ⲧ[ⲟⲕ]ϩⲱⲥⲧⲉ ⲛ̄ⲧⲉ[ⲧⲁⲅ]ⲅⲉⲗⲓⲕⲏ ⲧ[ⲏ]ⲣⲥ̄ [ϣⲧⲣ̄]ⲧⲣ̄. This disturbs the angelic host so that the angels and archangels flee for cover (113.24-26): ⲁ[ⲛⲁ]ⲅⲅⲉⲗⲟⲥ ⲙⲛ̄ ⲛⲁⲣⲭⲛⲁⲅⲅⲉⲗⲟⲥ ⲡⲱⲧ. But, the elders continue worshiping (ϩⲩⲙⲛ[ⲟⲥ...ⲡⲣⲉ]ⲥⲃⲩⲧⲉⲣ[ⲟⲥ] (114.35-36), singing hymns and casting their crowns down in front of the throne (cp. Rev. 4.2-10). Like Isaiah (*Asc. Isa.* 9.7-10; cf. *Dial. Sav.* 136.18-23; Rev. 6.9-11), they see the righteous receiving their 'robes' (113.38-43): ⲁ[ⲛⲉⲧⲟⲩ]ⲁⲁⲃ ⲧⲏⲣ[ⲟⲩ ϫⲓ ⲛⲉⲩ]ⲥⲧⲟⲗⲏ.

The Savior comes before the Father and tells him that he is 'greatly [distressed] (ⲉⲓⲙⲟ[ⲕ̄ϩ ⲛ̄ϩⲏⲧ ⲉ]ⲙⲁⲧⲉ)' because of the cup he has to bear. So he asks the Father, 'O my [Father], if [it is possible], let this [cup] pass by me (ⲱ̄ ⲡⲁ[ⲉⲓⲱⲧ] ⲉϣϫⲉ ⲟⲩⲛ̄[ϣϭⲟⲙ] ⲙⲁⲣⲉⲡⲉⲓⲁ[ⲡⲟⲧ ⲥ]ⲁⲁⲧ)' (114.2-9). A broken text follows in which the Father probably made a reply, confirming for Jesus that his action would bring 'salvation (ⲟⲩⲭⲁⲓ)' to 'the entire world (ⲙ̄ⲡⲕⲟ[ⲥⲙ]ⲟⲥ ⲧⲏⲣϥ̄)' (114.21-23). Thus, like the righteous martyr, Jesus 'bowed his knees [to] his Father' (ⲁⲡϣⲏⲣⲉ [ⲡ]ⲁϩⲧϥ̄ ⲉⲭⲛ̄ ⲙ̄ⲡⲁⲧ[ⲉ] ⲡⲉϥⲓⲱⲧ) and accepted his destiny: '[I am ready] to die with joy and pour out my blood upon the human race (†ⲥ[ⲃ̄ⲧⲱⲧ] ⲉⲙⲟⲩ ϩⲛ̄ ⲟⲩⲣⲁϣⲉ ⲁⲩⲱ ⲧⲁⲡⲱϩⲧ̄ ⲉⲃⲟⲗ ⲙ̄ⲡⲁⲥⲛⲟϥ ⲉⲭⲛ̄ ⲡⲅⲉⲛⲟⲥ ⲛ̄ⲛ̄ⲣⲱⲙⲉ)' (114.32-36). He expresses concern for the righteous men who died before him, hoping that they will be able to stand before him on the day of Judgment when Jesus will sit on his throne and '[judge] the world' (114.37-47): ⲁⲗⲗⲁ ⲉⲓⲡⲓⲙⲉ ⲙ̄ⲙⲁⲧ[ⲉ] ⲉ]ⲧⲃⲉ ⲛⲁⲙⲉⲣⲁ[ⲧⲉ] ⲉⲧⲉ ⲃⲁⲓ ⲛⲉ ⲁ[ⲃⲣⲁϩⲁ]ⲙ ⲙⲛ̄ ⲓ̈ⲥⲁⲁⲕ [ⲙⲛ̄ ⲓ̈]ⲁⲕⲱⲃ ϫⲉ ⲉ[ⲩⲛⲁ]ϣⲁϩⲉⲣⲁ[ⲧⲟ]ⲩ [ⲙ̄ⲡ]ⲉϩⲟⲟⲩ ⲙ̄ⲡϩⲁⲡ[ⲉ]ⲓ̈ⲛⲁϩⲙⲟ[ⲟ]ⲥ̄ ϩⲓⲡ[ⲁ]ⲑⲣⲟⲛⲟⲥ ⲧⲁ† ϩ[ⲁⲡ] ⲉⲡⲕⲟⲥⲙⲟⲥ.

A second time, the Savior comes before the Father and asks, 'O my [Father, if it is possible, let this cup] pass by me (ⲱ̄ ⲡⲁ[ⲓ̈ⲱⲧ ⲉ]ϣ[ⲱⲡ]ⲉ [ⲟⲩⲛ̄ϣϭⲟ]ⲙ [ⲙⲁ]ⲣⲉ [ⲡⲉⲓ̈ⲁⲡⲟⲧ] ⲥⲁⲁⲧ)' (*Gos. Sav.* 114.59-61). For the second time, the Father replies (114.62-64). Because page 115 is so fragmentary, the content of the reply is not made out. We do have a scrap of page 115, however, which suggests that, as in Matthew, the son came before the Father for a 'third time' to ask that the cup be removed (115.29-32).

g. *Ascent Narrative (Gospel of the Savior 14FH)*
We have a very fragmentary leaf in which the disciples and the Savior are having a vision of Jerusalem. Although the page is too fragmentary to place sequentially, it seems likely that it should be placed after page 115. It would make sense if it followed page 115, since Mt. 26.57 shifts the events to Jerusalem. The disciples, then, witness the Passion events while in a visionary state.

h. *Conclusion*
A preliminary interpretation of the *Gospel of the Savior* suggests that it is an early second-century Syrian text that was involved in the continuing debate between those Christians who identified themselves with the Syrian vision mystics and those Christians who supported the perspective of the Johannine faith mystics. Clearly this text is a vision mystic's esoteric exegesis of Mt. 26.26-46 based on Jewish mystical traditions similar to those which influenced the Thomasine Gospel. In addition, we can detect that the author of the *Savior* was familiar with the Johannine Gospel and used it in his exegesis. However, he often would not use the text in a straightforward manner, but instead 'corrected' the text in the places where he felt it erred. These occasions centered upon the visionary experience of the resurrected Jesus. The author of the *Gospel of the Savior* made it clear that the Johannine presentation of the resurrected Jesus to Thomas was incorrect. The reason for its inaccuracy, the author contended, was that John was afraid of the vision of Jesus in his full glory and did not understand the fiery nature of Jesus' transformed body.

3. *Apocryphon of James*

The *Apocryphon of James*[14] represents a position that can be called 'medial'. It is a text which attempts to preserve aspects of visionary

14. Harold Attridge, *Nag Hammadi Codex I (The Jung Codex): Introductions, Texts, Translations, Indices* (NHS, 22; Leiden: E.J. Brill, 1985), pp. 28-53.

mysticism welded with aspects of Johannine faith mysticism. First and
foremost, this text is a visionary text in that the disciples have a vision
of the resurrected Jesus who takes aside James and Peter to instruct
them privately in Christian esoterica (*Ap. Jas.* 2.15-34). Against the
Johannine perspective, the author of *James* has Jesus command these
two disciples to 'follow' him quickly (ⲟⲩⲱϩ ⲧⲏⲛⲉ ⲛ̄ⲥⲱ̈ⲓ ϩⲛ̄ ⲟⲩϭⲉⲡⲏ)
as he is about to ascend into heaven (*Ap. Jas.* 10.25-26). He not only
commands his disciples to immediately follow him into heaven, but he
has also taught them the secret passwords that are needed to success-
fully pass by the angelic guards (*Ap. Jas.* 8.34-36): ⲁϩⲓϩⲱⲛ ⲁⲧⲟⲟⲧⲕ̄
ⲁⲧⲣⲉⲕⲟⲩⲁϩⲕ̄ ⲛ̄ⲥⲱⲉⲓ ⲁⲩⲱ ⲁϩⲓ̈ⲧⲥⲉⲃⲉ ⲉⲓⲉⲧⲕ ⲁⲃⲁⲗ ⲁⲑⲩⲡⲟⲑⲉⲥⲓⲥ
ⲛ̄ⲛⲁϩⲣⲛ̄ ⲛ̄ⲛⲁⲣⲭⲱⲛ. He blesses 'those who are to ascend to the Father
(ⲥⲉⲛⲁϣⲱⲡⲉ ⲛ̄ⲙⲁⲕⲁⲣ[ⲓⲟ]ⲥ ⲛ̄ϭⲓ ⲛⲉⲧⲛ̄ⲛⲏⲟⲩ ⲁϩⲣⲏⲓ̈ ⲁⲣⲉⲧⲅ̄ ⲙ̄ⲡⲓⲱⲧ)' (*Ap.
Jas.* 13.11-13) and those who have seen themselves in the 'fourth
heaven' (ⲛⲉⲉⲓⲉⲧⲅ̄ ⲙ̄ⲡⲉⲛⲧⲁⲩⲛⲉⲩ ⲁⲣⲁⲩ ⲉⲩⲟⲉⲓ ⲛ̄ⲙⲁϩⲩⲧⲁⲩ ⲛ̄ϩⲣⲏⲓ̈ ϩⲛ̄
ⲙ̄ⲡⲏⲩⲉ) (*Ap. Jas.* 12.16).[15] So important is the ascent of the disciples
that Jesus blesses the believer who has 'seen' the disciples in God's
presence when the believer is 'proclaimed among the angels and glorified among the saints. Yours is life! Rejoice and be glad as sons of
God' (*Ap. Jas.* 10.35–11.1): ⲟⲩⲙⲁⲕⲁⲣⲓⲟⲥ ⲡⲉ ⲡⲉⲛⲧⲁⲩⲛⲉⲩ ⲁⲣⲱⲧⲛ̄
ⲛ̄ⲙⲙⲉⲩ ⲉⲩⲧⲁϣⲉ ⲁⲉⲓϣ ⲛ̄ⲙⲁⲩ ϩⲛ̄ ⲛ̄ⲁⲅⲅⲉⲗⲟⲥ ⲁⲩⲱ ⲉⲩϯ ⲉⲁⲩ ⲛⲉⲩ ϩⲛ̄
ⲛⲉⲧⲟⲩⲁⲁⲃ. ⲡⲱⲧⲛ̄ ⲡⲉ ⲡⲱⲛϩ̄ ⲣⲉϣⲉ ⲁⲩⲱ ⲧⲉⲗⲏⲗ ⲛ̄ⲙⲱⲧⲛ̄ ϩⲱⲥ ϣⲏⲣⲉ
ⲙ̄ⲡⲛⲟⲩⲧⲉ. Clearly this latter statement reflects knowledge of the transformative power of the visionary experience and the fact that Christians
are to anticipate this, probably as post-mortem event here. Their future
ascent is understood to mirror Jesus' own present ascent to the Father
which is described in the following (now familiar) mystical terms:

> But give heed to the Glory which awaits me, and having opened your
> hearts, listen to the hymns which await me up in heaven (ⲉⲣⲓ ⲡⲣⲟⲥⲉⲭⲉ
> ⲇⲉ ⲁⲡⲉⲁⲩ ⲉⲧϭⲱϣⲧ̄ ⲁⲃⲁⲗ ϩⲏⲧ ⲁⲩⲱ ⲉϩⲁⲧⲉⲧⲛ̄ⲟⲩⲏⲛ ⲁⲡⲉⲧⲛ̄ϩⲏⲧ ⲥⲱⲧⲙ̄
> ⲁⲛϩⲩ̈ⲙⲛⲟⲥ ⲉⲧϭⲱϣⲧ̄ ⲁϩⲣⲏⲓ̈ ⲛ̄ϩⲣⲏⲓ̈ ϩⲛ̄ ⲙ̄ⲡⲏⲩⲉ). For today I am obliged to
> take (my place) at the right hand of my Father (ⲁⲛⲁⲅⲕⲏ ⲅⲁⲣ ⲁⲣⲁⲉⲓ

---

15. The translation by Williams in Attridge, *Nag Hammadi Codex I*, p. 47,
'Blessed is he who has seen himself as a fourth one in heaven', does not make good
ideological sense. Thus, I propose that we amend the word order slightly. I think
that the ordinal number is modifying 'heavens': ⲛ̄ⲙⲁϩⲩⲧⲁⲩ ⲙ̄ⲡⲏⲩⲉ. The prepo-
sitional phrase, ⲛ̄ϩⲣⲏⲓ ϩⲛ̄, seems to have been inverted with ⲛ̄ⲙⲁϩⲩⲧⲁⲩ. This means
that the text probably should be translated: 'Blessed is he who has seen himself in
the fourth heaven.' This rendering certainly is more sensible than the previous one.

6. *Vision Mysticism in Early Syrian Christian Texts* 153

ⲙ̄ⲡⲟⲟⲩ ⲁⲧⲣⲁⲙⲟⲩϩ ⲛ̄ⲥⲁ ⲟⲩⲛⲉⲙ ⲙ̄ⲡⲁⲓ̈ⲱⲧ). Now I have said (my) last
word to you. I shall part from you. For a chariot of wind has taken me
up, and from now on I shall strip myself in order that I may clothe
myself (ⲁϩⲁⲟⲩϩⲁⲣⲙⲁ ⲅⲁⲣ ⲙ̄ⲡⲛ̄[ⲉⲩⲙ]ⲁ ϥⲓ ⲙ̄ⲙⲁⲉⲓ ⲁϩⲣⲏⲓ̈ ⲁⲩⲱ ϫⲓⲛ̄ ϯⲛⲟⲩ
ϯⲛⲁⲕⲁⲁⲕⲧ̄ ⲁϩⲏⲩ ϫⲉⲕⲁⲥⲉ ⲉⲉⲓⲛⲁϯ ϩⲓ̈ⲱⲱⲧ) (*Ap. Jas.* 14.26-36).

Immediately upon Jesus' ascension, James and Peter ascend after
him, sending their 'hearts up to heaven' (*Ap. Jas.* 15.6-9): ⲁϩⲛ̄ϫⲁⲩ
ⲙ̄ⲡⲛ̄ϩⲏⲧ ⲁϩⲣⲏⲉⲓ ⲁⲙⲡⲏⲟⲩⲉ. Just as we saw in the *Gospel of the Savior*,
Jesus' ascent causes disturbances in the lower realms. James and Peter
'heard' and 'saw' 'the sound of wars and a trumpet-call and a great
commotion' (*Ap. Jas.* 15.10-13), the beginning of the eschaton:
ⲁⲛⲥⲱⲧⲙ̄ ϩⲣⲏⲉⲓ ϩⲛ̄ ⲛⲉⲛⲙⲉϣϫⲉ ⲁⲩⲱ ⲁⲛⲛⲉⲩ ϩⲣⲏⲓ̈ ϩⲛ̄ ⲛⲉⲛⲃⲉⲗ ⲁⲡϩⲣⲁⲩ
ⲛ̄ϩⲙ̄ⲡⲟⲗⲉⲙⲟⲥ ⲁⲩⲱ ⲟⲩⲥⲙⲏ ⲛ̄ⲥⲁⲗⲡⲓⲅⲝ ⲙⲛ̄ ⲟⲩⲛⲁϭ ⲛ̄ϣⲧⲁⲣⲧⲣ̄. As they
passed beyond, ascending higher, they 'heard' and 'saw' 'hymns and
angelic praises and angelic jubilation' (15.15-23): ⲛ̄ⲧⲁⲣⲛ̄[ⲟⲩ]ⲟⲩⲱⲧⲃ̄
ⲁϩⲣⲏⲓ̈ ⲙ̄ⲡⲃⲗ̄ ⲙ̄ⲡⲙⲁ ⲉⲧⲙ̄ⲙⲉⲩ ⲁϩⲛ̄ϫⲁⲩ ⲙ̄ⲡⲛ̄ⲛⲟⲩⲥ ⲁϩⲣⲏⲓ̈ ⲛ̄ϩⲟⲩⲟ ⲁⲩⲱ
ⲁϩⲛ̄ⲛⲉⲩ ϩⲛ̄ ⲛⲉⲛⲃⲉⲗ ⲁⲩⲱ ⲁⲛⲥⲱⲧⲙ̄ ϩⲣⲏⲓ̈ ϩⲛ ⲛⲉⲛⲙⲉϣϫⲉ ⲁϩⲛ̄ⲩⲙⲛⲟⲥ ⲙⲛ̄
ϩⲛ̄ⲥⲙⲟⲩ ⲛ̄ⲛⲁⲅⲅⲉⲗⲟⲥ ⲁⲩⲱ ⲉⲩⲧⲉⲗⲏⲗ ⲛ̄ϩⲉⲛⲁⲅⲅⲉⲗⲟⲥ ⲁⲩⲱ ϩⲉⲛⲙⲛ̄ⲧⲛⲁϭ
ⲛ̄ⲙⲡⲏⲩⲉ ⲛⲉⲩⲣ̄ ϩⲩⲙⲛⲉⲓ ⲡⲉ ⲁⲩⲱ ⲁⲛ ⲁⲛ ϩⲱⲱⲛ ⲁⲛⲧⲉⲗⲏⲗ ⲙ̄ⲙⲁⲛ. Even
higher they ascended, desiring to send their spirits to stand before the
'Majesty', God (15.24-25): ⲙⲛ̄ⲛⲥⲁ ⲛⲉⲉⲓ ⲁⲛ ⲁϩⲛ̄ⲟⲩⲱϣⲉ ⲁϫⲁⲩ
ⲙ̄ⲡⲉⲛⲡⲛ[ⲉⲩⲛ]ⲁ ⲁⲡⲥⲁ ⲛⲧⲡⲉ ⲁⲣⲉⲧϥ̄ ⲛ̄ⲧⲙⲛ̄ⲧⲛⲁϭ. But their ascent to the
throne was cut off by the interruption of the other disciples who called
them back (15.26-34).

But how can these striking mystical themes be juxtaposed with the
seemingly Johannine statement also found in this text: 'Blessed are
those who have not seen [but] have [had faith] (ⲙ̄ⲙⲁⲕⲁⲣⲓⲟⲥ ⲛ̄ϭⲓ ⲛⲉⲧⲉ
ⲙ̄ⲡⲟⲩⲛⲉⲩ ⲁ[ⲗⲗ]ⲁ ⲁⲩ[ⲛⲁϩⲧⲉ])' (12.41–13.1)? Or how can these two
following sayings be interwoven with each other?

> And now, waking or sleeping, remember that you have seen the Son of
> Man, and with him you have spoken, and to him you have listened. Woe
> to those who have seen the Son [of] Man! (ⲉⲣⲉⲧⲛ̄ⲣⲁⲉⲓⲥ ⲁⲩⲱ
> ⲉⲣⲉⲧⲛ̄ⲛ̄ⲕⲁⲧⲕⲉ ⲉⲣⲓ ⲡⲙⲉⲉⲩⲉ ϫⲉ ⲛ̄ⲧⲱⲧⲛ̄ ϩⲁⲧⲉⲧⲛ̄ⲛⲉⲩ ⲁⲡϣⲏⲣⲉ ⲙ̄ⲡⲣⲱⲙⲉ
> ⲁⲩⲱ ⲡⲉⲉⲓ ⲁⲧⲉⲧⲛ̄ϣⲉϫⲉ ⲛⲙ̄ⲙⲉϥ ⲁⲩⲱ ⲡⲉⲉⲓ ⲁⲧⲉⲧⲛ̄ⲥⲱⲧⲙ̄ ⲁⲣⲁϥ ⲟⲩⲁⲉⲓ
> ⲛ̄ⲛⲉⲛⲧⲁϩⲛⲉⲩ ⲁⲡϣⲏⲣ[ⲉ ⲙ̄ⲡⲣ]ⲱⲙⲉ). Blessed will be those who have not
> seen the Man, and who have not consorted with him, and who have not
> spoken with him, and who have not listened to anything from him. Yours
> is life! (ⲥⲉⲛⲁϣⲱⲡⲉ ⲙ̄ⲙⲁⲕⲁⲣⲓⲟⲥ ⲛ̄ϭⲓ ⲛⲉⲧⲉⲙ̄ⲡⲟⲩⲛⲉⲩ ⲁⲡⲣⲱⲙⲉ ⲁⲩⲱ
> ⲛⲉⲧⲉⲙ̄ⲡⲟⲩⲧⲱϩ ⲛⲙ̄ⲙⲉϥ ⲁⲩⲱ ⲛⲉⲧⲉⲙ̄ⲡⲟⲩϣⲉϫⲉ ⲛⲙ̄ⲙⲉϥ ⲁⲩⲱ
> ⲛⲉⲧⲉⲙ̄ⲡⲟⲩⲥⲱⲧⲙ̄ ⲁⲗⲁⲁⲩⲉ ⲛ̄ⲧⲟⲟⲧϥ̄ ⲡⲱⲧⲛ̄ ⲡⲉ ⲡⲱⲛϩ̄) (3.12-25).

Such apparent contradictions sound nonsensical at first. But they do reveal a deep conflict that this author is having between visionary mysticism and faith mysticism.

I believe that one of the problems that developed in these vision-oriented communities was the absence of visions among its members and the need to provide an 'alternative' mystical encounter without expending the strong visionary soteriological model from their past. So minor adjustments in the model were made. In this case, the adjustments were particularly pertinent since the community seemed to be experiencing persecution and martyrdom (*Ap. Jas.* 4.23–6.20). Members wanted reassurance that their suffering and death would be worth it, especially those members who had not yet been blessed with an ascent and vision of God.

So, in this text, the Johannine idea of 'faith' is incorporated, although interpreted much differently from the Johannine author's original intent. According to James, other Christians will be 'enlightened' through James' own faith (*Ap. Jas.* 16.15) so much so that the piece opens with the proclamation: 'Blessed are those who will be saved through faith in this discourse' (*Ap. Jas.* 1.25-29). This suggests that if the believer has not been lucky enough to have had a visionary experience, then he should have faith in the visionary experiences of Jesus' disciples and the leaders of his community. In fact, their authority rested on the fact that they had had these mystical encounters. Such faith in the visions and authority of his leaders meant that upon the believer's own death (perhaps as a martyr), he could anticipate a similar ascent into heaven.

4. *Ascension of Isaiah*

This early Christian–Jewish text from Syria must also belong to the now established visionary mystical trajectory even though direct polemic against the Johannine views is not *immediately* observable nor are connections with the *Gospel of Thomas* detectable. So I include it in this chapter as additional textual evidence for the apparent common presence of vision mysticism early on in eastern Christian communities. My understanding of this text has been most influenced by the recent work of Robert Hall who examines the vision of God and its soteriological implications for Syrian Christians.[16]

16. R. Hall, 'Astonishment in the Firmament: The Worship of Jesus and

There are seven heavens replete with angels, thrones, and continual theophanies in the *Ascension of Isaiah*. At each level, the enthroned angel is God's 'stand-in', manifesting the Glory to the degree that the angels can perceive it at that level. The enthroned angel receives the praise and passes it on to the Great Glory in the seventh heaven. In the seventh heaven, the Beloved, the Angel of the Spirit, and the righteous dead worship God directly. Hall explains:

> In the seven throne angels, God's glory streams down to the lowest heaven (7.37) and in the praises from each heaven the glory returns to the highest throne. The vision of God creates a circulation of glory, a respiration of glory which orders and nourishes all the heavens.[17]

Hall notes that the vision of God and 'the consequent respiration of glory' stops at the lowest firmament because the angels of this world cannot see God's Glory:[18] they are fighting with each other, plundering and doing violence (*Asc. Isa.* 10.29-31). This disorder is mirrored on earth (7.10), making it impossible for humans to see God either. Thus, it is necessary for the Beloved to descend into the firmament and the world in order to manifest the vision of God to the lower angels and humans, who are unable to see God otherwise. Thus Hall concludes:

> In the *Ascension of Isaiah*, angels of the firmament and those below them cannot see the vision of God. Christ descends to reveal the glory of God, to provoke praise from human beings, and to unite them with the respiration which nourishes and orders them in heavenly life.[19]

In addition to the descent of Christ, the righteous people can ascend into heaven and report back to humans about their visionary experiences, thus also revealing the vision of God's Glory to this world (7.23; 11.34, 40). And finally, the Angel of the Spirit descends to manifest God's Glory to the righteous people living below the firmament (9.36; 10.6), opening the 'door' of heaven so that the praises of the righteous can ascend to God:

Soteriology in Ignatius and the *Ascension of Isaiah*', in C. Newman, J. Davila, and G. Lewis (eds.), *The Jewish Roots of Christological Monotheism: Papers from the St. Andrews Conference on the Historical Origins of the Worship of Jesus* (JSJSup, 63; Leiden: E.J. Brill, 1999), pp. 148-55; Hall, 'The Vision of God in the Ascension of Isaiah', in A.D. DeConick (ed.), *Early Jewish and Christian Mysticism: New Directions* (forthcoming).

17. Hall, 'Astonishment', p. 149.
18. Hall, 'Astonishment', p. 149.
19. Hall, 'Astonishment', p. 150.

And when they all heard the voice of the Holy Spirit, they all worshiped on their knees, and they praised the God of righteousness, the Most High, the one who dwells in the upper world and who sits on high, the Holy One, the one who rests among the holy ones, and they ascribed glory to the one who had thus graciously given a door in an alien world, had graciously given it to a man (*Asc. Isa.* 6.8-9).

This means, in Hall's words, that in the *Ascension of Isaiah*, 'the good news is the vision of God'.[20] Seeing God's Glory through Christ's revelation, the testimony of the mystic righteous, and the descent of the Holy Spirit enables humans to receive nourishment from the heavens. They are joined in a chain of life that connects them directly to God and immortality.

It is noteworthy that this brief summary of the ideology of this text suggests that the author was promoting celetial vision mysticism, but felt that the descent of the Beloved also provided the necessary theophany. This contrasts with John who argues that heaven's door remains closed to humans who must now rely solely on faith and the descent of the Spirit as visionary substitutes.

It is also significant that the *Ascension of Isaiah* preserves the Spirit's descent which we found to be so important in Johannine ideology. Here, the Spirit does not come in order to enable believers to love one another and thus manifest God to each other; rather, the Spirit descends in order to open heaven's door so that the worship of the righteous people can reach God!

In addition, the author of the *Ascension* builds a case in which post-mortem ascension is the *permanent* transforming experience for the believers. During Isaiah's pre-mortem ascent, he sees the righteous dead who have been transformed into angelic beings. Even though Isaiah begins to notice a transformation of the 'glory' of his face as he ascends (*Asc. Isa.* 7.25), he is not completely and permanently transformed to be equal to the dead righteous. He can only observe the glorified ones praising God (9.33). Although he glances at the Great Glory momentarily, his eyes become closed to this vision and he must be content to watch the dead righteous who continually partake of the great vision 'gazing intently upon the Glory' (9.37-38). Isaiah's angelic escort promises Isaiah while they are in the sixth heaven that, even though he has viewed sights unseen by other humans, he can only now *anticipate* becoming like the angels after death. His human days are not

20. Hall, 'Vision of God'.

yet complete (*Asc. Isa.* 8.23-28)! Thus Isaiah will not be immortalized until after he returns from his heavenly journey and dies a human death. Only then will he receive a garment and become like the angels. His angelic escort explains in 8.15:

> When from the body by the will of God you have come up here, then you will receive the robe which you will see (in the seventh heaven),...
> and then you will be equal to the angels who (are) in the seventh heaven.

It is not implausible that the author of this text may have been aware of Johannine theology and may have been creating his own Interpretative Trajectory and Synthetic End Point in response. At any rate, it now seems clear that many early Syrian Christians believed in a vision mystical soteriology, although some were modifying these Christian–Jewish traditions in order to allow for a more universal salvation experience in the face of community crisis: What happens to us, we can hear these Christians ask, if we aren't able to achieve a vision during our lifetimes? The righteous among us become reporters, the Spirit descends keeping the door to heaven open, and the immortalizing visions are postponed until after death.

5. *Dialogue of the Savior*

Although there is no explicit dialogue against the Johannine perspective in this text, I have argued elsewhere that this tract belongs to the Thomasine soteriological trajectory.[21] For this reason, I mention it here as another representative of the visionary mystical form of Christianity which seemed to be so threatening to the Johannine Christians. Because I have written at length on my interpretation of this text, I will only summarize relevant conclusions here.

According to my previous findings, the *Dialogue of the Savior* can be understood as a 'commentary' written in response to the type of vision mysticism associated with the *Gospel of Thomas*. Although the *Dialogue* is familiar with this soteriological scheme and agrees with it in most aspects, it finds one element disputable: that the transformative mystical experience is a *pre-mortem* encounter (*Dial. Sav.* 1–3; 20; 26–29; 56–57; 77; 96). Rather, the *Dialogue* insists that the 'great vision'

---

21. A.D. DeConick, 'The Dialogue of the Savior and the Mystical Sayings of Jesus', *VC* 50 (1996), pp. 178-99.

and immortalization cannot be realized until after the body has been discarded *at death* (*Dial. Sav.* 40; 42; 44; 52; 67–68; 84–85).

Thus this text represents a modified version of Thomasine soteriology popular perhaps in early second-century Syria as we have already seen in our analysis of the *Apocryphon of James* and the *Ascension of Isaiah*. It seems that the author of the *Dialogue* is at issue with the distinction between pre-mortem and post-mortem visions, promoting the eschatological premise rather than the ecstatic as *Thomas* had done. In order to understand the mystical scheme in this fashion, the author of the *Dialogue of the Savior* reinterpreted three themes that are central to *Thomas*: (1) the return to the 'Place of Life'; (2) the *visio Dei*; and (3) transformation.

a. *Return to the 'Place of Life'*

The *Dialogue of the Savior* opens with a saying of Jesus in which he acknowledges that the time has arrived for salvation when we will 'abandon our labor and stand at rest. For whoever will stand at rest will rest forever (ⲡⲉⲧⲛⲁⲱϣⲉ ⲉⲣⲁⲧϥ ϩⲛ̄ⲧⲁⲛⲁⲡⲩⲥⲓⲥ ϥⲛⲁⲙ̄ⲧⲟⲛ ⲙ̄ⲙⲟϥ ⲛ̄ϣⲁⲉⲛⲉϩ)' (*Dial. Sav.* 1).[22] This saying reflects a mystical soteriology where immortality is attainable in the present.

The author of the *Dialogue,* however, places this saying within a futuristic context that serves to interpret it in a futuristic manner. This context is that of the ascent of the soul at death. Comparable to Logia 49–50 of *Thomas*, Jesus announces that he has come to teach the 'elect and solitary' the way they will ascend to heaven, returning to God: 'When I came, I opened the path and I taught them about the passage which they will traverse, the elect and solitary' (*Dial. Sav.* 1). The author insists that the passage into rest, this ascent about which Jesus has come to instruct his followers, will occur at 'the time of dissolution (ⲡⲉⲟⲩⲟⲉⲓϣ ⲙ̄ⲡⲃⲱⲗ ⲉⲃⲟⲗ)' when one sheds the body and journeys to God past terrifying heavenly guards (*Dial. Sav.* 3). Since the Coptic phrase ⲡⲉⲟⲩⲟⲉⲓϣ ⲙ̄ⲡⲃⲱⲗ ⲉⲃⲟⲗ is a euphemism for death in classical and early Christian literature,[23] the author of the *Dialogue* intends his reader to understand that the ascent will be a post-mortem journey.

In vv. 1-3, the author of the *Dialogue* seems to be trying to resolve the tension that had developed as the inevitable result of mystical

22. S. Emmel, *Nag Hammadi Codex III,5: The Dialogue of the Savior* (NHS, 26; Leiden: E.J. Brill, 1984).

23. DeConick, 'Dialogue', pp. 182-83.

practices. The problem centers around the fact that if one believes that a person is deified as the result of a pre-mortem *visio Dei* as *Thomas* taught, then why did that person still die? The solution to this troubling dilemma, according to the *Dialogue*, was to emphasize that the immortalization is only a potential now which will not be fully realized until after death. Thus Jesus declares in the introductory verses that the time has arrived for salvation but that this state of rest will become permanent only after the dissolution of the body at death.

In v. 96, Jesus emphasizes the fact that this post-mortem journey to heaven is difficult, but 'you [will] go via [the path] which you have known'. So difficult is the journey to the highest heaven that Jesus exclaims in reference to his own post-mortem ascension, 'I [tell] you [that] it is difficult even [for] me [to reach] it!' This notion is extremely important to the author since he repeats Jesus' exclamation in v. 52. But Jesus insists that even though the way of ascent is very difficult and potentially dangerous, 'You will find the means to overcome the powers above as well as those below' (*Dial. Sav.* 20). These words must have been very reassuring to the readers of the *Dialogue*, encouraging those who were experiencing doubt and anxiety about the reality of their ascent to God and his 'place'.

The author makes it clear that the ascent cannot be expected to happen as long as one is embodied. This is poignantly stated in v. 28: 'Brother [Matthew], you will not be able to see it (the Place of Life) [as long as you are] carrying the flesh around'. Certainly the metaphor of shedding the body does not have to refer to removing the body *at death*, but in the context of the *Dialogue* it seems that this was the author's intention. Thus it is not surprising that in the succeeding v. 29, Matthew agrees with Jesus that, because he is still living in a human body, he cannot yet have the transforming vision of the place of pure light. Since he cannot ascend yet, he asks Jesus to at least help him to '[know it]' in the present.

b. *The visio Dei*

The *Dialogue of the Savior* distinguishes between two types of visions: 'transient' or 'ceasing' (ογωϲϥ) visions and 'the eternal (ϣλενεϩ) vision' (*Dial. Sav.* 44), which is 'the great (νοϭ) vision' of the 'Eternal Living One (πετϣοοπ ϣλνενεϩ)' (*Dial. Sav.* 42). This great vision is the transformative *visio Dei* which *Thomas* alludes to in Logia 15, 27, 37, 59, and 83. The author of the *Dialogue* insists that this great vision

of the divine cannot occur while one is carrying the flesh around. The
visions that occur during one's lifetime, he categorizes as only transient
visions which do not effect immortalization.

Such a vision is granted to Judas, Matthew, and Mary when they are
escorted by Jesus to the edge of heaven. They see an 'exceedingly high
place' and 'the place of the abyss below' (*Dial. Sav.* 36). They speak
with the Son of Man (*Dial. Sav.* 37) and watch a soul escorted by two
spirits ascend to heaven and be transformed when it meets its heavenly
counterpart (*Dial. Sav.* 40). Such visions are nowhere discouraged in
the *Dialogue*. But the point is made in the discussion between the
disciples and Jesus following this vision that these kinds of visions are
only transient visions. The 'great' vision of the Eternal Living One is
yet to come (*Dial. Sav.* 42).

c. *Transformation*
The *Dialogue* knows a tradition comparable to that found in *Thomas*
where a person would encounter his heavenly counterpart (L. 84). It
appears, however, that the author of the *Dialogue* understood this to be
a post-mortem experience. Thus in v. 40, the soul that ascends at death
apparently meets its heavenly counterpart which is described as 'big'. It
becomes this heavenly being, resembling the angels who receive it:
'The small one became like the big one. They were [like] those who
received them.' It may be that this verse is related to the tradition that
when someone ascends into heaven, he can anticipate being transformed into cosmic proportions (*Hist. Rech.* 5.3-4; *3 En.* 9.2). Significantly, Jesus' own post-mortem ascent and transformation are
described in comparable terms (*Acts Jn* 90; *Gos. Phil* 58.508).

This theme is expanded in verses 67-68 of the *Dialogue* where
Matthew asks: 'How does the small join itself to the big?' Jesus
responds by explaining that this state of rest can only be achieved when
'the works (ⲛ̄ⲛⲉϩⲃⲏⲟⲩⲉ) which will not be able to follow you' are
abandoned. Within the context of this encratic document,[24] 'works'
probably refers to sexual intercourse and procreation, the 'works
(ⲛ̄ⲛⲉϩⲃⲏⲟⲩⲉ) of womanhood' which are mentioned in v. 92. It seems
that the lifestyle that one must maintain in order to be immortalized
after death is characterized by encratism.

Not surprisingly, the transformation is described in terms of putting

---

24. On this, see my 'Dialogue', pp. 184-85.

on a garment. In fact, in the heavenly vision of Judas, Matthew, and Mary, when the two spirits bring the deceased to heaven, the command is made to give this soul its 'garment'. Then the soul is said to be transformed, becoming like its angelic counterpart. The employment of this image can be seen in v. 84 where Judas and Matthew want to understand what type of garment they will be given after they die: 'We [want] to understand the sort of garments we are to be [clothed] with [when] we come forth from the destruction of the [flesh] ([ϵ]ⲛϢⲁⲛⲉⲓ ⲉⲃⲟⲗ Ϩⲙ̄ⲡⲧⲁⲕⲟ ⲛ̄ⲧ[ⲥⲁⲣ]ⲝ)'. The Lord responds that 'the children of truth' will not continue to have 'transitory (ⲡⲣⲟⲥⲟⲩⲥⲉⲓϣ) garments' with which to 'clothe' themselves. Rather, this garment which represents the body, must be stripped off (*Dial. Sav.* 85).

It seems that in vv. 84-85, the *Dialogue* is stating that the 'transitory garments' will be destroyed and fall away at death, leaving room for the new garments replace them. This is the permanent instant of immortalization when the 'garments of life (ⲛ̄Ϩⲃ̄ⲥⲱ ⲙ̄ⲡⲱⲛϨ)' are donned (*Dial. Sav.* 52). Thus when Judas asks, 'How will [our] garments be brought to us', the Lord states:

> There are some who will provide for you, and there are others who will receive [you]. For [it is] they [who will give you] your garments. [For] who [will] be able to reach that place [which is the reward]? But the garments of life were given to man because he knows the path by which he will leave. And it is difficult even for me to reach it (*Dial. Sav.* 51-52)!

Here the donning of the garments is associated with ascent to heaven when the angelic officials will give the garments to the person who has been able to reach that 'place'. These garments are described as garments of 'life' because they represent the immortalization of the person.

The process of immortalization is the theme which is emphasized in the *Dialogue of the Savior*. This text attempts to provide the reader with the correct interpretation of Jesus' mystical sayings, an interpretation that would guarantee his or her spiritual transformation. Like *Thomas* Logion 1, Jesus says in the *Dialogue*, '[If you have understood] everything which I have [told you], you will [become immortal...]' (*Dial. Sav.* 82).

In the *Dialogue*, the author reassures his reader that he can anticipate a transformative ascent experience similar to that promoted by the *Gospel of Thomas*. The reader comes face to face with the powerful force of these hopes in v. 18: 'If someone [sets his soul] up high, [then he will] be exalted.' But, unlike *Thomas'* soteriological scheme which emphasized pre-mortem heavenly journeys, the *Dialogue* insists on the importance of the post-mortem journey, continually instilling in the reader his belief that the exaltation to the status of an immortal will only be fulfilled after the flesh is stripped off and destroyed at the moment of death.

6. *Conclusion*

This chapter has summarized several early second-century texts with Syrian provenance. It seems that, in Syria at least, there existed a form of Christianity which was mystically oriented, belonging to the trajectory of early Jewish and Christian mysticism. This 'type' of Christianity existed as early as the late first century as evidenced by the *Gospel of Thomas*. This ideology is preserved or slightly modified in other later Syrian texts like the *Preachings of John*, the *Gospel of the Savior*, the *Apocryphon of James*, the *Ascension of Isaiah*, and the *Dialogue of the Savior*.

It is plausible that these modifications in the earlier visionary soteriology were needed because the majority of believers were not experiencing celestial ascent journeys or the great *visio Dei* during their lives. Some community members may have even died without such experiences! We see such concerns expressed, for instance, in the disciple's comments in the *Dialogue of the Savior*: They ask Jesus to show them the vision of 'Him Who is Forever' (*Dial. Sav.* 137.10-13); they desire to 'see the place of life' (132.6-9); and they wonder how they will be transformed (138.20-21). The response of the author was to postpone the *visio Dei* until after death.

We noted similar concerns projected in the *Apocryphon of James* which provided an 'alternative' mystical encounter: Christians were blessed who had not received a vision or ascended as well as those who had! In addition, the absence of visions among members of the community were replaced by faith in the visions of those authorities who had gone before. Faith in the visions of the disciples and Christian leaders meant that, the believer could expect a comparable ascent into heaven at death.

The *Ascension of Isaiah* also modified the visionary scheme significantly. Like John, the author develops the theme that both Jesus and the Holy Spirit descended to earth to manifest God's Glory to humans:

Jesus during the historical period of his life; the Holy Spirit after Jesus' death. But, in contrast to John, the *Ascension* does not close off the possibility of heavenly journeys, especially for the righteous people in the community who returned from their journey to reveal God's Glory to Christians not fortunate enough to have their own mystical experience.

Evidence particularly from the *Preachings of John* and the *Gospel of the Savior* has suggested that the debate over vision mysticism and faith mysticism continued in early second-century Syria. Both of these texts paint a picture of John as a disciple who is greatly afraid of visions of Jesus as the Glory. John is portrayed as faithless because of this and the vision itself is lauded as the grounds for belief. It is probable that these texts echo the voices responding to the Gospel of John, the voices of the Syrian vision mystics who revered the disciple Thomas.

But, as history proceeded, their voice became the silenced voices and to this day we remember Thomas only as the 'Doubter' not as the mystic who learned from the mystic Jesus. It is worth observing that if the *Acts of John* or the *Gospel of the Savior* had been canonized rather than the Gospel of John, our expression today would not be the Doubting Thomas, but the Doubting John.

BIBLIOGRAPHY

Afzal, C., 'The Communal Icon: Complex Cultural Schemas, Elements of the Social Imagination (Matthew 10:32//Luke 12:8 and Revelation 3:5, A Case Study)', in V. Wiles, A. Brown, and G. Snyder (eds.), *Putting Body and Soul Together: Essays in Honor of Robin Scroggs* (Valley Forge, PA: Trinity Press International, 1997), pp. 58-79.

Anrich, G., *Das antike Mysterienwesen in seinem Einfluss auf das christentum* (Göttingen: Vandenhoeck & Ruprecht, 1894).

Ashton, J., *Understanding the Fourth Gospel* (Oxford: Clarendon Press, 1991).

—'Paraclete', *ABD*, V, pp. 152-54.

—'Bridging Ambiguities', in *idem*, *Studying John: Approaches to the Fourth Gospel* (Oxford: Clarendon Press, 1994), pp. 71-89.

Attridge, H., *Nag Hammadi Codex I (The Jung Codex): Introductions, Texts, Translations, Indices* (NHS, 22; Leiden: E.J. Brill, 1985).

Baarda, T., '2 Clement 12 and the Sayings of Jesus', in *idem*, *Early Transmission of Words of Jesus* (Amsterdam: VV-Uitgeverij, 1983), pp. 261-88.

Baldensperger, G., *Der Prolog des vierten Evangeliums* (Tübingen: J.C.B. Mohr, 1898).

Barrett, C.K., *The Gospel According to St. John* (London: SPCK, 1956).

—*The Gospel of John and Judaism* (London: SPCK, 1975).

Barrosse, T., 'The Relationship of Love to Faith in St. John', *TS* 18 (1957), pp. 538-59.

Baumgarten, J., 'The Qumran Sabbath Shirot and Rabbinic Merkabah Traditions', *RevQ* 13, (1988), pp. 199-213.

Behm, J., 'παράκλητος', *TDNT*, V, pp. 800-14.

Belleville, L.L., *Reflections of Glory: Paul's Polemical Use of the Moses-Doxa Tradition in 2 Corinthians 3.1-18*, (JSNTSup, 52; Sheffield: JSOT Press, 1991).

Berger, P., and T. Luckmann, *The Social Construction of Reality: A Treatise in the Sociology of Knowledge* (New York: Doubleday, 1966).

Bernard, J.H., *The Odes of Solomon* (Texts and Studies, 8.3; Cambridge: Cambridge University Press, 1912).

—*A Critical and Exegetical Commentary on the Gospel according to St. John* (ICC; New York: Charles Scribner's Sons, 1929).

Betz, H.D., 'The Delphic Maxim ΓΝΩΘΙ ΣΑΥΤΟΝ in Hermetic Interpretation', *HTR* 63 (1970), pp. 465-84.

—*The Greek Magical Papyri in Translation including the Demotic Spells* (Chicago: University of Chicago Press, 1986).

Betz, O., *Der Paraklet* (Leiden: E.J. Brill, 1963).

Bianchi, U., 'The Religio-Historical Relevance of Lk 20:34-36', in van den Broeck and Vermaseren (eds.), *Studies in Gnosticism and Hellenistic Religions*, pp. 31-37.

Bietenhard, H., 'ὄνομα, etc.', *TDNT*, V, pp. 242-81.

Black, M., *Apocalypsis Henochi Graece* (PVTG, 3.1; Leiden: E.J. Brill, 1970).

—*The Book of Enoch or 1 Enoch: A New English Edition* (SVTP, 7; Leiden: E.J. Brill, 1985).

Blanc, C., *Origène: Commentaire sur Saint Jean*, I (SC, 120; Paris: Cerf, 1966).

Blonde, G., 'Encratisme', in M. Viller, F. Cavallera and J. De Guibert (eds.), *Dictionnaire de Spiritualité*, IV (Paris: G. Beauchesne & Sons, 1960), pp. 628-42.

Bonnet, M., 'Acta Ioannis', in R.A. Lipsius and M. Bonnet (eds.), *Acta apostolorum apocrypha*, II/1 (repr., Hildesheim: Georg Olms, 1959), pp. 151-216.

Bonningues, M., *La foi dans l'évangile de Saint Jean* (Brussels: Pensée Catholique, 1955).

Borgen, P., *Bread From Heaven: An Exegetical Study of the Concept of Manna in the Gospel of John and the Writings of Philo* (NovTSup, 10; Leiden: E.J. Brill, 1965).

—'God's Agent in the Fourth Gospel', in Neusner (ed.), *Religions in Antiquity*, pp. 137-48.

—'Some Jewish exegetical traditions as background for Son of Man sayings in John's Gospel (John 3:13-14 and context)', *ETL* (1977), pp. 243-58.

—*Philo, John and Paul: New Perspectives on Judaism and Early Christianity*, (BJS, 131; Atlanta: Scholars Press, 1987).

—'The Gospel of John and Hellenism', in R. Alan Culpepper and C. Clifton Black, *Exploring the Gospel of John: In Honor of D. Moody Smith* (Louisville, KY: Westminster/John Knox Press, 1996).

Bornkamm, G., 'Die eucharistische Rede im Johannesevangelium', *ZNW* 47 (1956), pp. 161-69.

Bousset, W., 'Die Himmelsreise der Seele' (*ARW*, 4; Freiburg: J.C.B. Mohr, 1901), pp. 136-69, 229-73.

—*Die Religion des Judentums in späthellenistischen Zeitalter* (ed. H. Gressman; HNT, 21; Tübingen: J.C.B. Mohr, 1966).

—*Kyrios Christos* (trans. J.E. Steely; New York: Abingdon Press, 1970).

Bowker, J.W., 'Merkavah Visions and the Visions of Paul', *JJS* 16 (1971), pp. 157-73.

Bowra, C.M., *Pindar* (Oxford: Clarendon Press, 1964).

Boyancé, P., 'Sur les Mystères d'Eleusis', *REG* 75 (1962), pp. 460-82.

Braun, F.-M., 'Le don de Dieu et l'initiation chrétienne', *NRT* 86 (1964), pp. 1025-48.

Bremmer, J., *The Early Greek Concept of the Soul* (Princeton, NJ: Princeton University Press, 1983).

Broeck, R. van den, and M.J. Vermaseren (eds.), *Studies in Gnosticism and Hellenistic Religions, presented to Gilles Quispel on the Occasion of his 65th Birthday* (EPRO, 91; Leiden: E.J. Brill, 1981).

Brown, P., *The Body and Society: Men, Women, and Sexual Renunciation in Early Christianity* (Lectures on the History of Religions, 13; New York: Columbia University Press, 1988).

Brown, R., 'The Gospel of Thomas and St John's Gospel', *NTS* 9 (1962/63), pp. 155-77.

—'The Johannine Sacramentary Reconsidered', in *idem*, *New Testament Essays* (Milwaukee: Bruce, 1965), pp. 51-76.

—*The Gospel According to John* (2 vols.; AB, 29; Garden City, NY: Doubleday, 1966/70).

—*The Community of the Beloved Disciple: The Life, Loves, and Hates of an Individual Church in New Testament Times* (New York: Paulist Press, 1979).

Bultmann, R., *Die Geschichte der Synoptischen Tradition* (Göttingen: Vandenhoeck & Ruprecht, 1921).

—'Der religionsgeschichtliche Hintergrund des Prologs zum Johannes-Evangelium', in H. Schmidt (ed.), *Eucharisterion: Festschrift für Hermann Gunkel* (FRLANT, 37.2; Göttingen: Vandenhoeck & Ruprecht, 1923), pp. 3-26.

—'Die Bedeutung der neuerschlossenen mandäischen und manichäischen Quellen für das Verständnis des Johannesevangeliums', *ZNW* 24 (1925), pp. 100-46.

—*The Theology of the New Testament* (trans. K. Grobel; 2 vols.; London: SCM Press, 1955), II.

—'The Study of the Synoptic Gospels', in Bultmann, *Form Criticism: Two Essays on New Testament Research* (trans. F.C. Grant; New York: Harper & Row, 1966), pp. 11-76.

—*The Gospel of John: A Commentary* (trans. G.R. Beasley-Murray; eds. R.W.N. Hoare and J.K. Riches; Oxford: Basil Blackwell, 1971).

—*The Johannine Epistles*, (ed. R.W. Funk; trans. R.P. O'Hara, L.C. McGaughy and R.W. Funk; Hermeneia; Philadelphia: Fortress Press, 1973).

—*The Second Letter to the Corinthians* (ed. E. Dinkler; trans. R.A. Harrisville, Minneapolis: Augsburg Publishing House, 1985).

Burge, G., *The Anointed Community: The Holy Spirit in the Johannine Tradition* (Grand Rapids; Eerdmans, 1987).

Burkert, W., *Ancient Mystery Cults* (Cambridge, MA: Harvard University Press, 1987).

Cameron, R., *The Other Gospels* (Philadelphia: Westminster Press, 1982).

—'Ancient Myths and Modern Theories of the Gospel of Thomas and Christian Origins', *Method and Theory in the Study of Religion* 11 (1999), pp. 236-57.

Capart, J., 'Les anciens Egyptiens pratiquaient-ils déjà la lécanomancie?', *Chronique d'Egypte* 19 (1944), p. 263.

Chadwick, H., 'St. Paul and Philo of Alexandria', *BJRL* 48 (1966), pp. 286-307.

Chamay, J., 'Des défunts portant bandages', *Bulletin Antieke Beschaving* 52–53 (1977–78), pp. 247-51.

Charles, R.H., *The Ascension of Isaiah* (London: A. & C. Black, 1900).

—*The Testaments of the Twelve Patriarchs* (London: A. & C. Black, 1908).

—*The Greek Versions of the Testaments of the Twelve Patriarchs* (repr.; Oxford: Oxford University Press, 1960).

Charlesworth, J.H., *The Odes of Solomon* (Oxford: Clarendon Press, 1973).

—*The Beloved Disciple: Whose Witness Validates the Gospel of John?* (Valley Forge, PA: Trinity Press International, 1995).

Charlesworth, J.H. (ed.), *John and the Dead Sea Scrolls* (New York: Crossroad, 1991).

Chernus, I., 'Visions of God in Merkabah Mysticism', *JSJ* 13 (1983), pp. 123-46.

Collins, A.Y., 'The *Seven Heavens* in Jewish and Christian Apocalypses', in J.J. Collins and M. Fishbane (eds.), *Death, Ecstasy and Other Worldly Journeys* (Albany: State University of New York, 1995), pp. 62-87.

Colpe, C., 'Die "Himmelsreise der Seele" ausserhalb und innerhalb der Gnosis', in U. Bianchi (ed.), *Le Origini dello Gnosticismo, Colloquio di Messina 13–18 Aprile 1966* (Studies in the History of Religions; NumenSup, 12; Leiden: E.J. Brill, 1967), pp. 429-47.

Colson, F.H., *Philo*, IV (LCL; Cambridge, MA: Harvard University Press, 1932).

—*Philo*, IX (LCL; Cambridge, MA: Harvard University Press, 1941).

—*Philo*, X (Cambridge, MA: Harvard University Press, 1943).

Colson, F.H., and G.H. Whitaker, *Philo*, I (LCL; Cambridge, MA: Harvard University Press, 1929).

—*Philo*, III (LCL; Cambridge, MA: Harvard University Press, 1930).

—*Philo*, IV (LCL; Cambridge, MA: Harvard University Press, 1932).

—*Philo*, V (LCL; Cambridge, MA: Harvard University Press, 1934).

—*Philo*, II (LCL; Cambridge, MA: Harvard University Press, 1942).

Copenhaver, B.P., *Hermetica: The Greek Corpus Hermeticum and the Latin Asclepius in a New English Translation, With Notes and Introduction* (Cambridge: Cambridge University Press, 1992).

Corssen, P., 'Paulus und Porphyrios (Zur Erklärung von 2 Kor 3,18)', *ZNW* 19 (1920), pp. 2-10.

Crossan, J., *In Fragments: The Aphorisms of Jesus* (San Francisco: Harper & Row, 1983).

Culianu, I.P., ' "L'Ascension de l'âme" dans les mystères et hors des mystères', in U. Bianchi and M.J. Vermaseren (eds.), *La Soteriologia dei culti orientali nell' Impero romano* (Leiden: E.J. Brill, 1982), pp. 276-302.

—*Psychanodia I: A Survey of the Evidence Concerning the Ascension of the Soul and Its Relevance* (Leiden: E.J. Brill, 1983).

—*Expériences de l'extase* (Paris: Payot, 1984).

Cullmann, O., *'Eiden kai episteusen': Aux sources de la tradition chrétienne* (Paris: Mélanges Goguel, 1950).

—*Early Christian Worship* (SBT, 10; Chicago: Henry Regnery, 1953).

Cumont, F., *L'Egypte des astrologues* (Bruxelles: Edité par la fondation égyptologique reine Élisabeth, 1937).

Cunen, F., 'Lampe et coupe magiques', *Symbolae Osloensis* 36 (1960), pp. 65-71.

Dahl, N.A., 'The Johannine Church and History', in W. Klassen and G. Synder (eds.), *Current Issues in New Testament Interpretation* (New York: Harper, 1962), pp. 124-42.

Dart, J., 'Jesus and His Brothers', in R. Joseph Hoffman and G.A. Larue (eds.), *Jesus in History and Myth* (Buffalo, NY: Prometheus Books, 1986), pp. 181-90.

Davies, S., 'The Christology and Protology of the Gospel of Thomas', *JBL* 111 (1992), pp. 663-82.

Dean-Otting, M., *Heavenly Journeys: A Study of the Motif in Hellenistic Jewish Literature* (Bern: Peter Lang, 1984).

DeConick, A.D., 'Fasting From the World: Encratite Soteriology in the Gospel of Thomas', in U. Bianchi (ed.), *The Notion of 'Religion' in Comparative Research: Selected Proceedings of the XVI IAHR Congress* (Rome: 'L'Erma' di Bretschneider, 1994), pp. 425-40.

—'The Dialogue of the Savior and the Mystical Sayings of Jesus', *VC* 50 (1996), pp. 178-99.

—*Seek to See Him: Ascent and Vision Mysticism in the Gospel of Thomas* (VCSup, 33; Leiden: E.J. Brill, 1996).

—'Entering God's Presence: Sacramentalism in the Gospel of Philip', in *Seminar Papers for Society of Biblical Literature Annual Meeting 1998* (Atlanta: Scholars Press, 1998), pp. 483-523.

—'Heavenly Temple Traditions and Valentinian Worship: A Case for First-Century Christology in the Second Century', in C.C. Newman, J.R. Davila and G.S. Lewis (eds.), *The Jewish Roots of Christological Monotheism: Papers from the St. Andrews Conference on the Historical Origins of the Worship of Jesus* (JSJSup, 63; Leiden: E.J. Brill, 1999), pp. 308-41.

DeConick, A.D., and J. Fossum, 'Stripped Before God: A New Interpretation of Logion 37', *VC* 45 (1991), pp. 123-50.

Decourtray, A., 'La conception johannique de la foi', *NRT* 81 (1959), pp. 561-76.

De Jong, K., *Das antike mysterienwesen in religionsgeschichtlichen* (Leiden: E.J. Brill, 1909).

Delatte, A., *La catoptromancie grecque et ses derives* (Paris: E. Droz, 1932).

Deubner, L., *Attische Feste* (Berlin: H. Keller, 1932).

Dieterich, A., *Eine Mithrasliturgie* (Stuttgart: Teubner, 1966).

Dirkse, P.A., J. Brashler and D.M. Parrott, 'The Discourse on the Eighth and Ninth', in D.M. Parrott (ed.), *Nag Hammadi Codices V,2-5 and VI with Papyrus Berolinensis 8502* (NHS, 11; Leiden: E.J. Brill, 1979), pp. 341-73.

Dodd, C.H., *The Interpretation of the Fourth Gospel* (Cambridge: Cambridge University Press, 1953).

Doresse, J., *L'Evangile selon Thomas ou les paroles secrètes de Jésus* (Paris: Librairie Plon, 1959).

Draper, J.A., 'The Sociological Function of the Spirit/Paraclete in the Farewell Discourses in the Fourth Gospel', *Neot* 26 (1992), pp. 13-27.

—'Temple, Tabernacle, and Mystical Experience in John', *Neot* 32 (1997), pp. 263-88.

Dunderberg, I., 'John and Thomas in Conflict?', in J.D. Turner and A. McGuire (eds.), *The Nag Hammadi Library After Fifty Years: Proceedings of the 1995 Society of Biblical Literature Commemoration* (NHMS, 44; Leiden: E.J. Brill, 1997), pp. 361-80.

—'*Thomas* and the Beloved Disciple', in Uro (ed.), *Thomas at the Crossroads*, pp. 65-88.

—'*Thomas*' I-Sayings and the Gospel of John', in Uro (ed.), *Thomas at the Crossroads*, pp. 33-64.

Dunn, J., *Christology in the Making: A New Testament Inquiry into the Origins of the Doctrine of the Incarnation* (Philadelphia: Westminster Press, 1980).

—'Let John be John: A Gospel for Its Time', in P. Stuhlmacher (ed.), *Das Evangelium und die Evangelium: Vorträge vom Tübinger Symposium 1982* (WUNT, 28; Tübingen: J.C.B. Mohr, 1983), pp. 309-39.

Dupont, J., 'Le chrétien, miroir de la gloire divine d'après 2 Cor. III,18', *RB* 56 (1949), pp. 392-411.

Eagen, G., *Saint Ephrem: An Exposition of the Gospel* (CSCO, 5 and 6; Louvain: Secrétarit CSCO, 1968).

Elior, R., 'Mysticism, Magic, and Angelology—The Perception of Angels in Hekhalot Literature', *JSQ* 1 (1993/94), pp. 3-53.

—'From Earthly Temple to Heavenly Shrines: Prayer and Sacred Song in the Hekhalot Literature and its Relations to Temple Traditions', *JSQ* 4 (1997), pp. 217-67.

Elliot, J., *A Home for the Homeless: A Social-Scientific Criticism of 1 Peter, Its Situation and Strategy* (Philadelphia: Fortress Press, 1990).

Emmel, S., *Nag Hammadi Codex III,5: The Dialogue of the Savior* (NHS, 26; Leiden: E.J. Brill, 1984).

Festugière, A.-J., *Corpus Hermeticum. III. Fragments, Extraits de Stobeé I–XXII* (Paris: Société d'édition les belles lettres, 1954).

Fieger, M., *Das Thomasevangelium: Einleitung, Kommentar und Sytematik* (NTAbh, NS 22, Münster: Aschendorff, 1991).

Fitzmyer, J., 'The Oxyrhynchus *Logoi* and the Coptic Gospel According to Thomas', in *idem*, *Essays on the Semitic Background of the New Testament* (London: Geoffrey Chapman, 1971), pp. 355-433.

Fletcher-Louis, C., 'Ascent to Heaven and the Embodiment of Heaven: A Revisionist Reading of the Songs of the Sabbath Sacrifice' (SBLSP; Atlanta: Scholars Press, 1998), pp. 367-99.

Fossum, J., 'Jewish–Christian Christology and Jewish Mysticism', *VC* 37 (1983), pp. 260-87.

—*The Name of God and the Angel of the Lord* (WUNT, 36; Tübingen: J.C.B. Mohr, 1985).

—'The Magharians: A Pre-Christian Jewish Sect and its Significance for the Study of Gnosticism and Christianity', *Henoch* 9 (1987), pp. 303-44.

—'Colossians 1.15-18a in the Light of Jewish Mysticism and Gnosticism', *NTS* 35 (1989), pp. 183-201.

—'Glory כבוד δόξα', in K. van der Toorn *et al.* (eds.), *Dictionary of Deities and Demons in the Bible* (Leiden: E.J. Brill, 1995), pp. 1486-98.

—*The Image of the Invisible God: Essays on the Influence of Jewish Mysticism on Early Christology* (NTOA, 30; Göttingen: Vandenhoeck & Ruprecht, 1995).

—'Ascendio, Metamorphosis: The "Transfiguration" of Jesus in the Synoptic Gospels', in *idem*, *The Image of the Invisible God*, pp. 82-86.

—'In the Beginning was the Name: Onomanology as the Key to Johannine Christianity', in *idem*, *The Image of the Invisible God*, pp. 109-33.

—'*Portes posteriores dei*: The "Transfiguration" of Jesus in the Acts of John', in *idem*, *The Image of the Invisible God*, pp. 95-108.

—'The Son of Man's Alter Ego: John 1.51, Targumic Tradition and Jewish Mysticism', in *idem*, *The Image of the Invisible God*, pp. 135-51.

Gaffney, J., 'Believing and Knowing in the Fourth Gospel', *TS* 26 (1965), pp. 215-41.

Gager, J., *Kingdom and Community: The Social World of Early Christianity* (Engelwood Cliffs, NJ: Prentice–Hall, 1975).

Ganszyniec, R., 'Lekanomanteiva', PW, XII, pp. 1879-89.

Gärtner, B., *The Theology of the Gospel According to Thomas* (trans. E. Sharpe; New York: Harper & Bros., 1961).

Gaselee, S., *Achilles Tatius* (LCL; Cambridge, MA: Harvard University Press, 1984).

Gieschen, C., *Angelomorphic Christology: Antecedents and Early Evidence* (AGJU, 42; Leiden, E.J. Brill, 1998).

Goldberg, A., 'Der Vortrag des Ma'asse Merkawa: Eine Vermutung zur frühen Merkava-mystik', *Judaica* 29 (1973), pp. 4-23.

Goodenough, E.R., *By Light, By Light* (Amsterdam: Philo Press, 1969).

Goold, G.P., *Apuleius: Metamorphoses* (2 vols.; LCL; Cambridge, MA: Harvard University Press, 1989).

Grant, R., and D. Freedman, *The Secret Sayings of Jesus* (Garden City, NY: Doubleday, 1960).

Greimas, A., *Sémantique structurale: Recherche de méthode* (Paris: Larousse, 1966); ET; = *Structural Semantics: An Attempt at a Method* (trans. by D. McDowell, R. Schleifer, A. Velie; Lincoln: University of Nebraska Press, 1983).

Grelot, P., 'Le problème de la foi dans le quatrième évangile', *BVC* 52 (1963), pp. 61-71.

Grenfell, B., and A. Hunt, ΛΟΓΙΑ ΙΗΣΟΥ: *Sayings of Our Lord from an Early Greek Papyrus* (London: published for the Egypt exploration fund by H. Frowde, 1897).

Gruenwald, I., *Apocalyptic and Merkavah Mysticism* (AGJU, 14; Leiden: E.J. Brill, 1980).

Grundmann, W., 'Verständnis und Bewegung des Glaubens im Johannes-Evangelium', *KD* 6 (1960), pp. 131-54.

Haenchen, E., *Die Botschaft des Thomas-Evangeliums* (Theologische Bibliothek Töpelmann 6; Berlin: Alfred Töpelmann, 1961).

Hall, R., 'Astonishment in the Firmament: The Worship of Jesus and Soteriology in Ignatius and the *Ascension of Isaiah*', in C. Newman, J. Davila, and G. Lewis (eds.), *The Jewish Roots of Christological Monotheism: Papers from the St. Andrews Conference on the Historical Origins of the Worship of Jesus* (JSJSup, 63; Leiden: E.J. Brill, 1999), pp. 148-55.

—'The Vision of God in the *Ascension of Isaiah*', in A.D. DeConick (ed.), *Early Jewish and Christian Mysticism: New Directions* (forthcoming).

Halperin, D.J., *The Merkabah in Rabbinic Literature* (New Haven: American Oriental Society, 1980).

—'Ascension or Invasion: Implications of the Heavenly Journey in Ancient Judaism', *Rel* 18 (1988), pp. 47-67.

—*The Faces of the Chariot* (Tübingen: J.C.B. Mohr, 1988).

Harl, M., 'A propos des *Logia* de Jésus: Le sens du mot *monachos*', *REG* 73 (1960), pp. 464-74.

Harris, J. Rendel, 'The Origins of the Prologue to St. John's Gospel', *Expositor* 8.12 (1916), pp. 147-70, 314-20, 388-400.

Hawthorne, G.F., 'The Concept of Faith in the Fourth Gospel', *BSac* 116 (1959), pp. 117-26.

Hedrick, C.W., and R. Hodgson, Jr (eds.), *Nag Hammadi, Gnosticism, and Early Christianity* (Peabody, MA: Hendrickson, 1986).

Hedrick, C.W., and P. Mirecki, *The Gospel of the Savior: A New Ancient Gospel* (Sonoma, CA: Polebridge Press, 1999).

Helmbold, W.C., and W.G. Rabinowitz, *Plato's Phaedrus* (The Library of Liberal Arts, 40; Indianapolis: Bobbs–Merrill, 1968).

Hermann, I., *Kyrios und Pneuma* (Munich: Kösel, 1961).

Himmelfarb, M., 'Heavenly Ascent and the Relationship of the Apocalypses and the *Hekhalot* Literature', *HUCA* 59 (1988), pp. 73-100.

—*Ascent to Heaven in Jewish and Christian Apocalypses* (New York: Oxford University Press, 1993).

Hirshman, M., *Jewish and Christian Biblical Interpretation in Late Antiquity* (trans. B. Stein; Albany: State University of New York, 1996).

Hollander, H.W., H.J. de Jonge, and Th. Korteweg, *The Testaments of the Twelve Patriarchs: A Critical Edition of the Greek Text* (PVTG, 1.2; Leiden: E.J. Brill,1978).

Hopfner, T., *Griechisch-aegyptischer Offenbarungszauber* (Leipzig: W. Haessel, 2 vols.; 1921, 1924).

—'Mageia', PW XIV/1, pp. 301-93.

Horst, P.W. van der, 'Observations on a Pauline Expression', *NTS* 19 (1973), pp. 181-87.

Houghton, H.P., 'The Coptic Apocalypse', *Aegyptus* 39 (1959).

Howard, G., *The Teaching of Addai*, (Texts and Translations, 16; Early Christian Literature Series, 4; Chico, CA: Scholars Press, 1981).

Howard, W., *The Fourth Gospel in Recent Criticism and Interpretation* (London: Epworth Press, 1955).

Hugedé, N., *La métaphore du miroir dans les Epitres de saint Paul aux Corinthians* (Neuchâtel: Delachaux & Niestlé, 1957).

Isaac, E., 'Introduction' to the *Ethiopic Book of Enoch*, *OTP*, I, pp. 5-12.

Johannson, N., *Parakletoi: Vorstellungen von Fürsprechern für die Menschen vor Gott in der alttestamentlichen Religion, im Spätjudentum, und Urchristentum* (Lund: C.W.K. Gleerup, 1940).

Kanagaraj, J.J., *'Mysticism' in the Gospel of John: An Inquiry into its Background* (JSNTSup, 158; Sheffield: Sheffield Academic Press, 1998).

Kasser, R., *L'Evangile selon Thomas: Présentation et commentaire théologique* (Neuchâtel: Delachaux & Niestlé, 1961).

Kee, H., ' "Becoming a Child" in the *Gospel of Thomas*', *JBL* 82 (1963), pp. 307-314.

Kerényi, K., *Eleusis: Archetypal Image of Mother and Daughter* (London: Routledge & Kegan Paul, 1967).

Kinzer, M., 'Temple Christology in the Gospel of John' (SBLSP; Atlanta: Scholars Press, 1998), pp. 447-64.

Kittel, G., 'δόξα', *TDNT*, II, pp. 242-45.

Klijn, A.F.J., *The Acts of Thomas: Introduction—Text—Commentary* (NovTSup, 5; Leiden: E.J. Brill, 1962).

—'The "Single One" in the *Gospel of Thomas*', *JBL* 81 (1962), pp. 271-78.

—'John XIV 22 and the Name Judas Thomas', in *Studies in John presented to Professor Dr. J. N. Sevenster on the Occasion of his Seventieth Birthday* (NovTSup, 24; Leiden: E.J. Brill, 1970), pp. 88-96.

Klos, H., *Die Sakramente im Johannesevangelium* (Stuttgart: Katholisches Bibelwerk, 1970).

Knibb, M.A., and E. Ullendorf, *The Ethiopic Book of Enoch: A New Edition in the Light of the Aramaic Dead Sea Fragments* (2 vols.; Oxford: Clarendon Press, 1978).

Koester, H., 'Geschichte und Kultus im Johannesevangelium und bei Ignatius von Antiochien', *ZTK* 54 (1957), pp. 56-69.

—'GNOMAI DIAPHOROI: The Origin and Nature of Diversification in the History of Early Christianity', in J.M. Robinson and H. Koester (eds.), *Trajectories through Early Christianity* (Philadephia: Fortress Press, 1971), pp. 127-28.

—'Dialog und Spruchüberlieferung in den gnostischen Texten von Nag Hammadi', *EvT* 39 (1979), pp. 532-56.

—*Introduction to the New Testament*. II. *History and Literature of Early Christianity* (Philadephia: Fortress Press, 1982).

—'The History-of-Religions School, Gnosis, and the Gospel of John', *StTh* 40 (1986), pp. 115-36.

—'Gnostic Sayings and Controversy Traditions in John 8:12-59', in Hedrick and Hodgson, Jr (eds.), *Nag Hammadi*, pp. 97-110.

—*Ancient Christian Gospels: Their History and Development* (Philadelphia: Trinity Press International, 1992).

Kohler, K., 'Merkabah', *JewEnc*, VIII, p. 500.

Kretschmar, G., *Studien zur frühchristlichen Trinitätstheologie* (BHT, 21; Tübingen: J.C.B. Mohr, 1956), pp. 62-93.

Kuntzmann, R., 'Le temple dans le corpus copte de Nag Hammadi', *RSR* 67 (1993), pp. 15-37.

Kysar, R., *The Fourth Evangelist and His Gospel: An Examination of Contemporary Scholarship* (Minneapolis: Augsburg, 1975).

Lake, K., *Eusebius: The Ecclesiastical History* (LCL; Cambridge, MA: Harvard University Press, 1926), I.

Lattimore, R. (trans.), *The Odyssey of Homer* (New York: Harper & Row, 1967).

Layton, B., *Nag Hammadi Codex II,2-7 together with XII,2 Brit. Lib. Or. 4926 (1), and P. Oxy. 1, 654, 655. I. Gospel According to Thomas, Gospel According to Philip, Hypostasis of the Archons, and Indexes* (NHS, 20; Leiden: E.J. Brill, 1989).

Leipoldt, J., *Das Evangelium nach Thomas: Koptisch und Deutsch* (TU, 101; Berlin: Akademie Verlag, 1967).

Lelyveld, M., *Les Logia de la Vie dans L'Évangile selon Thomas* (NHS, 34; Leiden: E.J. Brill, 1987).

Léon-Dufour, X., 'Le signe du temple selon Saint Jean', *RSR* 39 (1951/52), pp. 155-75.

Levenson, J.D., 'The Temple and the World', *JR* 64 (1984), pp. 275-98.

—'The Jerusalem Temple in Devotional and Visionary Experience', in A. Green, *Jewish Spirituality From the Bible Through the Middle Ages* (World Spirituality, 13; New York: Crossroad, 1986).

Lewy, H., *Sobria Ebrietas* (BZNW, 9; Berlin: Alfred Töpelmann, 1929).

Lieb, M., *The Visionary Mode: Biblical Prophecy, Hermeneutics, and Cultural Change* (Ithaca, NY: Cornell University Press, 1991).

Lieber, A., *God Incorporated: Feasting on the Divine Presence in Ancient Judaism* (PhD dissertation, Columbia University, 1998).

Lindars, B., *Behind the Fourth Gospel* (London: SPCK, 1971).

Lipsius, R.A., and M. Bonnet, *Acta Apostolorum Apocrypha. II/2. Acta Philippi et Acta Thomae accedunt Acta Barnabae* (Leipzig: Hermannum Mendelssohn, 1903).

Lohse, E., 'Wort und Sakrament im Johannesevangelium', *NTS* 7 (1960–61), pp. 110-25.

Long, G., and A.J. Macleane, *The Phaedrus of Plato* (London: Whittaker, 1868).

Mack, B.L., *Rhetoric and the New Testament* (Minneapolis: Fortress Press, 1990).

Mahé, J.-P., *Hermès en Haute-Egypte*, II (BCNH, 7; Québec: Presses de l'Université Laval, 1982).

—'La voie d'immortalité á la lumière des *Hermetica* de Nag Hammadi et de découvertes plus récentes', *VC* 45 (1991), pp. 347-75.

—'Preliminary Remarks on the Demotic *Book of Thoth* and the Greek *Hermetica*', *VC* 50 (1996), pp. 353-63.

Maier, J., *Vom Kultus zur Gnosis* (Salzburg: Mueller, 1964).

Malatesta, E., *St. John's Gospel 1920–1965* (Rome: Biblical Institute Press, 1967).

Mann, U., 'Geisthöhe und Seelentiefe: Die vertikale Achse der numinosen Bereiche', *Eranos* 50 (1981), pp. 1-50.

Marcovich, M., 'Textual Criticism on the *Gospel of Thomas*', *JTS* 20 (1969), pp. 53-74.

Marjanen, A., 'Is *Thomas* a Gnostic Gospel?', in R. Uro (ed.), *Thomas at the Crossroads*, pp. 107-39.

Martyn, J.L., *History and Theology in the Fourth Gospel* (Nashville: Abingdon Press, 2nd edn, 1979).

—*The Gospel of John in Christian History* (New York: Paulist Press, 1979).

Meeks, W., *The Prophet-King: Moses Traditions and the Johannine Christology* (NovTSup, 14; Leiden: E.J. Brill, 1967).

—'Moses as God and King', in J. Neusner (ed.), *Religions in Antiquity: Essays in Memory of E.R. Goodenough* (NumenSup, 14; Leiden: E.J. Brill, 1968), pp. 354-71.

—'The Man from Heaven in Johannine Sectarianism', *JBL* 91 (1972), pp. 44-72.

Ménard, J., *L'Evangile selon Thomas* (NHS, 5; Leiden: E.J. Brill, 1975).

Meyer, M., *The Gospel of Thomas: The Hidden Sayings of Jesus* (San Francisco: HarperSanFrancisco, 1992).

—'Seeing or Coming to the Child of the Living One? More on *Gospel of Thomas* Saying 37', *HTR* 91 (1998), pp. 413-16.

Michaelis, W., *Die Sakramente im Johannesevangelium* (Bern: BEG-Verlag, 1946).

Milik, J.T., and M. Black, *The Books of Enoch: Aramaic Fragments from Qumran Cave 4* (Oxford: Clarendon Press, 1976).

Moloney, F.J., *The Johannine Son of Man* (Rome: LAS, 1976).

Morard, F.-E., 'Monachos moine, histoire du terme grec jusqu'au 4e siècle', *Freiburger Zeitschrift für Philosophie und Theologie* 20 (1973), pp. 332-411.

—'Encore quelques réflexions sur monachos', *VC* 34 (1980), pp. 395-401.

Morray-Jones, C., *Merkabah Mysticism and Talmudic Tradition* (PhD dissertation, University of Cambridge, 1988).

—'Transformational Mysticism in the Apocalyptic-Merkabah Tradition', *JJS* 48 (1992), pp. 1-31.

—'Paradise Revisited (2 Cor. 12.1-12): The Jewish Mystical Background of Paul's Apostolate. Part 1: The Jewish Sources' and 'Part 2: Paul's Heavenly Ascent and its Significance', *HTR* 86 (1993), pp. 177-217 and 265-92.

—'The Temple Within: The Embodied Divine Image and its Worship in the Dead Sea Scrolls and Other Early Jewish and Christian Sources', in *Seminar Papers 1998 for Society of Biblical Literature Annual Convention* (Atlanta: Scholars Press, 1998), pp. 400-31.

—*A Transparent Illusion: The Dangerous Vision of Water in Hekhalot Mysticism. A Source-Critical and Tradition-Historical Inquiry* (forthcoming).

Mullen, E. Theodore, *The Divine Council in Canaanite and Early Hebrew Literature* (HSM, 24; Chico, CA: Scholars Press, 1980).

Mussies, G., 'Catalogues of Sins and Virtues Personified (NHC II,5)', in van den Broek and Vermaseren (eds.), *Studies in Gnosticism and Hellenistic Religions*, pp. 315-35.

Nehamas, A., and P. Woodruff (trans.), *Plato: Phaedrus* (Indianapolis: Hackett, 1995).

Neusner, J., *A Life of Yohanan ben Zakkai: Ca. 1–80 CE* (Leiden: E.J. Brill, 2nd rev. edn, 1970).

Neusner, J. (ed.), *Religions in Antiquity: Essays in Memory of E.R. Goodenough* (NumenSup, 14; Leiden: E.J. Brill, 1968).

Newsom, C., *Songs of the Sabbath Sacrifice* (HSS, 27; Atlanta: Scholars Press, 1985).

—'Merkavah Exegesis in the Qumran Sabbath Shirot', *JSJ* 38 (1987), pp. 11-30.

—' "He Has Established for Himself Priests" ', in L. Schiffman (ed.), *Archaeology and History in the Dead Sea Scrolls* (Sheffield: JSOT Press, 1990), pp. 114-15.

Nitzan, B., *Qumran Prayer and Religious Poetry* (STDJ, 12; Leiden: E.J. Brill, 1994).

Nock, A.D., and A.J. Festugière, *Corpus Hermeticum. I. Traités I–XII* (Paris: Société d'édition les belles lettres, 1945).

—*Corpus Hermeticum. II. Traites XIII–XVIII, Asclépius* (Paris: Société d'édition les belles lettres, 1945).

Odeberg, H., *The Fourth Gospel Interpreted in its Relationship to Contemporaneous Religious Currents in Palestine and the Hellenistic-Oriental World* (repr. Amsterdam: B.R. Grüner, 1974 [1929]).

Pagels, E., 'Exegesis of Genesis 1 in the Gospels of Thomas and John', *JBL* 118 (1999), pp. 477-96.

Pascher, J., *Η ΒΑΣΙΛΙΚΗ ΟΔΟΣ Der Königsweg zu Wiedergeburt und Vergottung bei Philon von Alexandreia* (Studien zur Geschichte und Kultur des Altertums, 17.3-4; Paderbuorn: F. Schöningh, 1931).

Patterson, S., *The Gospel of Thomas and Jesus* (Sonoma, CA: Polebridge Press, 1993).

Pearson, A.C., *The Fragments of Sophocles*, III (LCL; Cambridge: Cambridge University Press, 1917).

Peterson, E., 'Einige Bemerkungen zum Hamburger Papyrusfragment der "Acta Pauli" ', in *Frühkirche, Judentum, und Gnosis* (Freiburg: Herder, 1959), pp. 182-208.

Philips, G., 'Faith and Vision in the Fourth Gospel', in F.M. Cross (ed.), *Studies in the Fourth Gospel* (London: Mowbray, 1957), pp. 83-96.

Podlecki, A.J., *Aeschylus: Eumenides* (Warminster: Aris & Phillips, 1989).

Potterie, I. de la, '*Oida* et *ginosko*, les deux modes de la connaissance dans le quatrième évangile', *Bib* 40 (1959), pp. 709-25.

Propp, V., *Morphologie du Conte* (Paris: Seuil, 1928, repr. 1965 and 1970).

Puech, H.-Ch., 'The Gospel of Thomas', in E. Hennecke and W. Schneemelcher (eds.), *New Testament Apocrypha*, I (ET R.McL. Wilson; Philadelphia: Westminster Press, 1963), pp. 278-307.

Quispel, G., 'Nathanael und der Menschensohn (Joh 1:51)', *ZNW* 47 (1956), pp. 281-83.

—'L'Evangile de Jean et la Gnose', in M.-E. Boismard (ed.), *L'Evangile de Jean: Etudes et problèmes* (RechBib, 3; Bruges: Desclé de Brouwers, 1958), pp. 197-208.

—'Gnosticism and the New Testament', in Quispel (ed.), *Gnostic Studies*, I, pp. 196-212.

—'John and Jewish Christianity', in Quispel (ed.), *Gnostic Studies*, II, pp. 210-29.

—'Love Thy Brother', in Quispel (ed.), *Gnostic Studies*, II, pp. 169-79.

—'Judaism, Judaic Christianity, and Gnosis', in A.H.B. Logan and A.J.M. Wedderburn (eds.), *The New Testament Gnosis: Essays in Honour of Robert McLachlan Wilson* (Edinburgh: T. & T. Clark, 1983), pp. 48-52.

—'The Study of Encratism: A Historical Survey', in U. Bianchi (ed.), *La Tradizione dell'Enkrateia, Atti del Colloquio Internazional—Milano 20–23 Aprile 1982* (Rome: Edizioni Dell'Ateneo, 1985), pp. 35-81.

—'The Gospel of Thomas and the Trial of Jesus', in T. Baarda, A. Hilhorst, G.P. Luttikhuizen and A.S. van der Woude (eds.), *Text and Testimony: Essays on New Testament and Apocryphal Literature in Honour of A.F.J. Klijn* (Kampen: Kok, 1988), pp. 193-99.

—'Qumran, John and Jewish Christianity', in Charlesworth (ed.), *John and the Dead Sea Scrolls*, pp. 144-46.

—'Hermes Trismegistus and the Origins of Gnosticism', *VC* 46 (1992), pp. 1-19.

Quispel, G. (ed.), *Gnostic Studies* (Nederlands Historisch-Archaeologisch Institut te Istanbul, 34; 2 vols.; Leiden: E.J. Brill, 1974).

Reitzenstein, R., *Poimandres* (Leipzig: Teubner, 1906).

—*Historia Monachorum und Historia Lausiaca: Eine Studie zur Geschichte des Mönchtums und der frühchristlichen Begriffe Gnostiker und Pneumatiker* (FRLANT, 24; Göttingen: Vandenhoeck & Ruprecht, 1916).

—*Hellenistic Mystery-Religions: Their Basic Ideas and Significance* (trans. J.E. Steely; PTMS, 15; Pittsburg: Pickwick Press, 1978).

Richardson, N.J., *The Homeric Hymn to Demeter* (Oxford: Clarendon Press, 1974).

Riley, G., *Resurrection Reconsidered: Thomas and John in Controversy* (Minneapolis: Fortress Press, 1995).

—'A Note on the Text of the *Gospel of Thomas* 37', *HTR* 88 (1995), pp. 179-81.

Robbins, V., 'The Dialectical Nature of Early Christian Discourse', *Scriptura* 59 (1996), pp. 353-62.

—*Exploring the Texture of Texts: A Guide to Socio-rhetorical Interpretation* (Valley Forge, PA: Trinity Press International, 1996).

—*The Tapestry of Early Christian Discourse: Rhetoric, Society and Ideology* (London: Routledge, 1996).

Robertson, R.G., *Ezekiel the Tragedian*, *OTP*, II, pp. 803-19.

Robinson, J. (ed.), *The Facsimile Edition of the Nag Hammadi Codices: Codex II* (Leiden: E.J. Brill, 1974).

Robinson, J.A.T., 'The Destination and Purpose of St. John's Gospel', in R. Batey (ed.), *New Testament Issues* (New York: Harper & Row, 1970), pp. 191-209.

Rowland, C., *The Influence of the First Chapter of Ezekiel on Jewish and Early Christian Literature* (PhD dissertation, Cambridge University, 1974).

—'The Visions of God in Apocalyptic Literature', *JSJ* 10 (1979), pp. 137-54.

—*The Open Heaven: A Study of Apocalyptic in Judaism and Early Christianity* (London: SPCK, 1982).

—'John 1.51, Jewish Apocalyptic and Targumic Tradition', *NTS* 30 (1984), pp. 498-507.

Schäfer, P., *Rivalitat zwischen Engeln und Menschen* (Berlin: W. de Gruyter, 1975).

—'Tradition and Redaction in Hekhalot Literature', *JSJ* 14 (1983), pp. 172-81.

—'Merkavah Mysticism and Rabbinic Judaism', *JAOS* 104 (1984), pp. 537-54.

—'New Testament and Hekhalot Literature: The Journey into Heaven in Paul and in Merkavah Mysticism', *JJS* 35 (1984), pp. 19-35.

—'The Aim and Purpose of Early Jewish Mysticism', in Schäfer, *Hekhalot-Studien* (Texte und Studien zum Antiken Judentum, 19; Tübingen: J.C.B. Mohr, 1988).

Schäferdiek, K., 'Johannesakten', in W. Schneemelcher (ed.), *Neutestamentliche Apokryphen*, II (Tübingen: J.C.B. Mohr, 1989), pp. 138-55.

Schenke, H.-M., 'The Function and Background of the Beloved Disciple in the Gospel of John', in Hedrick and Hodgson, Jr (eds.), *Nag Hammadi*, pp. 111-25.

Schiffman, L.H., 'Merkavah Speculation at Qumran: The 4Q Serekh Shirot 'Olat ha-Shabbat', in J. Renharz and D. Swetshchinski (eds.), *Mystics, Philosophers, and Politicians: Essays in Jewish Intellectual History in Honor of A. Altmann* (Durham, NC: Duke University Press, 1982), pp. 14-47.

Schiffman, L.H. (ed.), *Archaeology and History in the Dead Sea Scrolls* (Sheffield: JSOT Press, 1990).

Schnackenburg, R., *The Gospel According to St. John*, I (New York: Crossroad, 1982).

—*The Johannine Epistles* (New York: Crossroad, 1992).

Scholem, G., *Major Trends in Jewish Mysticism* (New York: Schocken Books, 1956).

—*Jewish Gnosticism, Merkavah Mysticism and Talmudic Tradition* (New York: Jewish Theological Seminary of America, 1960).

—*On the Kabbalah and its Symbolism* (trans. R. Manheim; New York: Schocken Books, 1965).

—*Kabbalah* (Jerusalem and New York: Meridian, 1974).

—*Origins of the Kabbalah* (ed. R.J.Z. Werblowsky; trans. A. Arkush; Princeton, NJ: Princeton University Press, 1987).

—*On the Mystical Shape of the Godhead: Basic Concepts in the KABBALAH* (ed. J. Chipman; trans. J. Neugroschel; foreword by J. Dan; New York: Schocken Books, 1991).

Schulz, S., *Untersuchungen zur Menschensohnchristologie im Johannesevangelium* (Göttingen: Vandenhoeck & Ruprecht, 1957).

Schweizer, E., 'Das Johanneische Zeugnis vom Herrenmahl', *EvT* 12 (1953), pp. 341-63.

Segal, A.F., *Two Powers in Heaven: Early Rabbinic Reports About Christianity and Gnosticism* (SJLA, 25; Leiden: E.J. Brill, 1978).

—'Heavenly Ascent in Hellenistic Judaism, Early Christianity, and their Environment', *ANRW*, II, pp. 1333-94.

—*Paul the Convert: The Apostolate and Apostasy of Saul the Pharisee* (New Haven: Yale University Press, 1990).

Segert, S., 'Observations on Poetic Structures in the Songs of the Sabbath Sacrifice', *RQ* 13 (1988), pp. 215-23.

Sell, J., 'Johannine Traditions in Logion 61 of The Gospel of Thomas', *Perspectives in Religious Studies* 7 (1980), pp. 24-37.

Sidebottom, E.M., *The Christ of the Fourth Gospel in the Light of First Century Thought* (London: SPCK, 1961).

Smith, J.Z., 'The Garments of Shame', *HR* 5 (1966), pp. 217-38.

Smith, M., *Clement of Alexandria and a Secret Gospel of Mark* (Cambridge, MA: Harvard University Press, 1973).

—'Ascent to the Heavens and the Beginning of Christianity', *Eranos* 50 (1981), pp. 403-29.

—'Two Ascended to Heaven—Jesus and the Author of 4Q491', in J.H. Charlesworth (ed.), *Jesus and the Dead Sea Scrolls* (New York: Doubleday, 1992), pp. 290-301.

Snell, B., *Tragicorum Graecorum Fragmenta*, I (Göttingen: Vandenhoeck & Ruprecht, 1971).

Stählin, O., *Clemens Alexandrinus, Werke II* (Die Griechischen christlichen Schriftsteller der ersten drei Jahrhunderte, 15 (Berlin: Akademie Verlag, 1962).

Steindorff, G., *Das Apokalypse des Elias: Eine unbekannte Apokalypse und Bruchstücke der Sophonias-Apokalypse* (TU, 17; Berlin: Akademie Verlag, 1899).

Stroumsa, G., 'Le couple de l'ange et de l'espirit: traditions juives et chrétiennes', *RB* 88 (1981), pp. 42-61.

—'Form(s) of God: Some Notes on Metatron and Christ', *HTR* 76 (1985), pp. 269-88.

Strugnell, J., 'The Angelic Liturgy at Qumran' (VTSup, 7; Leiden: E.J. Brill, 1960), pp. 318-45.

Swartz, M., *Scholastic Magic: Ritual and Revelation in Early Jewish Mysticism* (Princeton: Princeton University Press, 1996).

Tabor, J.D., *Things Unutterable: Paul's Ascent to Paradise in its Greco–Roman, Judaic, and Early Christian Contexts* (Lanham, MD: University Press of America, 1986).

Talbert, C., 'The Myth of a Descending–Ascending Redeemer in Mediterranean Antiquity', *NTS* 22 (1976), pp. 418-39.

Theissen, G., *The Sociology of Early Palestinian Christianity* (trans. J. Bowden; Philadelphia: Fortress Press, 1978).

—*Studien zur Soziologie des Urchristentums* (WUNT, 19; Tübingen: J.C.B. Mohr, 1979).

—*The Social Setting of Pauline Christianity* (trans. J. Schütz; Philadelphia: Fortress Press, 1982).

Thyen, H., 'Aus der Literatur zum Johannesevangelium', *TRu* 44 (1979), pp. 97-134.

Turner, J.D., *The Book of Thomas the Contender from Codex II of the Cairo Gnostic Library from Nag Hammadi (CG II,7): The Coptic Text with Translation, Introduction, and Commentary* (SBLDS, 23; Missoula, MT: Scholars Press, 1975).

Unnik, W.C. van, 'The Purpose of St. John's Gospel' (TU, 73; Berlin), pp. 382-411.

—' "With Unveiled Face", an Exegesis of 2 Corinthians iii 12-18', *NT* 6 (1963), pp. 153-69.

Urbach, E.E., 'Ha-Masorot 'al Torat ha-Sod bi-Tegufat ha-Tannaim', in A. Altmann (ed.), *Studies in Mysticism and Religion: Presented to G.G. Scholem on his Seventieth Birthday* (Jerusalem: Magnes Press, 1967), pp. 2-11.

Uro, R., 'Is *Thomas* an encratite gospel?', in R. Uro (ed.), *Thomas at the Crossroads*, pp. 140-62.

Uro, R. (ed.), *Thomas at the Crossroads: Essays on the Gospel of Thomas* (Edinburgh: T. & T. Clark, 1998).

Vaillant, A., *Le livre des secrets d'Hénoch: Texte slave et traduction française* (Paris: Institut d'études slaves, 1976).

Valantasis, R., *The Gospel of Thomas* (London: Routledge, 1997).

Vikan, G., *Byzantine Pilgrimage Art* (Washington, DC: Dumbarton Oaks Center for Byzantine Studies, 1982).

Wagner, C., 'Gotteserkenntnis im Spiegel und Gottesliebe in den beiden Korintherbriefen', *Bijdragen* 19 (1958), pp. 370-81.

West, D., *Virgil: The Aeneid* (New York: Penguin Books, 1990).

Widengren, G., *The Ascension of the Apostle and the Heavenly Book* (UUÅ, 7; Uppsala: Lundeqvist, 1950).

Wilson, R. McL., *Studies in the Gospel of Thomas* (London: Mowbray, 1960).

Windisch, H., *Der zweite Korintherbrief* (Göttingen: Vandenhoeck & Ruprecht, 1924).

—*The Spirit-Paraclete in the Fourth Gospel* (trans. J. Cox; Philadelphia: Fortress Press, 1968).

Winston, D., 'Was Philo a Mystic?', in J. Dan and F. Talmadge (eds.), *Studies in Jewish Mysticism* (Cambridge, MA: Association for Jewish Studies, 1982), pp. 15-41.

Wolfson, E.R., *Through a Speculum that Shines: Vision and Imagination in Medieval Jewish Mysticism* (Princeton, NJ: Princeton University Press, 1994).

Wuthnow, R., *Communities of Discourse* (Cambridge, MA: Harvard University Press, 1989).

Zandee, J., ' "The Teachings of Silvanus" (NHC VII,4) and Jewish Christianity', in R. van den Broek and M.J. Vermaseren (eds.), *Studies in Gnosticism and Hellenistic Religions presented to Gilles Quispel on the Occasion of his 65th Birthday* (Leiden: E.J. Brill, 1981), pp. 498-583.

INDEXES

INDEX OF REFERENCES

OLD TESTAMENT

OLD TESTAMENT APOCRYPHA AND PSEUDEPIGRAPHA

NEW TESTAMENT APOCRYPHA AND NAG HAMMADI CODICES

OTHER ANCIENT SOURCES

INDEX OF AUTHORS